Chains of Fear

AMERICAN RACE RELATIONS SINCE RECONSTRUCTION

Michael J. Cassity

Grass Roots Perspectives on American History, Number 3

GREENWOOD PRESS
WESTPORT, CONNECTICUT • LONDON, ENGLAND

Library of Congress Cataloging in Publication Data

Cassity, Michael J.
   Chains of fear.

   (Grass roots perspectives on American history,
ISSN 0148-771X ; no. 3)
   Includes bibliographical references and index.
   1. United States—Race relations. 2. Afro-Americans
—History. 3. Slavery—United States—History.
I. Title. II. Series.
E185.C37   1983   305.8'00973   82-21092
ISBN 0-313-21324-0 (lib. bdg.)

Library of Congress Catalog Card Number: 82-21092
ISBN: 0-313-21324-0
ISSN: 0148-771X

First published in 1984

Greenwood Press
A division of Congressional Information Service, Inc.
88 Post Road West
Westport, Connecticut 06881

Printed in the United States of America

10 9 8 7 6 5 4 3 2 1

For my parents

Contents

Part III: The Malaise of Race and Society in Modern America   229

Acknowledgments

As is altogether appropriate upon the completion of a project such as this, one feels small. The influence, the assistance, the encouragement and support, and the direction provided by so many others, directly and indirectly, have come so generously that perhaps all that remains of my own contribution are the errors of fact and judgment. These, and a little of what is good in these pages, I claim as my own.

David P. Thelen provided his usual incisive and penetrating criticism and pointed commentary on the specific documents and arguments I presented; he also demonstrated a persistent attitude of encouragement and indulgence at the right times. I am grateful that he is a friend as well as a critic. Numan V. Bartley also read through the entire manuscript, found much to disagree with, and, like Thelen, tried to save me from the error of my ways in style and substance. His numerous suggestions and questions provided me significant opportunity to improve my work. This is not the first time that I have benefited from these two individuals. I hope to continue to do so.

I am happy to acknowledge other debts as well. Lynn Questel provided enormous assistance in the seemingly endless task of locating and gathering important source materials. The late John C. Rainbolt, some time ago, taught me by his own example ways to extract the maximum meaning from any particular bit of evidence by seeking a broader historical context. Danney G. Goble, as true a friend as could ever be hoped for, inspired some of my interpretations of specific documents and events although he will be quick to deny this.

Gilbert C. Fite, Paul C. Nagel, and Lester D. Stephens in their successive terms as head of the history department at the University of Georgia not only tolerated but actively encouraged my efforts in this study through the supportive allocation of resources and time. All the secretaries in the history department who shared the burden of typing the manuscript proved to be efficient and good humored in the performance of their task. I also want to thank the large group of individuals who allowed me to use material that they have written or that they control and whom I have acknowledged at the appropriate points in the collection of documents, and the many people on the staffs of various libraries and research collections who have provided so much help in my quest for source material.

My parents, Ralph O. Cassity and Elizabeth L. Cassity, and my brother, Joe Cassity, all understand the debt I owe them; they also understand that it is a debt that can never be repaid. I hope that the scars left in the growth of my daughters Rebecca Rose and Jessica Mariah by my work on this project can in sufficient time heal. As always, my wife Constance helped me gain perspective not only on the past but on the present. I hope I have kept that perspective and that I will not lose it. That is, after all, what it is all about.

Introduction

The beginning point for this inquiry into the origins of modern American race relations is a plain question: Why have Americans often feared that greater freedom for others necessarily implies a loss for themselves? At its broadest this is obviously not a question confined to relations between black and white Americans, or between rich and poor, or between male and female. It is a question that reaches into a variety of relationships of authority, public policy, and popular sentiment. Yet it is a question of particular relevance to the study of American race relations since the rationale for racial subjugation has often involved an answer, however crudely put, to precisely this question, and since alternative visions of society seeking the realization of justice, equality, and freedom and the elimination of racial discrimination must confront that dilemma. It is also a question that requires more than a consideration of the words of particular spokesmen, whether self-appointed or proclaimed by "society," and more than a consideration of the problem of justice framed in the terms of modern jurisprudence. Thus stated, the problem involves two factors: (1) a perception of the American people, black and white, as agents of history often independent of the courses urged upon them by their leaders in the shaping of American race relations; and (2) a historical awareness in which the opportunities, limitations, aspirations, frustrations, and hopes and fears of the American people are continually transformed and are not assumed to be unchanging phenomena through the centuries. Put quite another way, this is an effort to explore the social and historical context of particular events in the lives of the American people that either shaped the course of development of American race relations, or that reveal the subtle forces at work and how people managed to cope with them on their own terms.

Any effort to explore American race relations faces a variety of problems of focus, theory, evidence, and perspective, each of which can serve to illuminate the issue at hand or to make its interpretation that much more tentative. One obstacle is the tendency to separate race relations from other social relationships with the consequence being all too often a distortion of focus and a neglect of the active forces shaping those relationships. By integrating the pattern of race relations into the larger structure of life that gives them their particular forms and logic, however, it is possible to avoid isolating the issue solely as a narrow struggle between the races, between racial subordination and equality— the kind of framework that lends itself more to moralizing than to understanding. A major goal of this study is to suggest some ways in which American race relations emerged from certain patterns of life and social organization and how those patterns are related to the larger society.

If this quest for social context is to be useful it must be something more than a colorful backdrop against which significant developments can be seen. In this study that social context is sought in the effort to locate the material social environment and the particular traditions and legacies of the past which together inform and restrict the behavior of individuals. In concrete terms this effort to locate actions in their appropriate contexts usually involves the examination of experiences of identifiable people in the circumstances in which they were lived by those people. Human beings—black and white—are placed in circumstances which they have not always chosen; are confronted by forces not of their own making; and are faced with the day-to-day demands of life, demands that are themselves intimately related to the larger society. This volume is an effort to understand the material forces shaping the choices available to people and the ever growing and changing relationships of race and class and community—indeed, of love and deference and freedom.[1]

By considering the changing pattern of social organization, that social context also becomes a historical context. Of special importance in the effort to identify this historical context is the concept of the market as a set of changing social relationships. It is the market that permits a focus on relationships of scarcity consciousness and competitiveness that loom large in questions of equality and subordination. What is so valuable about this notion, though, is not its application to the question as an economic formula in the production and distribution of goods but its larger implications as a framework and reference point for the organization of society. While medieval society and even to some extent early American society tended to restrict the acquisitive passions of man through devices like the just wage, just price, and usury laws—and also through paternalistic provision for community needs through some of the same mercantilist arrangements—the erosion of those controls and the consequent liberation of individual energy through contracts, corporations, and individualistic conceptions of rights, especially in the nineteenth century, unleashed or propelled into society exactly those same acquisitive passions.[2] The reverberations of the change were enormous as the structure of society altered, and as its proclaimed object became the protection, not of the commonwealth, but of individual freedom. The organizing principles of society were revolutionized and in this change the whole realm of social relations was transformed, with race relations being but one of many elements caught up in the transformation of a pre-market society to a society dominated by the market and industrial patterns of organization. The implications in terms of work processes, in terms of distribution of rewards, in terms of materialistic domination of values and priorities, in terms of individual relationships, in terms of the fate of pre-market cultures, in terms of competition for pride, dignity, and self-respect, dominate the relationships between the races and challenge whole ways of life.

Despite this emphasis on social context in the search for the meanings of specific events or actions, and despite the emphasis on the market as a historical force shaping that social context, there is no intention here to ascribe the course of race relations in America to a deterministic, inevitable pattern of change. Indeed, one basic theme of this presentation is exactly the opposite: people, in active relationship with their environments, have made conscious decisions, the consequences of which we now live with; and just as those decisions were made by men and women, so too can men and women move the relationships of their society today in the directions they most want. To view the problem otherwise is to accept either a view of man as a powerless captive of external forces or to attribute to him free will in transcending the forces shaping his society. In 1943, Francis Downing explored the problem of racial violence in Detroit and confronted exactly that dilemma of origins and also the way in which authorities continually sidestepped the question of origins and responsibility. In his assessment (reprinted below in Document 36) Downing offered this reminder: "Despite some of our alleged philosophers, there are still causes for things. And results are still their fruits." And that is exactly the issue involved in the search for the origins of American race relations.

The emancipation of the slaves did not automatically mean the end of oppression. Social and racial tensions persisted though often greatly altered in form. The institutional and cultural manifestations of the new forms of bondage and subjugation had been well anticipated by those who, whether friends or antagonists of slavery, had predicted earlier that the new freedom to be experienced would be essentially a market-bound conception that valued neither the creative potential nor the free individualistic nature of man but instead stressed the individual's responsibility for his own fate. This notion of self-reliance in other contexts could be benign; it could even be noble if logically carried forward to complete independence. But in the context of a society where individuals were free to sell their labor as a commodity, and in which access to land was limited to those who had sufficient resources so that they did not need to sell their labor as a commodity, those freedmen would be dependent first on a market for their labor and second on those who had land. This could mean, as one planter put it, the bleak freedom to starve.

Even before the end of the Civil War the military authorities and the friends of the freedmen in areas dominated by Union forces anticipated the contours of the social and economic revolution about to proceed. With the necessity of the wage stimulus, the sanctity of the contract, the obligation to work for survival (indeed the notion that idleness was a crime), and the government as the supervising and enforcing agent of the new work relationships all in mind, it was then obvious that freedom, the freedom of the marketplace, came not as a vast release from oppression but as an alternate system of restraints and that in fact the new work relationship was to be reduced to that of a wage relationship instead of being part of a broader traditional social system of obligations and responsibilities.[3]

At the same time that this new society based upon the market system of relations was emerging, it also became obvious that many of the social implications of slavery would be in doubt with the demise of that core institution. Perhaps chief among these implications were those affecting race relations; under slavery, even if a black was among those who were free, there could be no doubt of social position since caste and race had long ago merged to form permanent barriers and privileges. Perhaps what was so alarming to many whites in this transition was not that they would now be competing with blacks for limited economic rewards, but that the market pattern of relationships itself threatened old verities. The central assumed truth was the superiority of white people to blacks. Thus when racial violence erupted it would often take the form of a pogrom to prove this point, possibly to the blacks but more likely to the whites themselves. In this sense what was being suppressed was not so much the black populations of Memphis and other communities which happened to be the convenient and unfortunate victims, but the assumptions, hopes, and theoretical promises of the market.[4]

The promises of this market-conceived freedom demanded for their fulfillment, paradoxically, the repudiation of other forms of freedom and the acceptance of the social and psychological restraints appropriate to the development of self-discipline and calculating acquisitiveness. Hence the freedmen were urged by their friends not to be too free, to produce for the market instead of for subsistence, to inculcate the habits of sobriety and productivity and the values of possessive individualism, and to forsake their own culture (or, as it appeared to the well-meaning northern missionaries to the freedmen, their *lack* of culture, so different was it from their own) for something more civilized and reserved.[5] The impact of this proselytizing is difficult to calculate. Some would say, in an effort to bolster their racial views, that it had no impact and that the black population remained uncivilized and perhaps proved the difficulty (or, again, the impossibility) of improving the race. Others, like the missionaries themselves, while experiencing frustrations, remained optimistic. As for the blacks themselves, the impact came mainly in the form of a tension between two cultures, one having its origins in the relationships of the market, the other in pre-market habits and relations, even in Africa. The tension compounded with the additional factor that to move in either direction could be interpreted by white people on one side or the other as confirming hidden fears about the nature of the Negro, or even about themselves. At a minimum, the acculturation effort seems to have succeeded largely in forcing black culture into less outward and visible forms, even to the point of denying its existence.

So would be the future for blacks: caught between the grinding and opposing forces of the market and the resistance to that market. In economics the market reshaped the institutions of the South. The supply of black labor and the demand for that labor by landowning planters created a system of sharecropping which amounted to a form of wage labor, with the wage in this capital-scarce region consisting of a share of the crop at the end of the year; and later a system of tenancy dominated by the crop-lien, a system more individualized but with the same effect in terms of bondage to the land.[6] In both systems continual indebtedness replaced the chains of slavery. But with the crop-lien system of tenancy even the landlord found his power slipping away, not to his tenants, but to his source of capital, usually a local merchant or banker, with the ultimate source resting in the northern banks and industries. As power and status waned resistance increased. In the by now characteristic pattern of American race relations, that problem would seldom be challenged directly in political and economic terms. The penetration of the market, with its blessings going to those with the greatest resources, spurred negative reactions against the most visible beneficiaries of this system—those black people who no longer bore the chains of slavery and who, during Reconstruction at least, attempted to participate in the political process. Thus the disfranchisement of blacks by violence and intimidation, and a more general subjugation of blacks who only sought to vote or merely to get by in normal ways during the course of a day or who encountered whites—proceeding sometimes under the guise of the Ku Klux Klan or other clandestine organizations and sometimes without formal direction—seeking a victim. The combination of economic pressures and social coercion meant, of course, the complete return to a caste system—a return to a pre-market social arrangement without, in the process, dividing along class lines, a prospect that would have meant poor white and black against the white planter class or, increasingly, against the merchant and business class. The difficulty with that approach, aside from the human toll, was that it only stifled people who shared the same problems and who were equally resistant to the ravages of the market. This stability came at the expense of those black and white people who already were the victims of the system.

The impulse toward segregation could obviously fit into this pattern of resistance to the potentially atomizing and individualizing force of the market. Indeed, such often appears to have been the case, as can be seen in the early instances of segregation in the free North during the days of slavery. The existence of a social chasm during slavery could be universally assumed despite the closest contact between masters and slaves, even to the extent of slave and mistress sharing the same sleeping quarters, but in a society where that chasm could not be assumed it had to be created to avoid the possibility of assumptions of equality becoming too widespread. These impulses surfaced in the South on an irregular and uneven basis in private policy and practice and gradually by law as well. Two perspectives are especially revealing in this growth of Jim Crow society. One involves the flexibility of the system, a flexibility that sometimes made it possible for blacks to cross the white barrier (as in Document 7) when the rules prohibited interracial contact and that made it possible for officially open doors for both races to be subverted (as in Document 6). How universal the effort to secure Jim Crow proved to be is one question that remains to be answered; how universally those practices were observed is another. By the same token the lack of formal strictures in a particular part of society should not be taken to be evidence of openness.

The other perspective on the problem of segregation moves to another level. Inasmuch as segregation could be a device geared for the suppression of the black population it appears as an irony that the same system could serve contrary purposes. Yet just as close contact between the races during slavery served as an instrument of social control, so too could separation of the races mean a blow for autonomy and against domination. One potentially powerful agent of control lay in religion. With enormous energy ministers mined the preachings of the Apostle Paul to declare the sanctity and duty of obedience of slave to master throughout the centuries. They never tired of it. Upon emancipation one of the quickest moves for independence, cultural and physical, came in the emigration of blacks from those churches where they had been captive congregations. One church history noted that the blacks left the church and when the churchmen offered them the gospel again, "they declined it as coming from us" (Document 4). In its place followed the line of the African Methodist Episcopal Church. But even there when the leadership seemed to be aiming more at acculturation than at traditional forms of salvation the independent spirit reigned in the local congregations unchecked by hierarchical pressure (Document 5).[7]

Aside from massive exodus from the South, itself a possibility that carried no promises of true freedom, the options available to secure equality seemed limited. Some leaders of the commercially alert "New South" like Lewis H. Blair insisted that only two choices could be made: either promote market forms of relationships and ruthless competition for jobs among all men which would generate economic growth for the South and individual freedom for blacks, or retain a caste-bound society that permitted no growth and oppress the black population more fiercely to keep them subservient. That the options Blair posed had been narrowed to an artificial Hobson's choice disconnected from real issues of freedom became evident from the perspectives of workers in the South in the 1880s and 1890s. Those views (as expressed in Document 8) suggested that a variety of experiences for both black and white could lead to the same conclusion: the real goal of freedom could not be found in either the oppression of one race by another or in the equal freedom of all to be exploited in a competitive market. Freedom could be found, these miners argued, only in the brotherhood of man and the liberation of all from the pressures generated by a compelled struggle for the right to survive.[8] Indeed, the market in this view, instead of being the liberator of man from social repressions, became but another huge system of gain for a few at the expense of the many. And racial competition, as much as individual competition, served to perpetuate the power of the few by preventing a real brotherhood of man from becoming an effective political and social force. Not surprisingly, given the origins of the system of race relations in America, this issue had been apparent in the making of slavery in the South two centuries earlier. The efficacy of this system of racial subordination had been proven beyond a doubt.

By the end of the nineteenth century a maze of internal contradictions plagued the nation and especially the South. The market provided both opportunity and oppression. It carried hopes and fears with it into the South with manifestations in the crop-lien system and farm tenancy and the gradual migration of blacks to the cities and the North in search of better lives. And an economy that had come to depend on the market in the 1890s found itself ravaged by depression. It is precisely at that moment of general social debilitation that new forms of oppression were launched against blacks. The ferocious wave of extralegal violence directed at blacks in intense and repeated surges had been unprecedented in that it was sustained over a period of years. Jim Crow became a permanent fixture. The law now countenanced the disfranchisement of black voters. In institutional forms and in behavioral aspects the contact between the races at the end of the nineteenth and the beginning of the twentieth centuries resembled closely the forms of tribal warfare in a situation of colonial oppression. As Frantz Fanon suggested, the viciousness involved usually centered around quests for dignity and self-respect; the external situation of the colonized peoples permitted very little of that pride.[9] That this phenomenon could extend across the South suggests one dimension of the problem. That it could occur in the urban centers of the North (as in Document 12) suggests another. The source of the problem lay partly in regional power struggles and oppression but more fundamentally in a larger struggle over the structure and purpose of organized society. Again the larger context of this pattern of race relations suggests their efficacy for the perpetuation of this system.

At the same time that white people often relied on primitive forms of resistance to the transformation wrought by the market in their social relations, blacks also exhibited a rejection of the market by the creation or perpetuation of cultural forms that carried either pre-market themes or anti-market tensions. With the characteristically romantic appeal of the exotic and the natural, many of those cultural strains also found appeal among whites. Thus the aura of the supernatural seemed at first glance to be the exclusive province of the blacks, yet its mysteries and magic aroused more intensive attention and comment among whites than among blacks where that supernatural world could be assumed (Document 13). Black music also testified to the vibrance of black culture and certainly to its depth in more than a set of compensations for economic losses. So complete was this rejection of the material world that many blacks would shun the songs that crossed the line from the spirituals, which alone held legitimacy. For a religious person to sing a secular song would be to sin (Document 14). The appeal of the Negro spiritual to white audiences is legendary. The rise of black secular song, though, in the forms of ragtime and blues especially, often attracted other audiences and attracted people with frustrations akin to those that helped form the culture in which the music was born.[10] Whether or not those white aficionados could ever capture the soul that blacks applied to their music would remain the lesser issue; the distinctiveness of that culture and its significance as a repudiation of the restraints and confines of the culture of the market would be of greater importance.

That importance loomed even larger as the force of the market altered substantially the material circumstances of life for white and black Americans. Especially pronounced was the increased migration of black people out of the South. Pushed by the bleak possibilities for improvement on any level given the sustained, institutionalized, and intensified persecution mounted against blacks in the South, by the forces of nature in floods and boll weevils, and by larger economic slumps, and pulled by the growth of the industrial machines of the urban centers of the North, by the hopes, even if often illusory, of better treatment in those areas of the country not bound to a slaveholding tradition, and especially by the opportunities generated by the mobilization of the economy in those urban areas for World War I, black people moved in dramatic numbers to a new promised land. This demographic shift, of course, failed to bring the measure of relief many anticipated as jobs proved to be more competitive as more people applied for employment and as fundamental problems of housing and survival were transformed but not alleviated by an urban existence. Nor did the military side of Wilson's war to make the world safe for democracy prove to be any more fulfilling for black people. While the war generated both outrage and violence at home and then oppression of that dissent, the soldiers who were some-times caricatured as cannon fodder for the corporations could only justify their actions in the military in terms of the rhetoric produced by the President and the Committee on Public Information. For black soldiers that rhetoric proved to be much more glaring an affront than was evident to even some of those in the states who were prosecuted for their crit-icism of the war. Assigned a wartime mission and then constantly de-nigrated and systematically discriminated against in the routine matter of accomplishing that mission, black soldiers noted a particular hollow-ness in the high-sounding rhetoric from Washington. While the bene-ficiaries of the war were few and the benefits they reaped huge, the crystallization of a distinctly modern and powerful centralized social organization during the war meant that the demands that system could make on the individual could be equally large, and the implication of that tension for race relations could be just as portentous as the war itself.

Some of the portent could be seen in the years of the accelerated migration and of the war. In East St. Louis it was obvious to the congres-sional committee investigating the savage rioting that plagued the city in 1917 that a system designed to benefit the few at the expense of the least powerful would have such dire results (Document 17). The rioting in Washington and Chicago in 1919 bore similar if less explicit connec-tions between the distribution of power and the operation of the orga-nized system.[11] That urban violence was not new. What was striking in the developments of these years was that blacks were fighting back with whatever means it took, be they violent or political, be they in the urban centers of the nation or in the backwash of the market in the rural South. And this resistance probably was not new. But it certainly was more widespread and visible. The challenge for the future would be that of transforming such resistance to an offensive and of defining freedom in a meaningful way. Both problems would be compounded by the chang-ing structure of American society itself.

While the process had significant and subtle development ahead of it, the basic contours of the rise of modern society were evident at least by the end of the first world war. With the expansion of market relationships; the depersonalization of social relations; the fragmentation of society and the economy into competing groups seeking increased rewards and power for their own sectors; and the growth of a national political economy and an accommodating social structure that embodied a transfer of social, political, and economic authority from local to central levels, the outlines of the modern organization of society became clear. While such a pattern of organization facilitated commercial interests and activities, and thereby reflected its material origins, purposes, and justifications, it also exacted a price. In the fragmentation of society into competing groups, the price involved the forsaking of other, less economically derived loyalties in the name of interest group specialization and the reduction of competition. In the centralization of power the price was a loss of local authority to increasingly remote levels of the economy and the government, whether to large businesses, unions, or public agencies. The apprehensions of dispossession, both cultural and material, generated by this process of change go far in contributing to an understanding of the course of race relations in twentieth century America.

Such a context makes more comprehensible the racial and ethnic repression evident in the years following Wilson's war as many felt themselves dispossessed by the alterations in the social structure and then sought to return to earlier patterns of social organization that emphasized not fluidity and uncertainty and powerlessness for individuals, but instead venerated traditional conceptions of morality and propriety in social relations. Such attempts to revive the caste patterns of the past, to replace relativistic ethics with absolute truths, and even to romanticize the days that were no more in various forms of cultural revitalization point to not only the disintegration of those pre-modern social arrangements but the unsatisfying nature of the new forms as well. This process had not only created a new society but had made the "Nordic" American, in the words of the Ku Klux Klan, "a stranger in large parts of the land his fathers gave him" (Document 21). What such lamentation bespoke most, of course, was the dispossession of a heritage in the name of economic growth.[12]

One consequence of such a process was to push blacks further down; another was to make their culture that much more distinctive and attractive to white adventurers. In the growth of the popularity of jazz the unrestrained and natural and spontaneous aura, as it widely became characterized, expressed key and integral elements of black culture and paved a cultural road for the expression of other associated arts emanating from black life. Jazz, with its complete spontaneity and its lack

of externally imposed discipline and tight patterns of artificial synchro-
nization, offered a repudiation of the key elements of an increasingly
"rationalized" society and proved successful in so doing. The ubiquitous
jazz, the growth of Harlem, and the vitality of the Harlem Renaissance
should probably first be recognized for their quintessential expressions
of black culture in America and second for the enormous popularity of
that culture among whites.[13] In that white popularity can be seen the
dichotomy generated by the course of society and modernization; non-
material, unrestrained impulses could be found mainly in the licensed
culture of black Americans. Black culture was not, however, thereby
legitimized. The process worked the other way: in the popular mind
perhaps it was the new order that lacked real legitimacy.

At the same time it would be a mistake to identify only a single black
culture in the urban centers. As life varied according to racial values
and identities, income levels, kinds of work, religion, and social expectations it became that much more obvious that blacks were themselves
divided, and had been, in ways comparable to white society. What this
demonstrated was in part the penetration of the market system of values
into black society, in part the vitality of the independent strains of black
culture that had been nourished and perpetuated through previous generations, and in part the fragmenting tendency of modern society. The
dynamics of social tensions would dictate that racial tensions between
black and white would either become diffused in the array of competing
loyalties, become more sharply focused as a result of racial identification,
or yield to class tensions given the commonality of experience along
class lines. The outcome was by no means certain in a modernizing
society. Nor would the dilemma regarding the course of race relations
be restricted to the new urban black population. Black people in the city
and the country, in the North and the South, like white people across
the nation, faced the future with trepidation.

The depression by its very nature tended to intensify the scarcity
consciousness that already had caused people to view their fellow citizens as competitors for limited rewards. But in race relations that may
not have been the chief effect. Instead, it appears to have driven some
to acts of violence fed by the frustration, not just of unemployment, but
of the system that would generate such unemployment itself and indeed
such competition. The alternative, misguided though it be, seemed to
be the resurrection of a caste system that knew no systematic individual
competition. And (as in Document 28) sometimes the despair of the
situation drove races together. When the Bonus Marchers converged on
Anacostia Flats, as Roy Wilkins reported, Jim Crow did not join the
protest against the system of power in the nation that left out these
heroes and cannon fodder of a decade and a half before. Given this
example of cooperation, the consequence of promoting group compe-

tition and heightened scarcity consciousness would likely be exacerbated race relations or at least the perpetuation of the system that generated such racial tension.

The system of power in the nation underwent alterations through the development of the New Deal. Instead, however, of a new responsiveness to popular needs and broadly felt frustrations, the main pattern of change followed the lines of centralization of power in both economy and government and the continued, indeed, the enforced, fragmentation of the public into competing groups. Combined, the two forces signalled the responsiveness of government to the most powerful interest groups. For black people as for most white workers, this meant not a burden lifted but a redefinition of the problem of powerlessness to narrower job-defined approaches. In the factories of the nation, the National Recovery Administration set about to bring industrial recovery by eliminating competition between companies already aware of their community of interests, thereby to raise prices and profits with hopes (ultimately) of a "trickle-down" of benefits to workers. It neglected the plainly observable fact that purchasing power had already been devastated by inflated prices in the twenties and that now unemployment caused substantial difficulty in theory and actually increased the problems for the poor in reality. Even in those situations where workers might be able to press for a larger share of the fruits of their labor in Blue Eagle industries, black workers seemed almost systematically excluded through wage differentials and alternate schedules, as explained by a group of black workers to a government representative in Document 29. Likewise in agriculture the New Deal moved with the greatest vigor to bail out the largest farms and systematically pushed sharecroppers and tenants off the farm as the need for their labor was eliminated by reduced production and by subsidies which could finance tractors and thereby push other laborers off the land.

The solution to the problems of those at the bottom lay, according to the Roosevelt administration, not in attacking the concentrated economic and political power many believed to be responsible for the depression and the chasm between rich and poor but in organizing groups to press, in the political and economic arenas, for greater rewards for the members of those mutually exclusive interest groups, such rewards to come from the other parts of society that lacked the political and economic power to withstand the onslaught. Such a formula could work if its goal were limited to generating temporary social stability. It was less well suited to meeting the needs of citizens who lacked money and power.

Even when the government responded directly to the problems of black people the benefits sometimes carried dubious fruits. In the matter of relief, the problem of discrimination in its distribution aside, the adequacy of welfare in its direct or work-relief forms can be questioned in terms of its sheer sufficiency in helping people pay bills and buy food as well as in the number of people actually reached through the programs. But a deeper dilemma lay in the system even when it worked at its best. Critics like Herbert Hoover were quick to point to the possible dependence on the government that such relief could generate for the poor. Indeed, in the case of the business community, that habitual dependence upon government support seemed to prove that it was a likely possibility. In fact, it may be argued that in the circumstances of despair, where life itself was an uncertainty, the sustenance provided could be worth the price of abnegation and the risk of further dependence. Ironically, however, that assistance could also generate not just dependence but support; by providing a pittance whose life-giving value could easily be appreciated by the recipient the political economy actually provided those who benefited the very least, indeed who were the major casualties of the system of power, reason for becoming its most ardent enthusiasts.[14] In the 1930s black people turned Abraham Lincoln's picture to the wall and joined the congeries of interest groups making up the Roosevelt coalition of the Democratic Party.

In many ways it is accurate to view World War II as a continuation of the trends pressing forward under the name of the New Deal. Like the first world war it brought a centralized social system and a regimented economy, with all the sacrifices and inequities those developments could imply. The industrial machinery of the nation finally returned to pre-depression production levels and then moved beyond. The agriculture of the nation experienced its second revolution in machinery. During the Civil War horse and mule drawn machinery transformed the farms of the nation; during World War II tractors performed the same function. The result, however, proved not to be universally beneficial. As industries produced more, workers in those plants failed to see the justice of their sacrifices in terms of wages and hours, the right to strike, and industrial control when compared to the mounting profits of the corporations. As more people went to work in the cities those cities became crowded and strained and housing became a scarce commodity. As consumers cut their diets and lived with rationing, the "dollar a year" men seemed to experience no want for themselves or their corporations. Beyond these strains the problems facing black workers included first, the inability to find employment, second, the inability to enter unions, and, third, the inability to find housing. The main product of A. Philip Randolph's threatened march on Washington, the Fair Employment Practices Commission, may have helped alleviate some of the discrimination; more often it served as a lightning rod to prevent too vigorous an attack on the administration for tolerating such discrimination. The gains for blacks came not from government decree or intervention. They came from an expanding economy.

But perhaps the most telling developments of the war at home were the eruptions of violence that the war seemed to produce in major cities of the nation. On the one hand, the war was being waged in the name of freedom and especially against a racist nation in Europe. On the other hand, black people, including soldiers in still segregated units, witnessed every day the lack of freedom in their own land and institutions. The issues precipitating the violence involved housing in Detroit and an altercation between a white policeman and a black soldier in Harlem but the significance emerges most in the response of the two communities to the violence (see Documents 36 and 37). Detroit used martial law. New York used a more sophisticated approach, utilizing black leaders and black Military Policemen to help quell the turbulence. The recognition given to the black community in Harlem served baldly as an agency of social control, one more effective than force. In all this the cause of the distress, the objective problems facing black and white Americans, the problems that caused white people to feel threatened by the changes that black advances represented and that caused black people to believe (as expressed in Document 38) that the white worker encountered "no unjust limitation upon the advancements which he may attain," remained untouched. As had been the case for centuries, one of the most effective instruments of fundamental social control continued to be antagonism between black and white, at the expense of common social goals.

Oddly enough, sometimes the erosion of that animosity itself presented yet a different obstacle to black quests for equality. The righteous concern for black people could sometimes assume the form of a rank paternalism wherein black needs and aspirations would be assumed rather than investigated, as in Document 40. That these white people would in turn see themselves as the agents of deliverance for their less fortunate and less independent brethren involved not so much an act of brotherhood as an act of condescension and, what was more deeply hidden, as an act of control. The larger political manifestation of this in post-World War II America came in the effort, however ineffectual, of the Democratic Party to embrace the cause of civil rights, with those civil rights ordinarily defined in terms of entry into white society and institutions and with the condition of assimilating market goals and values always as the prerequisite. The disturbing and frightening memories of the riots during the war apparently lingered long after the smoke lifted.

Two major developments transformed the struggle for racial equality in the 1950s. The first was that of the 1954 Supreme Court decision in *Brown* v. *Board of Education* which, like its adamant restatement the following year, obliterated the chief institutional prop that had contributed to the perpetuation of discrimination: the constitutional notion of separate but equal facilities for the races. By so mandating individual equality in the eyes of the law and forbidding racial distinctions in public education, the legacy of caste, in its formal and public manifestations, received a fatal blow, although much time would pass before the accomplishment of that objective could be realized. In its place would come a system of relations that ostensibly valued an individual according to merit and character. Yet the second development undermined the virtues of such a system. The emergence in the post-World War II period, and especially in the 1950s, of the phenomenon often labelled the "new mass culture" signalled the incursion of modernization into cultural areas in ways that proved both threatening and powerful in race relations. Contemporary social critics from William H. Whyte to C. Wright Mills noted the erosion of individualism in the pressure to conform to material standards of success and character. The pressures of conformity to such uniform standards were naturally subtle. David Riesman explained, for example, that the process of socialization in traditional societies involved the internalization of old verities and morals in preparation for adulthood; in modern society, he suggested, the process of socialization consists mainly of the sensitizing of one's self to the expectations of others. Where the sin in traditional societies was to be wrong, the sin in modern society is to be unpopular.[15] In race relations this meant, first, the homogenization of society implicit in the elimination of racial and cultural distinctions. In that sense the *Brown* decision reflected the fundamental trend. But hidden in the impact lay the potential counterproductivity of the process: in the reduction of cultural differences to a single norm compatible with the material goals of society, a powerful quest for a sense of purpose beyond material gain, usually in the realm of moral views of human relations, began to surge forward. While the basic structural trend encouraged conformity, some people responded by affirming their humanity by undertaking a crusading effort to secure justice and freedom for black people. Others responded by attempting to hold on to the system of caste and segregation being challenged. This confrontation between the forces of the past and the present provides the context for understanding the conflict in much of the civil rights struggle whether in Montgomery, Little Rock, or other parts of the South. Both sides seemed to be combatting modernization.

The more success achieved in the civil rights movement, the more the limits of that movement became apparent. This was evident in the mid-1960s. Even when the laws could be changed, either by creating new protections or by removing old barriers, racial discrimination persisted. The prominence of *de jure* segregation had in fact deflected attention from the fundamental social problems to the more manageable and soluble legal expressions of those problems. Moreover, the ability to take advantage of new opportunities in education and commerce opened by civil rights pressures often fell beyond the reach of the masses of black people. Expensive stores and state universities might be opened but the potential black clientele included only the already well-to-do blacks. In fact the very goal of the civil rights movement, one generally expressed as increased opportunities for black people, turned out to be an idea founded in a market conception of the American dream: material acquisition as the goal of life and the measure of success and character. Given this larger limiting framework it is not surprising in addition that this movement was unable to shake a certain measure of white domination, well-meaning though it was. One Mississippi black woman engaged in the voter registration campaign of the Student Nonviolent Coordinating Committee (SNCC) (in Document 48) bemoaned the dependence on that white leadership. In a political analysis it could be argued that the federal government, and especially the Democratic Party, had assumed that paternalist function. But even that is to view the problem too narrowly. This paternalism was more broadly social rather than racial in origin; race relations, however, may have been the most visible manifestation of a larger paternalism in American society assumed by various elites in the therapeutic state. What was going on was the entry of blacks into the same paternalistic framework that already engulfed white people. The fight against that paternalism ordinarily involved assertions of racial pride.

Increasingly blacks took over their movement for equality. Increasingly they turned the direction of the movement toward a revitalization of the black community. Increasingly they advocated enlarged militance in the pursuit of their goals. With the black takeover of SNCC, the white liberal Democrats' rejection of the Mississippi Freedom Democratic Party, and the rioting in Watts, the course of the future dramatically changed. Again, massive assistance from the federal government in the form of the War on Poverty seemed likely to forestall a major outbreak.[16] Indeed, the War on Poverty produced the intended goals as it generated competition between various black organizations and constituencies seeking support for one kind of assistance over another and thereby fragmented the black community further, as indicated in Documents 52 and 53. The government jobs created also managed in some instances to lure activists away from their independent efforts, as in the case of the Mississippi Freedom Democratic Party discussed in Document 54. Despite that effort, the black community persisted in an independent direction, sometimes contrary to its own leaders, and black brotherhood and nationalism and independence and power became the defining elements of the new effort to secure justice and equality. Militance became its hallmark as major rioting in the largest cities became common and predictable, culminating in the wave of riots sparked by the assassination of Martin Luther King in 1968. By the same token, that rioting itself produced even stronger feelings of black solidarity. It appeared by 1968 that a significant movement was taking shape which directed its attention not at the symptoms of the problems facing black people, but at the basic forces generating those problems, those forces generating dependence, abnegation, and competition.

The discontent and outrage of black Americans merged with that of many others in the late 1960s and early 1970s as a protest against exploitative and alienating institutions and relationships provoked by an unpopular war in Vietnam and consequent distorted priorities at home. College students, blacks and other minorities, and women pushed and protested against the established system of power. Jerry Farber's famous essay, "The Student as Nigger," suggested the commonality of experiences for the two core groups in this movement and made it clear that subtle and bald forms of paternalism provided the targets of the various efforts.[17] But blacks and students seldom completely joined hands in this cause. There remained, for one thing, the black suspicion of well-meaning whites; too often their liberators had knocked at their doors holding new kinds of chains. Indeed, many of the early student radicals came to their convictions after working in the civil rights movement. This could provide cause for more suspicion and distrust or it could be cause for celebration given the vastly different orientations in the two protests. Another factor preventing a complete fusion of black and white activism revolved around the fear and distrust of institutions. Too often in this country have institutions—political parties, government agencies, churches, universities, labor organizations, reform groups—been formed in the purest and noblest of faiths and causes only to assume a life of their own independent of the original needs of their creators, and indeed to also make demands of and attempt to control for their own perpetuation those individuals who looked to them for salvation. And many, therefore, figured the basic problem not to have an institutional solution. An uneasy alliance but a mutual respect took the place of formal connections and coordinated activity. That mutual respect, however, ordinarily based upon theories of capitalist domination and exploitation and the concomitant apprehension of common experiences and legacies in resistance to that combination, proved to be an accomplishment of major significance. The prospect of greater freedom for both blacks and whites came not to those protestors of each race with fear and trepidation but with enthusiasm and the belief that it would contribute to a greater freedom for all. It would be, indeed, a moment of broader liberation. In all this a sensitivity to the core issues affecting black and white people alike had surfaced on a wide front for perhaps the first time in the nation's history. The competitive and paternalistic assumptions that had maintained the antagonism between the races as a system of social control, if not overcome, were certainly challenged with great vigor. A new era had begun. The hopes and promises for the future appeared bright to many not so much because of the power these groups wielded but because of the theoretical possibilities for fundamental social change.

While the power of the movement urging alterations in the organization of society could be disputed, the accomplishments were notable. The Vietnam War, probably the central catalyst of the widespread revolt, did come to an end, even if it was too long in coming. So too did the draft. In a period of around six years two powerful presidents were forced from office. Cities that had experienced major throes of violence, or had been threatened, moved to increase the number of black elected officials and the number of black police officers. Governmental assistance, in what was often called its "human resources" programs, began to achieve positive results in terms of black income, education, employment opportunities, housing, physical health, and government decision-making considerations. From a variety of perspectives it would appear that the proponents of social change had not just achieved significant reforms but had achieved the fulfillment of their dreams.

But the opposite proved to be the more accurate assessment. Success came to others. Perhaps the most succinct characterization of the changes can be found in President Ford's remark about the ignominious departure of Richard Nixon from Washington and his own ascendancy to the Presidency (and before he pardoned his uncontrite patron); it showed, Ford said, that the system worked. The changes, desired and welcome though they were, did not necessarily, however, prove the success of the system in responding to the fundamental needs of the nation. Instead those changes found their origins in an even more sophisticated political paternalism that focused on symptoms of problems rather than on the problems themselves. One result was that the problems remained while the protest was diffused. Presidents came and went but their official policies remained virtually indistinguishable. Black people administered the cities and donned police uniforms, but the ghettoes remained and the incidence of black crime did not diminish.[18] The draft ceased to make its demands on America's youth (for the time being) and the percentage of blacks in the Army climbed as a reflection of pervasive limitations on blacks in civilian society. The need to which these changes responded appeared to be that of stability more than the fundamental wrongs generating such widespread public disaffection.[19]

A further consequence of this form of response lay not just in the deflection of insurgent discontent from its objectives but in the actual increase of paternalism and the promulgation of greater public dependence on experts and bureaucrats, on the established system. In welfare this dependence has been made explicit by critics whose political views range broadly as well as by the recipients themselves, and it has been obvious for decades. The system of welfare also contributed to the de-

cline of the family, especially the black family. Viewed in a broader
framework this was part of a long, subtle process in which the functions
of the family, such as production, education, and moral inculcation, had
been assumed by the larger society and especially by public institutions,
providing less reason for the family's existence beyond companionship.[20]
Traditionally outside the framework of that modernizing machinery,
black families had experienced neither the gradualness of the process
nor the full dependence on it until the advances of the civil rights movement opened up those opportunities; and the high incidence of black
unemployment included that many more black families in the process.
The result, as Documents 59 and 60 suggest, was the precipitous decline
of the black family and the increase in government paternalism, in its
most condescending forms. This "problem" then generated additional
rationale for greater involvement by experts and social agents in the
affairs of these people. The black community did not reciprocate the
paternalism nor did it always shun it, given the limited choices available.
But neither did they suffer the illusions of participation in the process
of decision-making, whether before a Senate committee (Document 59)
or in the larger political arena. Black voting in the South declined to
levels below those of years before the enactment of the Voting Rights
Act of 1965 (Document 61). While the reasons offered for such non-
voting varied, the general sentiment suggested that it did not matter.
Blacks, like women and eighteen-year-olds, got the right to vote and
then discovered that it did not make much difference, so powerful was
the new paternalism.[21]

The revival of racial animosity and violence in the 1970s fit neatly into
this pattern of modernization. Along with the loss of individual authority
(and responsibility) to the centralized system came the renewed fragmentation of the public. Two explosive issues demonstrated the contours
of this process. In the effort to achieve racially balanced school systems,
the courts ordered the busing of school children from various schools
where one race predominated to other schools. Consequently violence
occasionally erupted, as in Boston (Document 62) between the advocates
and opponents of busing. The artificiality of the issue quickly becomes
apparent. Few people would disagree with the fundamental goal, equal
educational opportunity for all. Yet by turning the issue into a contest
between those who advocated racial equality and those who proclaimed
the importance of freedom of choice and neighborhood autonomy the
system was able to warp the issue. Nobody, but nobody, could win
such a struggle without major sacrifice of dignity and essential values.
The original purpose became clouded, then lost. So too with the second
issue, affirmative action. By instituting a system of preferences for employment consideration or admission into professional schools, many
advocates of racial equality hoped to undo the wrongs inflicted and

perpetrated through centuries of discrimination. And many agreed that something needed to be done along this line to provide genuine opportunity for blacks to enter business and the professions. Yet once again the very context was so limited that it could not help but generate racial tension. Given a limited number of jobs or positions in school, the competition became not one centering on merit but on race. For every black person so blessed by affirmative action there came to be a white person who felt deprived of his birthright. The irony was that in a nation that needed more jobs for all people and in a nation that needed, specifically, more doctors, the resentment was not only unnecessary but the system that generated it even cruel.[22] Like quality of education, the development of an economy that functioned to meet people's needs need not threaten anyone. But the issue, as it always had been, was placed in such a narrowed and artificial context that racial conflict proved inevitable.

Much of the problem rests in the fact that the solution to the tensions evident in American race relations defies a traditional institutional focus and cure. At best such an approach could trade one set of problems for another. At worst it could exacerbate the very tensions it purports to assuage. In either case it will miss the fundamental problem and likely forestall any focused debate on that issue that could produce meaningful results. The origins of modern American race relations, after all, lie in a social structure that is itself founded upon a scarcity consciousness which demands a competitive struggle for the determination of material rewards, social status, and even individual dignity, and in the efforts of the masses of American people to cope with such a system, resisting it in ways that might be noble and direct or mean, ugly, and indirect throughout its centuries of growth in this country. When this issue has been reduced and narrowed to a struggle in race relations, it has involved repeated irony as efforts to solve the problem of racial inequality have often made the solution a more remote possibility; as efforts to deny liberty to one group have meant the forging of chains for the oppressors; as efforts to liberate black people have meant the denial of the legitimacy of black culture; as whites have imputed to blacks the cultural qualities they most yearn for themselves and then oppress them for it; as blacks, in order to secure freedom, have sacrificed pride; and as a nation committed in its founding documents to freedom and justice for all has persisted in denying it for most. It also has involved a certain tragedy. The central issue surrounding the purpose of organized society and the distribution of power and dispensation of justice in the nation as a broad social issue and not as a narrowly defined racial issue has been persistently clouded and its public perception undermined and deflected into narrower channels in order to avoid a confrontation over the heart of the problem. For it is in the perception of that issue that it becomes apparent that greater freedom for others need come as a threat to no one. So long as people fear that greater freedom and justice for others mean an automatic loss for themselves, so long will those same people remain unfree. When the issue is perceived, in many respects it is resolved.

Notes

1. This approach to the analysis of social and cultural issues that are broadly political in their implication rests in part on the formulations found in Raymond Williams, *The Long Revolution* (New York, 1961), pp. 48-71; Raymond Williams, *Culture and Society 1780-1950* (New York, 1958); E. P. Thompson "Anthropology and the Discipline of Historical Context," *Midland History*, 1 (Spring 1972): 41-55; Anthony F.C. Wallace, "Revitalization Movements," *American Anthropologist*, 58 (April 1956): 264-81; and Karl Polanyi, *The Great Transformation* (Boston, 1957).

2. Two analyses of this conceptualization of the market that have been especially provocative are C. B. Macpherson, *The Political Theory of Possessive Individualism: Hobbes to Locke* (New York, 1962), and James Willard Hurst, *Law and the Conditions of Freedom in the Nineteenth-Century United States* (Madison, Wis., 1956).

3. In addition to the various formulations of the significance of the Civil War see especially Barrington Moore, Jr., *Social Origins of Dictatorship and Democracy: Lord and Peasant in the Making of the Modern World* (Boston, 1966), pp. 111-55.

4. Anthony F. C. Wallace's discussion of similar forms of social action provides a valuable conceptualization of the phenomena; Wallace, "Revitalization Movements."

5. Lawrence Levine, *Black Culture and Black Consciousness* (New York, 1977), pp. 136-55.

6. Joel Williamson, *After Slavery: The Negro in South Carolina During Reconstruction 1861-1877* (Chapel Hill, 1965), pp. 164-75, contains a cogent discussion of the initial steps in the change in agriculture.

7. Williamson, *After Slavery*, pp. 180-208.

8. Herbert G. Gutman, "The Negro and the United Mine Workers of America: The Career and Letters of Richard L. Davis and Something of Their Meaning: 1890-1900," reprinted in Gutman, *Work, Culture, and Society in Industrializing America: Essays in American Working-Class and Social History* (New York, 1976).

9. Frantz Fanon, *The Wretched of the Earth* (New York, 1963), pp. 93-95; J. Glenn Gray, "Understanding Violence Philosophically," in *On Understanding Violence Philosophically and Other Essays* (New York, 1970). This problem is discussed further in the headnote to Document 11. While George M. Frederickson, *The Black Image in the White Mind: The Debate on Afro-American Character and Destiny, 1917-1941* (New York, 1971), and C. Vann Woodward, *American Counterpoint: Slavery and Racism in the North-South Dialogue* (Boston, 1971), pp. 243-46, approach this problem in their use of Pierre L. van den Berghe's notion of "*Herrenvolk* democracy," they emphasize the importance of competition between black and white instead of the emergence of a competitive, market society which dislocates both.

10. Levine, *Black Culture and Black Consciousness*, pp. 190-217.

11. William M. Tuttle, Jr., *Race Riot: Chicago in the Red Summer of 1919* (New York, 1970); Elliott Rudwick, *Race Riot at East St. Louis July 2, 1917* (Carbondale, Ill., 1964).

12. See, again, Wallace's formulation of "Revitalization Movements," and also Richard Hofstadter's intriguing but sketchy discussion of the Ku Klux Klan in Hofstadter, *The Age of Reform: From Bryan to F. D. R.* (New York, 1955), pp. 293-97.

13. On this see especially Gilbert Osofsky, *Harlem: The Making of a Ghetto: Negro New York, 1930-1980*, 2d ed. (New York, 1971), which presents a penetrating analysis fusing social, economic, and cultural developments using Harlem as a way of focusing large historical questions; Levine, *Black Culture and Black Consciousness*, pp. 217-97; and LeRoi Jones (Imamu Amiri Baraka), *Blues People: Negro Music in White America* (New York, 1963).

14. The larger framework for this phenomenon obviously includes more than black people; indeed, it helps one understand the basic trends in modern American culture and society. See Erich Fromm's contemporary analysis of the problem of social abnegation in Fromm, *Escape from Freedom* (New York, 1941).

15. William H. Whyte, *The Organization Man* (New York, 1956); David Riesman *et al.*, *The Lonely Crowd: A Study of the Changing American Character* (New Haven, 1950); C. Wright Mills, *White Collar: The American Middle Classes* (New York, 1951); Herbert Marcuse, *One-Dimensional Man: Studies in the Ideology of Advanced Industrial Society* (Boston, 1964).

16. Theodore Lowi, *The End of Liberalism: Ideology, Policy, and the Crisis of Public Authority* (New York, 1969); Sar Levitan, *The Great Society's Poor Law* (Baltimore, 1969); Richard A. Cloward and Frances Fox Piven, "The Urban Crisis and the Consolidation of National Power," *Proceedings of The Academy of Political Science*, 29 (1968): 159-68.

17. Jerry Farber, "The Student as Nigger," in Farber, *The Student as Nigger: Essays and Stories* (New York, 1969). The theoretical and practical contours of this revolt and the alliances and tensions within it can be gleaned most readily from the pages of *Ramparts* magazine in the late 1960s and early 1970s.

18. Symptomatic of this phenomenon would be the effort of some black leaders like Congressman John Conyers of Detroit and Mayor Maynard Jackson of Atlanta to secure the abolition (or rigid control) of civilian use of handguns in an effort to deter crime, which is especially endemic in the black community. The main historical precedents for such controls can be found first in the attempts of the Ku Klux Klan after the Civil War to disarm blacks and in the efforts of the corporations at the end of the nineteenth and the beginning of the twentieth century to disarm workers (having their greatest success in New York's Sullivan Law). The question, though, is not so much that of historical precedent but partly that of the right of people in high crime areas to defend themselves and partly that of the creation of a greater dependency on the agencies of the state for protection, ineffective though they be.

19. See the political and economic critique of this process from the perspective of one who had been involved in central aspects of its evolution: Fred R. Harris, *The New Populism* (New York, 1973).

20. While Christopher Lasch would dissent from aspects of this discussion,

his treatment of the problem of social control through the therapy of the family provides perhaps the most subtle inquiry into the general issue available; in particular see his discussion of the Moynihan Report on the black family. Lasch, *Haven in a Heartless World: The Family Besieged* (New York, 1977), pp. 157-66.

21. Again, the long-range process involved in the loss of individual responsibility and then the development of narcissistic or "irresponsible" patterns of behavior by those people has received its most sensitive and sustained analysis by Christopher Lasch. Lasch, *The Culture of Narcissism: American Life in an Age of Diminishing Expectations* (New York, 1979).

22. See the editorial on the *Bakke* decision in *The Progressive*, September 1978, pp. 7-8: "Until we change the context in which we address the issues of inequality in this country, we can expect such muddled decisions as *Bakke* and a multitude of suits asking how much affirmative action is enough. A Supreme Court decision that approves of affirmative action programs only up to a point misses the point altogether and, by accepting the pitting of minority groups against each other and against poor whites, leaves the civil rights cause in disarray."

I

The Market and the Conditions of Freedom

1   The Burden of Teaching Freedom's Ways

In the following extract from the diary of Laura M. Towne, one of a number of anti-slavery advocates who went into the Union-occupied sea islands of South Carolina to work with the freed slaves, the difficulties of teaching proper habits of agriculture and economics are developed. There were, no doubt, great difficulties involved in teaching the freedmen that they were no longer to allow *any masters* to claim them at the same time that they begged those now in authority over them for the privilege of growing corn, something practical and edible, instead of cotton, something marketable. The logic of the system of production for the market rather than for subsistence and of being paid on account and then having to pay high prices for the goods made of the cotton no doubt struck many of the former slaves as strange if not thoroughly tainted. Yet this was definitely more than an economic endeavor, for the economics were yet again bound up in a larger pattern of civilization that stressed discipline and reserve and work. Their own religion, nurtured for generations in the slave quarters, was as incomprehensible to women like Laura Towne as was the Yankee religion to the blacks. It was no exaggeration from either perspective when the one black man rose to say, "The Yankees preach nothing but cotton, cotton," and when Towne herself described the religious shout as "savage" and "a regular frolic." A conception of freedom that included both the material and spiritual world was evident time and again and was dominated in both areas by a spirit of productivity and discipline, by the subordination of other freedoms to the demands of the market and indeed to a market definition of man.

Source: Rupert S. Holland, ed., *Letters and Diary of Laura M. Towne Written from the Sea Islands of South Carolina 1862-1884* (Cambridge, Mass., 1912), pp. 18-20.

The blessed soldiers, with all their wrong doing, did this one good thing—they assured the negroes that they were free and must never again let their masters claim them, nor any masters. I think it is very touching to hear them begging Mr. Pierce to let them cultivate corn instead of cotton, of which they do not see the use, since they worked it last year for pay which has not come yet, while their corn has saved them from starvation. Next week they are to be paid a dollar an acre for cotton they have planted under Mr. Pierce. They do not understand being paid on account, and they think one dollar an acre for ploughing, listing, or furrowing and planting is very little, which of course it is. Mr. P. wants to make it their interest to tend the cotton after it is planted, and so he pays on it just as little as he can, until it is all ready for the market. Meanwhile, if the masters drive us off, no return will ever be made for their work, to the people who are planting for us. Nothing is paid for the cultivation of the corn, and yet it will be Government property. The negroes are so willing to work on that, that Mr. P. has made it a rule that till a certain quantity of cotton is planted they shall not hoe the corn. This they take as a great hardship, for the corn wants hoeing. Several boxes of clothing have lately come here for distribution, and from early morning till evening the negroes are flocking here to buy. I do not like the prices fixed on the goods at all. They are in some cases higher a good deal than the retail Philadelphia prices.

* * *

The church was in the midst of splendid live-oak trees hanging with moss, and the services were impressive only because they were so unusual, especially the singing. The garments seen today were beyond all description. One man had a carpet, made like a poncho, and he stalked about in such grandeur. There was an old woman there who came from Africa in a steamship. Her face was tattooed a little. Mr. Horton, who was one of our fellow passengers on the Oriental, a Baptist minister, preached a sermon upon true freedom, and I think the negroes liked it. We heard of one old negro who got up in meeting, when one of the young superintendents was leading the services, and said, "The Yankees preach nothing but cotton, cotton." The fact is that every man has thought it his duty to inculcate the necessity of continuing to work, and the negro can see plainly enough that the proceeds of the cotton will never get into black pockets—judging from past experience.

Tonight I have been to a "shout," which seems to me certainly the remains of some old idol worship. The negroes sing a kind of chorus,—three standing apart to lead and clap,—and then all the others go shuffling round in a circle following one another with not much regularity, turning round occasionally and bending the knees, and stamping so that the whole floor swings. I never saw anything so savage. They call it a religious ceremony, but it seems more like a regular frolic to me, and instead of attending the shout, the better persons go to the "Praise House." This is always the cabin of the oldest person in the little village of negro houses, and they meet there to read and pray; generally one of the ladies goes there to read to them and they pray.

2 The Catechism of Citizenship

Edward L. Pierce, another of those who went to the sea islands to teach and organize the freedmen, described some of his frustrations and successes in 1863 in the *Atlantic Monthly*. Familiar themes and issues of cultural contact emerge yet again, but Pierce takes pride in the successes of the efforts undertaken to inculcate proper ideas and habits. Again, the content of the values taught and the lessons prescribed focused largely upon productivity, as the catechism he employed in his examination of school children demonstrated. After that experience he had no doubt about the ability of this race to "acquire with maturity of years the ideas and habits of good citizens." So important was this teaching mission that school itself sometimes interfered with the real substance of what was being taught; it was not to be allowed "to interfere in any way with industrious habits." Thus the school children went into the fields, a task more important than those associated with the schoolhouse. Perhaps Pierce's greatest pride was evident in his proclaimed success that these people had inculcated acquisitive habits of ownership and desires for material comforts that would both generate and be served by a market system. In those habits they had finally recognized the difference between slavery and wage-labor, although the precise difference is never made entirely clear by Pierce. One final duty and habit of citizenship enters the scene obliquely: the draft had taken the men and in that way permitted the women to learn the virtues of honest work by laboring in the fields.

Source: Edward L. Pierce, "The Freedmen at Port Royal," *Atlantic Monthly*, 12 (September 1863): 306-7, 308-9, 310-11.

Though I have never been on the school-committee, I accepted invitations to address the schools on these visits, and particularly plied the pupils with questions, so as to catch the tone of their minds; and I have rarely heard children answer with more readiness and spirit. We had a dialogue substantially as follows:—

"Children, what are you going to do when you grow up?"

"Going to work, Sir."

"On what?"

"Cotton and corn, Sir."

"What are you going to do with the corn?"

"Eat it."

"What are you going to do with the cotton?"

"Sell it."

"What are you going to do with the money you get for it?"

One boy answered in advance of the rest,—

"Put it in my pocket, Sir."

"That won't do. What's better than that?"

"Buy clothes, Sir."

"What else will you buy?"

"Shoes, Sir."

"What else are you going to do with your money?"

There was some hesitation at this point. Then the question was put,—

"What are you going to do Sundays?"

"Going to meeting."

"What are you going to do there?"

"Going to sing."

"What else?"

"Hear the parson."

"Who's going to pay him?"

One boy said,—"Government pays him"; but the rest answered,—"We pays him."

"Well, when you grow up, you'll probably get married, as other people do, and you'll have your little children; now, what will you do with them?"

There was a titter at this question; but the general response came,—

"Send'em to school, Sir."

"Well, who'll pay the teacher?"

"We's pays him."

One who listens to such answers can hardly think that there is any natural incapacity in these children to acquire with maturity of years the ideas and habits of good citizens.

The children are cheerful, and, in most of the schools, well-behaved, except that it is not easy to keep them from whispering and talking. They are joyous, and you can see the boys after school playing the soldier, with corn-stalks for guns. The memory is very susceptible in them,—too much so, perhaps, as it is ahead of the reasoning faculty.

The labor of the season has interrupted attendance on the schools, the parents being desirous of having the children aid them in planting and cultivating their crops, and it not being thought best to allow the teaching to interfere in any way with industrious habits.

* * *

Next as to *industry*. The laborers, during their first year under the new system, have acquired the idea of ownership, and of the security of wages, and have come to see that labor and slavery are not the same thing. The notion that they were to raise no more cotton has passed away, since work upon it is found to be remunerative, and connected with the proprietorship of land. House-servants, who were at first particularly set against it, now generally prefer it. The laborers have collected the pieces of the gins which they destroyed on the flight of their masters, the ginning being obnoxious work, repaired them, and ginned the cotton on the promise of wages. Except upon plantations in the vicinity of camps, where other labor is more immediately renumerative, and an unhealthy excitement prevails, there is a general disposition to cultivate it. The culture of the cotton is voluntary, the only penalty for not engaging in it being the imposition of a rent for the tenement and land adjacent thereto occupied by the negro, not exceeding two dollars per month. Both the Government and private individuals, who have become owners of one-fourth of the land by the recent tax-sales, pay twenty-five cents for a standard day's-work, which may, by beginning early, be performed by a healthy and active hand by noon; and the same was the case with the tasks under the slave-system on very many of the plantations.

* * *

The laborers do less work, perhaps, than a Yankee would think they might do, but they do about as much as he himself would do, after a residence of a few years in the same climate, and when he had ceased to work under the influence of Northern habits. Northern men have sometimes been unjust to the

South, when comparing the results of labor in the different sections. God never intended that a man should toil under a tropical sun with the same energy and constancy as in our bracing latitude. There has been less complaint this year than last of "a pain in the small of the back," or of "a fever in the head,"—in other words, less shamming. The work has been greatly deranged by the draft, some features of which have not been very skilfully arranged, and by the fitfulness with which the laborers have been treated by the military authorities. The work both upon the cotton and the corn is done only by the women, children, and disabled men. It has been suggested that field-work does not become women in the new condition; and so it may seem to some persons of just sympathies who have not yet learned that no honest work is dishonorable in man or woman. But this matter may be left to regulate itself. Field-work, as an occupation, may not be consistent with the finest feminine culture or the most complete womanliness; but it in no way conflicts with virtue, self-respect, and social development. Women work in the field in Switzerland the freest country of Europe; and we may look with pride on the triumphs of this generation, when the American negroes become the peers of the Swiss peasantry. Better a woman with the hoe than without it, when she is not yet fitted for the needle or the book.

* * *

Another evidence of developing manhood appears in their desire for the comforts and conveniences of household life. The Philadelphia society, for the purpose of maintaining reasonable prices, has a store on St. Helena Island, which is under the charge of Friend Hunn, of the good fellowship of William Penn. He was once fined in Delaware three thousand dollars for harboring and assisting fugitive slaves; but he now harbors and assists them at a much cheaper rate. Though belonging to a society which is the advocate of peace, his tone is quite as warlike as that of the world's people. In this store alone—and there are others on the island, carried on by private enterprise—two thousand dollars' worth of goods are sold monthly. To be sure, a rather large proportion of these consists of molasses and sugar, "sweetening," as the negroes call it, being in great demand, and four barrels of molasses having been sold the day of my visit. But there is also a great demand for plates, knives, forks, tin ware, and better clothing, including even hoopskirts. Negro-cloth, as it is called, osnaburgs, russet-colored shoes,—in short, the distinctive apparel formerly dealt out to them, as a uniform allowance,—are very generally rejected. But there is no article of household-furniture or wearing apparel, used by persons of moderate means among us, which they will not purchase, when they are allowed the opportunity of labor and earning wages. What a market the South would open under the new system! It would set all the mills and workshops astir. Four millions of people would become purchasers of all the various articles of manufacture and commerce, in place of the few coarse, simple necessaries, laid in for them in gross by the planters. Here is the solution of the vexed industrial question. The indisposition to labor is overcome in a healthy nature by instincts and motives of superior force, such as the love of life, the desire to be well clothed and fed, the sense of security derived from provision for the future, the feeling of self-respect, the love of family and children, and the convictions of duty. These all exist in the negro, in a state of greater or less development. To give one or two examples. One man brought Captain Hooper seventy dollars in silver, to keep for him, which he had obtained from selling pigs and chickens,—thus providing for the future. Soldiers of Colonel Higginson's regiment, having confidence in the same officer, intrusted him, when they were paid off, with seven hundred dollars, to be transmitted by him to their wives, and this besides what they had sent home in other ways,—showing the family-feeling to be active and strong in them. They have also the social and religious inspirations to labor. Thus, early in our occupation of Hilton Head, they took up, of their own accord, a collection to pay for the candles for their evening meetings, feeling that it was not right for the Government longer to provide them. The result was a contribution of two dollars and forty-eight cents. They had just fled from their masters, and had received only a small pittance of wages, and this little sum was not unlike the two mites which the widow cast into the treasury. Another collection was taken, last June, in the church on St. Helena Island, upon the suggestion of the pastor that they should share in the expenses of worship. Fifty-two dollars was the result,—not a bad collection for some of our Northern churches. I have seen these people where they are said to be lowest, and sad indeed are some features of their lot, yet with all earnestness and confidence I enter my protest against the wicked satire of Carlyle.

Is there not here some solution of the question of prejudice or caste which has troubled so many good minds? When these people can no longer be used as slaves, men will try to see how they can make the most out of them as freemen. Your Irishman, who now works as a day-laborer, honestly thinks that he hates the negro; but when the war is over, he will have no objection to going South and selling him groceries and household-implements at fifty per cent advance on New York prices, or to hiring him to raise cotton for twenty-five or fifty cents a day. Our prejudices under any reasonable adjustment of the social system, readily accommodate themselves to our interests, even without much aid from the moral sentiments.

Let those who would study well this social question, or who in public trusts are charged with its solution, be most careful here. Every motive in the minds of these people, whether of instinct, desire, or duty, must be addressed. All the elements of human nature must be appealed to, physical, moral, intellectual, social, and religious. Imperfect indeed is any system which, like that at New Orleans, offers wages, but does not welcome the teacher. It is of little moment whether three dollars or thirty per month be paid the laborer, so long as there is no school to bind both parent and child to civil society with new hopes and duties.

3 Toward a New System

In the postwar South it was not inevitable that any specific system of organization of the economy and society would emerge. Yet a new system of agriculture emerged that focused upon the devices of the market-place: (1) the contract as the connection between workers and owners; (2) government officials serving as enforcers of the terms of the contract; (3) the withholding of payment for work until the crop was harvested, farm laborers being charged interest in the interim on the provisions they purchased. While the parties to the contract would change before too long to farm workers and commercial operators, the following letters make clear that in the years immediately following the war the owners of the land, though clearly beset by a lack of capital and a change in social relations, still commanded power over their plantations. Even so, the need for money through loans from Charleston indicates a dependence on a commercial class even at this point. Of course, it would then be the croppers at the bottom who payed the final interest on that money. And just as the first letter printed below carries with it the recurrent theme of a labor shortage, the observation is equally clear that only the doling out of rations by the government kept the freedmen from all going to the planters who were more capable of paying them. The rations were what seem to have saved at least these planters precisely because they averted the natural force of the market in labor. The labor situation itself is curious, though. Part of the shortage appears to have been due to the fact that the blacks were unacquisitive. They were content to plant but small patches; they were at best reluctant to contract. Part of that reluctance may have been due to the actual terms of the contract as spelled out in the letter. With the itemized deductions from their share the workers would do well to receive a third of the value of the crop that they planted and harvested. Of course out of that third would come their living expenses which, as the second letter confirms, were indeed exorbitant and wilfully applied to the blacks. Throughout, both letters reveal a changing social system in which the economics of the market increasingly determine the relations between the races in the most material sense. The new system of sharecropping is replacing that of slavery. The chief difference between the two systems appears ever so discreetly: the responsibility for the bottom-most place of the blacks in the system is the responsibility not of the system into which they were born but of their individual and collective laziness.

Source: William Elliott to his mother, March 25, 1866, and Mrs. (Hattie) A.J.G. to her mother, May 3, 1868, Elliott-Gonzales Papers, #1009, Southern Historical Collection, The University of North Carolina at Chapel Hill. Printed with the permission of the Director of the Southern Historical Collection.

"The Ruins" March 25th 66

My Dearest Mother

Your letter reached me in Charleston; too late, however, to undo what had already been done, for I had already contracted with the hands at Cheeka. To have asked your opinion first would have lost too much time.— I will briefly state the circumstances which you could not know or judge of at such a distance. lst I found it extremely hazardous to plant here, from cattle being every where. If kept out of the home field they would most certainly destroy town hill & the two Cypress fields. The poor people own them *and in spite of any law* cannot if they would inclose them for *want of the labor*. That they have no intention of attempting it even is indicated by their burning of all the pine barrens in the neighborhood. That Major King & Clement have no faith in their ability or intention to enclose them is shown by the fencing they are putting up. Now even with hands t'would be too late for me to make fences. But I have been unable to get them. One promised to come with two others & failed. When Dick came on the 15th, I sent Jacob on a mule to try & procure them. He failed. All the labor of the neighborhood except disbanded soldiers has been absorbed. Jacobs six or seven relatives have not appeared and he, I am compelled to think is indifferent in the matter. He wishes to squat on the place and have lions share of everything he may make. I offered him half of everything if with Rose he would plant 5 or 6 acres of Sea Island Cotton. He prefers planting two & having all the provisions he may make for himself—this in consideration of his past important services to the family. I told him I thought the obligation lay the other way. He is eaten up with self esteem & selfishness. He thinks it hard provisions are not to be advanced him. This I'll not make a stumbling block if funds are furnished. I say to him—"get two or three hands & you can plant the home field so your mistress have some income from the place." He insists they cannot be got. —"The place has no houses, no mill." Everybody of course has got the start of me by several weeks & by first supplying themselves with provisions attracted labor.

I was very loth to give up what I should have been proud to accomplish. I have sacrificed thereby comfort-convenience & inclination but it was no time to stand still. I must try Cheeka where the hands already were. Accordingly on Sunday last I rode over on mule back carrying Jacob. The Negroes were civil but would not come over having already planted their patches. They had also listed several Acres of Cotton land. I must therefore plant there or not at all. Now the idea that you would [receive] anything from their crop will vanish, when you know that the Bureau had issued them only two weeks rations—that rations were then ordered to be discontinued to all able bodied negroes, by the govmt—and the negroes were [receiving] a scanty & uncertain subsistence by working sometimes for people in the neighborhood. This labor then would not have been devoted to the "Bluff" but absorbed by the Rhetts & others capable of feeding them, and sadly in want of hands. They had no cotton seed & no money (as far as I could learn) to buy it. They meant to squat on patches. Would the Est get anything think you? I thought (as others tell me) there was a far *better* chance for a crop there even if the impossibility of getting hands for this place did not exist. Passing through Wm Mears. Lt. Rhett only was there & told me of the terms of contract adopted by the neighborhood. Well they give half the crop & advance the provisions, the percentage charged the negroes on which is enormous. I spent a day and a half explaining to them the advantages of a contract. They objected to nothing but that they could not have Saturday. I put my foot down against that & sent for the Lieut at Corn bakes who sent a letter he desired I should read them & which stated he allowed no such squandering of time in any contract that "they must sign it "t'was best for them"&&. It had the desired effect—and your letter found me in Charleston getting corn implements (the last I could not get before) and *a loan* of $200 til 23d April from Willis & Chisolm, part of which I retain & the rest has been bestowed in a way to be accounted for. You have purchased the seed (tho it has not yet arrived) was I to throw it away? Nearly everybody here is planting Friff seed. Now the money for Oak Lawn would plant the Bluff with better results. Even with another mule the cost would scarcely be over $800,—I'd undertake it with $500. There is no danger of your having to part with Oak Lawn my dear mother. All this may be a great error or folly on my part but it is too late to recede. To go backward would be ruinous. Tis not so clear that the opposite course would. I've undergone great fatigue but no exposure & the change of air has much benefitted my cough. My plan is not fully developed as yet but I expect to be there during April—until the crop is sown. I may then return to Adams Run for the summer—going over once a fortnight & making Johnson (negro with the pleasant countenance) the foreman—report to me here every other week. Or if neighbours are found Chisolmville may do for part of the summer. Dick left this morning with wagon and provisions & I go by train far as Ashepo [?] Ferry on Tuesday. There are many Neighbours at the Bluff all planting & no cattle near—land looks fresh—not requiring manure or very little-some could be planted today if the seed had come. The gang eleven & expecting two more—small but prime. I'll turn over Myrtle Bank to the Est before you shall lose Oak Lawn. Dick will put me up a shantie over there. I consulted with that ingenious mechanic about this outhouse—and agreed with him that for $150.00 it could be put in excellent order. The upper rooms are quite comfortable & both stories have good fireplaces. Now with repairs of Boards paint & papering and thorough refitting & cleaning it would be good enough for a small white family to live in

twice as good as Balls used to be. This in case there were not time or means to
build a cottage next winter. I will do what I can to make a crop for that end,
feeling an interest in the place & being very grateful for your and my sisters
kindness to me & wish Gods blessing I may succeed. I expect to make 4 bags
to the hand which at 20 cts will give 44 bales multiplied by 80 = $3250. Divide
by two = $1760, half the crop. Now at least $230 will come out of the other half
from percentage, sickness, paying for 1/2 mule feed, injury to tools & & all
deducted from their share. You have there $2000, clear—added to prime cost
of provisions of course much more from the lowest probable price next year. I
beg then if you get the loan you will help instead of blaming me. Everybody is
at work and more despondent. I've done what I believe best for your interests—
I would not see you dependent without a cent of income from three (4) plantations.
Others perhaps may see their interest in this and take an especial pleasure in
seeing the tables turned & prey upon your necessities. Humiliating twould be
to be assisted now—far deeper & more grinding another year.———

Social Hall May 3d [1868]

Dearest Mama

* * *

We are not quite as energetic as you are & seldom finish breakfast before half
past seven—but then we are busy quite late every evening, hands coming for
rations & buying provisions, all the workman at the farm but one are paid in
provisions or cloth—I determine the prices of the last—the Gen thinks I am too
exorbitant but I tell him I *am sure* the nigs do not do 'full work'—a piece of nice
blue check which cost 22 cts by the piece, your Jewess' of a daughter gets 60
cts for—& the freedmen get 12 yds at a time—& I have now a box of assorted
candy to tempt them—but as these articles are paid for in work of course my
satisfaction at getting high prices is greatly diminished. Dont imagine that I
allow my children to be with negroes out of my presence—on one occasion only
have they been so with my knowledge—I was too glad to get the boys out of
Charleston—the boys there are so profane & vulgar— Good by dear Mama

Hattie

4 Steps toward Segregation

While a distinctive system of production was emerging in the postwar South, so too were social relations in the process of change in a variety of areas of activity. The courses taken at this early moment of opportunity could be especially revealing of the origins of habits of race relations that would become entrenched in custom and that later would often be written into law. It has been noted that the races in the "free" North had been frequently separated before the Civil War; likewise the proximity of the races, albeit with no pretense of equality, appears to have been the dominant pattern in the South. The logic of the choices made in this moment of determination is often a curious one, at least to the sensibilities of modern generations accustomed to the rantings of apartheid advocates here and around the world. The following item is a case in point. This history of the Presbyterian Church in South Carolina notes that church officials after the Civil War attempted to halt the flight of blacks from the church. While blacks composed about half the membership, they "were almost entirely dependent on our people for moral advancement and spiritual culture." On the part of the blacks, "the Gospel was offered them but they declined it as coming from us." In their effort to keep the freedmen in the congregation the whites were attempting in an honest and explicit way to exercise a form of social control which they recalled from days of slavery. The blacks initiated separatism, in this area, precisely to avoid that social control. While the move may not have struck a blow for racial equality, it did repudiate paternalism in spite of the good intention in which it was clothed.

Source: F. D. Jones and W. H. Mills, eds., *History of the Presbyterian Church in South Carolina Since 1850* (Columbia, S.C., 1926), pp. 119-23.

Harmony Presbytery in October, 1865, sent to the General Assembly a memorial as to the duty of maintaining and perpetuating our present ecclesiastical organization. Some were ready to conclude that as the political bonds which formerly bound the South and North together were being reestablished, so the ecclesiastical bonds which had been severed should also be restored. But this was regarded as an unwarranted deduction.

One reunion was to be regarded as brought about by the providence of God, while the same providence stood directly in the way of the other reunion. The memorial recounts the actions of the Northern General Assembly in receiving private members. That Assembly was charged not only with excommunicating us from fellowship but with inaugurating measures which aimed at our overthrow, as a Christian Church. Another ground of complaint was found in the legislation of the Northern Church in regard to political matters. The best thing to be done was to stand in our lot, feeling assured that God would never forsake us. A very fine and earnest pastoral letter was issued by the Presbytery to its own churches. The difficulties of the situation were set forth, the desolating effects of war, the loss of members, the infidelity and immorality which threatened to invade us. Personal religion was to be guarded, the Church of God to be cared for, reclaiming the wandering, encouraging the doubting, supporting the feeble, stimulating attendance. The claim of the ministry for a support was to be urged and feeble churches and missionary stations were to be strengthened. The colored members, now intoxicated with their first experience of liberty, were to be dealt with gently, forbearingly and patiently. "Let us remember their infirmities and not be too hasty." The *Narrative* presented a report in which the shadows prevailed. Preaching had been regular, but the attendance had been interfered with by the ravages of war, the falling off of the colored members had been considerable. "The reaction from the restraints and excitement of war shows itself in some by the inactivity of despair, others resort to dishonest gains, while others seek relief in the frivolities and dissipations of the world." There was a call for liberality on the part of churches in supporting the ministers and a call for self-denial on the part of the latter. The *Narratives* of this period were written largely in Biblical language, and made free use of Biblical figures. This one concludes, "Finally, brethren, all that remains for us is to go down into the swelling of the floods of this Jordan, bearing the ark of Jehovah's covenant; doubtless we shall pass over and possess the fair land of our inheritance."

The Presbytery resolved that notwithstanding the change in the social and political condition of our colored people, "we regard our obligations to impart to them the blessings of the Gospel as unimpaired, and enjoin on ministers and churches to continue to instruct them by preaching, catechetical teaching, and all other means of improving their spiritual condition." About one-half the membership in the churches of this Presbytery was then composed of negroes, who were almost entirely dependent on our people for moral advancement and spiritual culture.

The churches were urged to impress upon the colored people that their obligations to God and the Church were not weakened by the change in their civil relations, that this change laid them under greater obligation to contribute to the support of the ministry. Their marriages were to be celebrated by regularly ordained ministers, and "Christian parents were to remember their duty to consecrate their infant children to God in baptism." The treasurer of Presbytery was to be freed from any obligations to pay out funds received in Confederate money, which had now become worthless. A good deal of calculation was necessary to adjust the debts incurred by the Presbytery to its evangelists and home missionaries, in accordance with the change of currency. The current "greenbacks" varied so much in value, owing to the high cost of gold, that the amount due in United States currency had to be ascertained.

The *Narrative* for October, 1868, was more hopeful. "The cloud is beginning to pass away." Worldly-mindedness and love of gain are still prevalent but some churches had been revived, and conversions had been made. A severe drought had cut off supplies. Some pastors, both old and young, had been removed or laid aside by illness and in the financial straits of the period, the support of the latter class was precarious. Attention had been given to the "Freedmen," a new term in phraseology! They were manifesting some disposition to return to our communion, after a temporary alienation from us. Several mission stations had been established for their benefit, and it was hoped that a regular missionary for them might be employed.*

The Home Mission report mentioned the various stations which had been established for the Freedmen, six in all, supplied usually by the nearest white pastors and having an attendance of from eighty to one hundred and fifty persons. At these stations, some white people had also attended, such as had rarely gone to any place of worship.

Three of these stations were afterwards given up to the colored people. "They were too unsettled, politically and religiously, to inaugurate any permanent plan of religious instruction among them, separate from the old plan. The pastors must still do all they can in the midst of manifold discouragements." The anomalous condition in which these people find themselves, the inducements held out to them to tear them away from their former relations by designing emissaries from abroad and designing persons at home make the fact that they are conducting themselves with any prudence or propriety at all more surprising than the excesses into which they have run. We can never forget the time when they crowded to our sanctuaries, when they listened to the Gospel as preached to their owners, and then to the additional discourse designed especially for themselves. We can never forget the communion table spread for master and servant; the bread and the wine administered to each by the same hand and from the same vessels and at the same table. These are all pleasant memories and they greatly comfort us amid the surrounding desolations, giving us the

---

*Probably no greater harm was done the Presbyterian Church than the loss of its influence over the colored people, arising from the estrangement and bitterness of the reconstruction period. It has been shown how conscientiously and affectionately the religious interests of the negroes had been looked after, and what testimonials were given as to their consistent lives. Politics came in to separate the races, to break up forever the old tie of personal affection between master and servant, to substitute a hireling spirit and a bitter prejudice, the results of which are still felt, after fifty years.— THE AUTHOR.

assurance that we had attempted to do something for this unfortunate race in their highest interests.

In October, 1867, the Presbytery had thirty-two ministers, thirty-nine churches, three licentiates, seven candidates, and 3,276 communicants. There had been received on profession 333, and by letter 45. To foreign missions had been given $541; to home missions, $591; to education, $426.

The *Narrative* for April, 1868, reported nothing very encouraging. Some pastors had been supported, others had been compelled to seek other fields of labor. Little had been done for the instruction of the colored people. Only one preaching station was now open for them. "The Gospel was offered them but they declined it as coming from us. They have turned to other teachers, and for the most part, to such of their own class as are utterly ignorant, some of them not being able even to read God's Word. When the blind leads the blind, the result is inevitable. We ought to be sure, however, that we leave no opening unoccupied, no proper means untried to gain access to them with the Gospel."

5   "By Their Fruits Ye Shall Know Them"

Black people themselves were not unified in religious sentiments. In 1878 Bishop Daniel Alexander Payne of the African Methodist Episcopal Church noted the prevalence of forms of worship that deeply offended his religious sensibilities. In many ways this is the same conflict between the form of worship practiced in the slave quarters and the religious habits characterized by restraint and solemnity urged upon blacks by whites. The significance of the competition may be seen first in the persistence of long held religious customs that were less than orthodox. But by the last quarter of the nineteenth century the division in the religious forum may signal the strains placed upon the black community, and even a fragmentation or at least a split in that community. One side, represented by people like Bishop Payne, may have viewed itself to be, as he put it, "the most thoughtful and intelligent," but was characterized more by the acceptance of a narrow orthodoxy that emphasized discipline and restraint. The other side, deriving possibly from Africa, even to the point of being associated with voodoo, focused upon salvation (through the rings) and an emotional excitement that, as Payne tersely observed, left them "unfit for labor" the following day. The religious issue involved far more than worshipping beside whites; it indeed followed the same dialectic as the issue of freedom.

Source: Bishop Daniel Alexander Payne, *Recollections of Seventy Years* (Nashville, 1888), pp. 253-57.

In May it was my privilege to visit the Sunday-school of Old Bethel, in Philadelphia, and at a meeting of the Sunday-school teachers I conducted responsive reading of the First and Second Psalms of David. I showed them how England had become great by habitually making her people read the Scriptures on Sunday in the great congregation; and how the colored race, who had been oppressed for centuries through ignorance and superstition, might become intelligent, Christian, and powerful through the enlightening and sanctifying influences of the word of God. I also stated that thereafter, by my orders, every pastor occupying the pulpit of Bethel should make responsive readings of the Holy Scriptures a part of the public worship. Bethel Church about this time had set about furnishing the music-room at our university, which they completed by June.

I have mentioned the "Praying and Singing Bands" elsewhere. The strange delusion that many ignorant but well-meaning people labor under leads me to speak particularly of them. About this time I attended a "bush meeting," where I went to please the pastor whose circuit I was visiting. After the sermon they formed a ring, and with coats off sung, clapped their hands and stamped their feet in a most ridiculous and heathenish way. I requested the pastor to go and stop their dancing. At his request they stopped their dancing and clapping of hands, but remained singing and rocking their bodies to and fro. This they did for about fifteen minutes. I then went, and taking their leader by the arm requested him to desist and to sit down and sing in a rational manner. I told him also that it was a heathenish way to worship and disgraceful to themselves, the race, and the Christian name. In that instance they broke up their ring; but would not sit down, and walked sullenly away. After the sermon in the afternoon, having another opportunity of speaking alone to this young leader of the singing and clapping ring, he said: "Sinners won't get converted unless there is a ring." Said I: "You might sing till you fell down dead, and you would fail to convert a single sinner, because nothing but the Spirit of God and the word of God can convert sinners." He replied: "The Spirit of God works upon people in different ways. At camp-meeting there must be a ring here, a ring there, a ring over yonder, or sinners will not get converted." This was his idea, and it is also that of many others. These "Bands" I have had to encounter in many places, and, as I have stated in regard to my early labors in Baltimore, I have been strongly censured because of my efforts to change the mode of worship or modify the extravagances indulged in by the people. In some cases all that I could do was to teach and preach the right, fit, and proper way of serving God. To the most thoughtful and intelligent I usually succeeded in making the "Band" disgusting; but by the ignorant masses, as in the case mentioned, it was regarded as the essence of religion. So much so was this the case that, like this man, they believed no conversion could occur without their agency, nor outside of their own ring could any be a genuine one. Among some of the songs of these "Rings," or "Fist and Heel Worshipers," as they have been called, I find a note of two in my journal, which were used in the instance mentioned. As will be seen, they consisted chiefly of what are known as "corn-field ditties:"

"Ashes to ashes, dust to dust;
If God won't have us, the devil must.
"I was way over there where the coffin fell;
I heard that sinner as he screamed in hell."

To indulge in such songs from eight to ten and half-past ten at night was the chief employment of these "Bands." Prayer was only a secondary thing, and this was rude and extravagant to the last degree. The man who had the most powerful pair of lungs was the one who made the best prayer, and he could be heard a square off. He who could sing loudest and longest led the "Band," having his loins girded and a hankerchief in hand with which he kept time, while his feet resounded on the floor like the drumsticks of a bass drum. In some places it was the custom to begin these dances after every night service and keep it up till midnight, sometimes singing and dancing alternately—a short prayer and a long dance. Some one has even called it the "Voudoo Dance." I have remonstrated with a number of pastors for permitting these practices, which vary somewhat in different localities, but have been invariably met with the response that he could not succeed in restraining them, and an attempt to compel them to cease would simply drive them away from our Church. I suppose that with the most stupid and headstrong it is an incurable religious disease, but it is with me a question whether it would not be better to let such people go out of the Church than remain in it to perpetuate their evil practice and thus do two things: disgrace the Christian name and corrupt others. Any one who knows human nature must infer the result after such midnight practices to be that the day after they are unfit for labor, and that at the end of the dance their exhaustion would render them an easy prey to Satan. These meetings must always be more damaging physically, morally, and religiously than beneficial. How needful it is to have an intelligent ministry to teach these people who hold to this ignorant mode of worship the true method of serving God. And my observations lead me to the conclusion that we need more than an intelligent ministry to cure this religious fanaticism. We need a host of Christian reformers like St. Paul, who will not only speak against these evils, but who will also resist them, even if excommunication be necessary. The time is at hand when the ministry of the A.M.E. Church must drive out this heathenish mode of worship or drive out all the intelligence, refinement, and practical Christians who may be in her bosom.

So far from being in harmony with the religion of the Lord Jesus Christ, it antagonizes his holy religion. And what is most deplorable, some of our most popular and powerful preachers labor systematically to perpetuate this fanaticism. Such preachers never rest till they create an excitement that consists in shouting, jumping, and dancing. I say systematically do they preach to produce such results, and just as systematically do they avoid the trial of persons accused of swindling, drunkenness, embezzling, and the different forms of adultery. I deliberately record that which I know, and am prepared if necessary to prove.

To these sensational and recreant preachers I recommend the careful and prayerful study of the text: "To the unknown God, whom ye ignorantly worship, him declare I unto you." (Acts xvii. 23.) The preachers against whom I make this record are intensely religious, but grossly immoral. "By their fruits ye shall know them."

6
Early Integration: An Uneasy Truce

While federal law until 1883 prohibited racial discrimination in public accommodations, the pattern of acceptance, resistance, and enforcement is far from clear in the postwar South. The following account of a trip on a steamship from Charleston to Beaufort, South Carolina, indicates the difficulty in generalizing about the openness of race relations, or for that matter, the rapid emergence of segregation. While blacks and whites were both present on this trip, ways could be found to subvert the spirit of equal treatment if sufficiently desired. And in such an apprehensive atmosphere ways could be found to interpret any action—or inaction—as hostile. Most likely the closest appreciation of the situation could be found in Elizabeth Hyde Botume's summary comment: "We seemed to be living over a volcano." And possibly the issue was one that could be resolved only at each point it was raised. Precedents abounded for either course.

Source: Elizabeth Hyde Botume, *First Days Amongst the Contrabands* (Boston, 1893), pp. 267-69.

As we were returning South in the fall of 1868, we heard disheartening stories about the freedmen. We were told in Washington they were becoming usurpers. They realized their power, and began to feel they could do without white influence. It was said they had taken the entire direction of their schools, putting into office colored trustees and a colored superintendent, and they had removed several white teachers and put inefficient colored teachers in their places.

Miss Amy Bradley, who was giving her life to help the "poor whites" in Wilmington, N.C., spoke to us of the arrogant assumption of the negroes around her as a serious evil.

In Charleston we heard of riots in different parts of the State, excited certainly by what Governor Andrew had already predicted, the unwillingness of the old slave-holders to recognize free labor. We feared there was a growing hostility between the two races, *as races*.

We took a small steamer from Charleston for Beaufort. Here we found a decided change since we went North. Then no colored person was allowed on the upper deck, now there were no restrictions,—there could be none, for a law had been passed in favor of the negroes. They were everywhere, choosing the best staterooms and best seats at the table. Two prominent colored members of the State Legislature were on board with their families. There were also several well-known Southerners, still uncompromising rebels. It was a curious scene and full of significance. An interesting study to watch the exultant faces of the negroes, and the scowling faces of the rebels,—rebels still against manifest destiny and the new dispensation. Until now we had but little understood these portentous changes, the meaning of which we must study out for ourselves.

We were summoned to dinner. When we reached the table we found there only colored people occupying more than half the seats on each side. They were doing the honors with something of an air that said, "Receive this from me or go without." In all respects, however, they were courteous and attentive. There was no loud talking or laughing.

The stewardess came behind us, and leaning over whispered we had better wait a little, as they were obliged to give the colored passengers the first table. The white passengers would come to the second. We thanked her, but preferred to keep our seats. A few Northerners joined us. One, who we know had been a first-class Democrat, and "down on the niggers," was obliged to leave us and sit next to a man as black as ink. He swallowed his prejudices and took his seat, and fraternized with his neighbor to the best of his ability; besides, it was no longer a question of inclination, it was business. This was the point in which our fears were most aroused. The freedmen, no longer slaves, were fast becoming tools.

The negro who sat not far from me was an immense fellow, seemingly an iron man, with powerful physique and indomitable will. He had made an incendiary speech in July, telling his people this was their government, and they no longer needed or had any use for white people. All the morning he had walked around scanning and apparently marking the passengers. His looks seemed to say, "If you are with us, well and good; if not, stand back." Whilst the scowling faces and muttered words of the Southerners implied, "If you stand back, well and good; if you fraternize with the niggers, be —."

The little group of Northerners noted and translated what they saw. Each one watched his neighbor. I now understood why we were so frequently asked in Charleston if we were not afraid to return to Beaufort just now. Some friends had earnestly urged us to wait until after election on Tuesday, but that was the time we wanted to be with the people in our own district. We had no fears for ourselves, but grave apprehensions for our friends. These were exciting times. We seemed to be living over a volcano.

7 Early Integration: An Amicable Conflict

While sometimes potentially explosive relations emerged where integration was the rule, so too could sometimes friendly relations emerge where segregation was the rule. In the following document a black man joins whites on a railroad car which is by rule separate. In the very form of the encounter a pattern of race relations in the Gilded Age again proves elusive. But in the substance of the report several related points emerge. One concerns the conflict between theory and practice on the railroad. While the stated policy was segregation by race in separate cars, the actuality appeared to be more a class division. So too in the theaters discussed: the policy was flexible, depending upon the specific circumstances. It is difficult to determine if the black traveler on the car at the beginning of the account is accepted because he is recognized or because of his education and attire. But furthermore, in the discussion of the two whites and the one black, a certain ritual appears to emerge, one that would come to dominate race relations among the most articulate elements of the nation. After stating their positions on the race question facing the nation with fair candor, the friendly discussion could have been on the verge of an abrupt termination or unfriendly confrontation as it drifted closer to the inevitable consideration of possible solutions to the problems facing black people. Deftly the black spokesman placed the responsibility for change not on his white adversaries but on the blacks themselves. To secure morality and education for his people was the main task. After having recited the injustices done to blacks with exceptional vigor and wit, this was a curious turn. In fact it would not be unreasonable to suggest that it was a turn against his own people by the terms of his own logic. Yet, there may be more to it than this. There is something to be said for the strategic, or in this case tactical, qualities evident in this traveler's demeanor and for the actual content of his argument. It may not have been such a turn against his own people after all. Just as August Meier in his *Negro Thought in America 1880-1915* has probed the ambiguities of the apparently accommodating philosophy of Booker T. Washington and found a complex array of hopes and commitments, so too may it be possible to inquire, or suggest, more in this particular incident. On one level obviously the black man's audience no doubt felt more comfortable when he turned his attention to the foibles and shortcomings of his own race. The burden appeared to have been taken from the backs of white people. But that same shifting of the burden served another purpose, one possibly less benign had his listeners perceived it. It was a thorough rejection of white paternalism and an assertion that blacks could and would make it by themselves—without the aid of the white man. They would not beg. It must still be recognized, however, that this approach undeniably carried the unfortunate consequence of confirming in the white mind the idea that the whites had no social responsibility for the fate of the blacks, and also the possible sacrifice of the present generation for the benefit of future generations. Even so, in this brief encounter between the races the black protagonist made one further point that was fraught with implications: "Gentlemen, you do not care if we are degraded and worthless; but it's bad for you, too, if the negro is a brute." In this it was true that he had a "comprehension of the subtle bonds that unite men in their moral destiny, and make the strong and fortunate in some ways dependent on the fate of the lowly," but was this a subtle appeal to their self interest or was it possibly even a veiled threat? Oppress the black man further only at your own risk. In either case it offered a recognition that there was indeed a limit to the autonomy and self-help that could be effectively developed by any subjugated people. But the ambiguity of the message, racial autonomy reconciled with accommodation to white values, institutions, and relations—those of the market and Social Darwinism at that—remains perhaps the intriguing puzzle of Gilded Age race relations.

Source: J. B. Harrison, "Studies in the South," *Atlantic Monthly*, 50 (November 1882): 625-27.

A negro came in, and was recognized by two gentlemen as having in his childhood belonged to some one whom they knew, and they bade him sit down and give an account of himself for the long time that had passed since their last meeting. They were all evidently glad to see each other, and the conversation that ensued evinced reciprocal regard and respect. One gentleman was a merchant from Nashville; the other I understood to be a physician from Mississippi. Both showed good manners, wide information, and much interest in public affairs. They appeared to be business men of high character, energetic and practical. They were democrats; the negro was a republican.

They soon launched broadly into a discussion of the whole question of the character, capabilities, and interests of the negro race in this country, and of the various problems growing out of the relations between the negroes and the white people. There was the utmost courtesy on both sides, but I was astonished at the ability and the boldness of the negro. He seemed to know and remember every political blunder and fault of the party in power in Alabama since its first organization after the war, and every instance of injustice done to the people of his race. Several times the gentlemen thought him in error regarding matters of fact, but he took a ponderous memorandum book out of his pocket, filled with newspaper cuttings, notes, and references, and showed in each case that he knew what he was talking about. For more than two hours there was such an exhibition of argument, wit, apt reply, and incisive repartee as I have rarely heard anywhere. There was great fairness and entire good humor all around. The two white men were evidently delighted with the ability shown by their antagonist, and when he was too strong for them they "owned up" heartily. He was nearly always too strong for them. He had evidently given most of the points discussed far more attention than they. I have scarcely ever heard his readiness of reply equaled. Both his opponents together were no match for him. As they concluded, he said, "Gentlemen, we give you notice that we intend to have our rights, all that the law gives us, and that we are going to fight for them—not with our hands, but with our mouths and our brains—till we obtain them. Sooner or later we shall have them, and you might as well understand it first as last."

Both gentlemen said, "That's right. We don't blame you. We like your spirit. Of course we would do the same in your place." Then one added, and the other expressed hearty assent and approval, "But I'll be damned if I'll ever sit down to the table with a nigger." The negro laughed, and taunted them with the far more intimate relations which white men frequently form with negro girls. All this talk was open and public. There were no ladies in the car, and the men gathered around to hear. The negro's account of the condition of his own race was very depressing, and he plainly felt that the chief obstacles in the way of their advancement were to be found, not in the opposition or injustices of the white people, but in the low qualities and tendencies of the negroes. He did not seem to be hopeful, but was full of spirit, and was plainly resolved to make a gallant fight for the improvement of his people, whatever the odds against him. In the course of the talk he described his efforts to put down vice and disorder among the colored people in the town where he lived. He had on a certain occasion organized and supervised a picnic for his own people, and when some vicious colored girls had intruded upon the company, he had forcibly expelled them from the grounds. They made a charge of assault and battery against him, and the affair cost him many hundreds of dollars. He confessed that he had violated the law in kicking and striking those disorderly women, but he had done so in protecting his own wife and daughters from insult and violence.

He thought that disorderly and licentious white men incited the baser class of the negroes to invade and disturb his picnic, and that even the good white people did not give him any sympathy or moral support in his efforts to maintain order and suppress vice among the colored people. Said he, "Gentlemen, you do not care if we are degraded and worthless; but it's bad for you, too, if the negro is a brute." His comprehension of the subtle bonds that unite men in their moral destiny, and make the strong and fortunate in some ways dependent on the fate of the lowly, would have delighted the heart of Carlyle. He said, "There are three hundred and sixty-two lewd colored girls in my town. It's a shame and a curse for us. Do you think it's nothin' for you?"

This negro seemed a born leader of men. He was fully alive to the faults and weaknesses of the negro character, and appeared to be less hopeful regarding the future of his race in this country than were his white antagonists; but he loves struggle and conflict, and will, no doubt, contend bravely to the end for what he regards as the rights of his people. I had some talk afterward with his friendly opponents. They spoke of him in terms of admiration, and said that he had the reputation of being one of the best public speakers in the State, and they had no doubt it was deserved. Then they added that if a hotel, theatre, or church, or any place of entertainment, amusement, or public resort in the South, should be conducted on the plan of really making no distinction on account of color or race, no white person of good character would attend it, or support it in any way whatever. This is doubtless true at present, in the main, at least.

Civil Rights

On most of the railroads in the South the negroes were expected and told to take a particular car in each train, and they usually did so, but the rule did not appear to be strictly enforced. (Indeed, I could not see that anything was done strictly in the South.) Well-dressed negroes sometimes traveled in the same car with "first-class" white people, ladies and gentlemen; and there were usually some white people, poor whites or working folk, in the negro car. In Norfolk, Virginia, the colored people were directed to a particular gallery or part of the house at all lectures or public entertainment, but I do not think they had been, of late, forcibly prevented from taking seats in the body of the house. In Richmond, Virginia, at the time of my visit to that city, two young colored men bought tickets for a public lecture, and attempted to enter the main audience room. The usher very courteously suggested that they would find seats in the gallery. They objected, and asked, "Do you forbid us to go into the best part of the hall?" "Not at all, gentlemen," he replied; "on the contrary, I call every one present to witness that I do not forbid you to go there. At the same time, I think you would better go into the gallery." Just then the manager of the lecture course came in, and the usher appealed to him. He smiled, and passed the negroes into the principal auditorium, and they took seats at one side and in the rear, where there would be nobody near them.

If there had been a crowd, the manager would not have authorized them to go in; and if the negroes had insisted on seating themselves among the white people, everybody in that part of the hall would have left it. Similar conditions and feelings appeared to prevail everywhere in the South in regard to these matters. There was a universal disposition on the part of the white people to avoid difficulty and conflict with the colored people respecting their civil rights, and the negroes were, in general, not disposed to contend for them. But a few colored men are inclined to insist upon enjoying whatever rightly belongs to them under the law, because they believe that any concessions on the part of the black people, or surrender of their legal rights, would invite and produce new injuries and oppressions. It is likely that some degree of irritation will often result from the attitude of the two races regarding this matter of the civil rights of the negroes.

8 A Slave Line Rather Than a Color Line

That there was indeed another option available besides racial equality through competition and market relations, or racial suppression through acceptance of market values and resentment toward those who seemed to resist, was evident in the following letters from workers, black and white, to the *United Mine Workers' Journal* in 1892 and 1893. These letters are important for their common theme, the possibility and often necessity of interracial cooperation to address common problems, and also for the diversity in which that position is developed. The perspectives range from the common heritages of blacks and whites as serfs or slaves to the practical necessity of cooperation against the same enemy and system of corporate greed. They provide examples of interracial brotherhood as well as lectures on the need to overcome prejudice. The recurring point so often, however, is simply that a divided community of workers benefits neither whites nor blacks but only the owners and that racial prejudice and competition serve only the interests of a system that exploits both. Whether the workers found hope in the United Mine Workers or the Knights of Labor or simply in the actions of their fellows in the cause, their affirmation of relations properly conceived as brotherhood and cooperation indicates a rejection of the market system itself.

Source: *United Mine Workers' Journal*; dates of publication noted with each selection.

[April 14, 1892]
. . . I am an Afro-American myself, and have lived all my life in the South but the last eight months, and if the Afro-Americans are union men for principle, as I believe they are, then it is more than the most of the whites were when it became necessary to remove a colored mine foreman and checkweigher, as all

of the power that the president and secretary-treasurer of District 19 could not avoid it. You are right, no true union man will stop reading the JOURNAL, but what we want is to test them and get the tried and true ones. My object in speaking of the Memphis and all other such outrages was to call organized labor's attention to them as both parties have said by their ways, that they cannot bring the violators to justice, while if it was for the benefit of Mammon, and to oppress labor all the detectives of the county and the State militia to assist them would be brought out as at this time in Tennessee, and as to the votes that they get don't deserve them by one-half. Brother W. R., would the United Mine Workers or the Knights of Labor be guilty of passing a law as is being done in Kentucky and in force in Tennessee that will not let an Afro-American ride in the same car as a white person, even though one is President and the other Secretary-Treasurer of District 19? I am sure it would not and you are welcome to write all you can and I shall take pleasure to read it. I am also proud that you can fill the position you have, also one that is higher than the pick or shovel either. As to the declaration of independence it is so in theory only and I trust that you will read the Knights of Labor platform before you act critic, as I stand upon Section 1 and then all that is just. Now what is needed most is principle and discipline and in conclusion, brothers, buy and read a few Afro-American papers, to see just what the negro has to fight, as I believe that brothers are so far behind they don't know how to start to catch up from the resolution that was tabled at Columbus.

Willing Hands.

[May 5, 1892]

. . . I will make this statement, that there is no color line at all, but simply the slave line; and, to sustain my assertion, I will say that I have known men and women of other nationalities who were nearly as black, a great deal more ignorant, and four-fold more degraded than the very meanest "nigger" I ever saw, yet they never had that infernal curse of slavery upon them, and they were received by some of the kickers against the black man with open arms as their social equals. "Oh, consistency thou art a jewel." Now, the fallacy of such things is really sickening to a person of any thought, no matter whether he be black or white.

Just to illustrate the matter I will suppose that a citizen (white or colored) of the United States should go to Africa and happen to be nabbed as was the colored man and become a slave for years and should then escape and get back to his native heath, would he be received as one below the general order of humanity or as a hero? A hero by all means. Well, why is not the colored man as much a hero who escaped the tyranny of slavery in this country? Now I will make another assertion, viz., that some of the smartest men we have in this country are men whose skins are black, whether so by nature or by climatic influences for centuries I will not discuss, but I say that a few days ago I heard a colored man illustrate the cause of his condition in a manner that for simplicity of understanding and correctness of detail was ahead of any definition of the cause I ever heard. He said: "I was a bound slave, my master controlled me and my wages, he was a smart man and they could not fool him. Now I am a free slave, I am ignorant and at the mercy of the rich man and cannot help myself; they made me so on purpose to rob me." But, he said, "through organization I know I can better my condition," although, he continued, "no man can be a true Knight of Labor man and be either a Democrat or Republican." Now I would like to know which is the best and smartest man, this poor old slave or the white gentlemen who on election day will carry around a body full of whiskey and hurrah for some low-down drunken ward politician? If I was not afraid of getting on dangerous ground I would say that in a great many places the worst line that is drawn is the political line. When men who are white do not like to sit in the same assembly with the colored man, yet are glad to welcome him into the political club room just before election day and pat him on the back and call him a good fellow and then after the election; my Lord! why they just can't stand a nigger. Another thing let me tell you, but I want you to remember not to say anything about it, the party that is in the majority or minority is the one that is most likely to do this. The K. of L. declares that it abolishes races, creeds and colors and the man who can't stand that kind of doctrine, let him just get up and git. Now, I will say in conclusion that I would like for some one to tell me the difference between a negro who has seven-eighths of white blood in him and a white man with one-eighth of negro blood? " 'Tis place not blood that makes the man," and if we could have a few transpositions of souls or at least the cultivated brain of James G. Blaine placed in the being of a colored man who had been blacklegging and vice versa, what would be the consequences? Why you would have a colored man with capabilities to be secretary of state and a white man who would blackleg. So I can say let politics go to thunder, stick to the principles of the K. of L., do all we can for one another, irrespective of race, creed or color. If we do this when we come to the jumping off place we will most likely go to a country where in reality there is no color line, if they do think there is one here.

Wm. Camack.

[June 9, 1892]

When visiting this community previously I found a compact, well-united and disciplined body of workingmen enjoying the privileges and conditions incident to well organized communities; contented and happy enjoying equal advantages, a means at hand to rectify any disadvantages or inequalities existing, no trouble with the free click, no favorites to whom the boon of free click must be granted and their word had no charm nor portent in them days, for the law of common rights, equal privileges and the brotherhood of miners, was the rule by which miners measured their conduct to each other, and man scorned any advantages secured at a disadvantage to his fellow-man: "Then man to man was true," then was a prosperous community, all were happy, all basking in the sunshine of prosperity, all made an attempt to better their condition. Every man's ambition was to better his condition socially and financially, and with that end in view land lots were purchased by the hundreds, homes were built, the people expected to make of the community their permanent dwelling place so long as life lasted. It was their ambition to labor for the means to make themselves homes, while, if not imposing and grand should at least be comfortable. They had a right to expect this. Had not men who counted their wealth by the millions, men who were honored by the fellow-men and who were trusted and looked up to as the very personification of business rectitude and commercial honesty invested a considerable portion of their wealth there? Had they not issued manifesto after manifesto drawing attention to the superior advantage offered by them to investors? Had they not proclaimed how comparatively easy it was for an industrious community to build up a very Eden of comfort and enjoyment under the beneficial and munificent plans adopted by them? Hundreds of our fellow craftsmen under the promise of good and steady work invested their all, little dreaming that the unwritten law concerning the conditions under which all the promised blessings and prosperity was to be secured was the deprivation of every privilege as a man, that any independence on his part was to be the sign for dismissal from his employment or an introduction of a system of espionage so tyrannical on his action that his further continuing in their employment was an impossibility. And to further assist in the work of destruction, men who were willing to lend themselves to the schemes of employers were selected as the recipients of free-click and these vampires readily caught at the opportunity to injure their fellowman, and, like Judas of old, "these fellows whose every true interest lay in being true to their fellow-miners, forgot every obligation, obliterated every consideration, save the fact that they were the recipients of the favors of the employers, not because they were loved better than others, but because they were less manly than others and could be used for a purpose that no true man could be used for, namely, the disruption and destruction of the miners hopes, their methods and plans lay in creating factions among them that would prevent that degree of unification that could successfully cope with the needs of the mining community. Well, do these people understand that a house divided against itself cannot stand! When will the miners and mine workers realize the fact that factional fights of all kinds must cease and the house united so that it may offer effective resistence to unjust encroachment from any quarter offered, whether it be from the free-click quarter or whether it be from national and religious prejudices, which it is evident is being done in this community. Under our American constitution there is no room for such prejudices to exist, there should be no room in our craft affairs for such prejudices, and where they do or might exist they can only do so at the expense of the craft, and he who would stir them up whether employer or employee must be regarded as the worst enemy of our craft, and dealt with accordingly. I am reminded when such tales are told me of the man who having been caught with a chicken on his person which he had undoubtedly purloined, upon giving his explanation of how it got on his person said that the man who put it there was no friend of his, and my fellow-craftsmen the recipients of free-click at the expense of your more manly brother miner, the man who given it to you is not your friend any more than he is your friend when stirring up your national or religious prejudices. Twenty to one he don't care a fig what your national pride or religious prejudices are and in his sleeve is laughing at your silly, senseless action in allowing yourselves to be betrayed unto factions, which gives him all the advantages and you all the disadvantages. Cease giving him gratification by creating factions among you. Close up your ranks as of old; direct your efforts against a common enemy. Let there be no Irishman, no Welshman, no Scotchman, no Italian, no

German, no Bohemian and no Polander; no Catholic, no Presbyterian, no Baptist and no Methodist with their peculiar prejudices, but let there be one brotherhood of miners under a fatherhood of God, who made all men equal in their privileges, no matter what is our individual preference as to methods of worship. Let the glad anthem of unification be sung by a united craftsmen all over the mining communities of this country and if the reign of peace and the millenium is to be established when each man can sit under his own vine and fig tree it will be when the factions cease from troubling and the disrupter and designer is laid at rest under the' contempt and ridicule of the regenerated craftsmen, secured by the unification of the whole and let the miners of Spring Valley and every other valley, as well as mountain top and plain, come unto the chariot of organization and it will carry you to the Mecca of success without doing violence to any of our national religions and denominational prejudices. Then will the bright sun of prosperity cast its beneficient rays upon us, filling all our homes with comforts and blessing. So may it be.

Thomas W. Davis.

[June 9, 1892]

. . . a word about the traveling accommodations in this part of the country for one of my race. I will say that had it not been for Brother E. E. Page, traveling salesman of the West Virginia Cut and Dry Tobacco Co., of Wheeling, and Brother Moran, this boy would have seen a hard time of it on last Saturday and Sunday, on my way from Pocahontas to the New river regions. I will try to give your many readers a short description of it: We left Pocahontas at 3:30 P.M. on Saturday, May 28, and arrived at Peterstown at about six o'clock, in time for supper. After washing and getting ready for eating as I thought, the colored man who worked there came to me and told me that he would show me my room, and just to think taking me to my bed before eating my supper. Well, I went with him, and where do you suppose he took me? Away, away from the main building, out in the wood yard, to an old dilapidated log cabin. I looked in and saw the bed. I turned to the man and asked him was it intended that I should sleep there? He said yes, that he slept there. I told him that he might sleep there but I wouldn't, that I would walk to Lowell, 30 miles away, that night first. About that time Brother Page came and took an observation of my bedchamber. He went away and held a consultation with the proprietor, which resulted in my getting about the best bed in the house and I would not be afraid to bet that I am the first negro to eat at the table in that man's dining room. Well, the next morning we started for Lowell across the mountains in a hack, we got to Red Sulphur Springs about 10 o'clock and stopped for dinner, but I was told that I could not eat in that house. My dinner was prepared outside. I lost my appetite and told him no, I didn't want anything to eat. We started from there a little after two o'clock and arrived at Lowell at about 6 o'clock. Brother Moran asked the proprietor, could I get supper there, and his answer was, oh, yes, but lo, when the bell rang and I was about to enter the dining-room, he caught me by the shoulder and told me to wait awhile. Brother Page turned around to him and told him that I was with them. He looked as though he was thunderstruck and of course I got my supper, but had it not been for those two white brothers I don't know but that I would have been by this time behind the bars, for I would have got tired had I been by myself and I don't know what the consequences would have been, for I felt like cursing and I would have used cuss words had I been by myself.

R. L. Davis

[May 25, 1893]

The race problem, or what aught or should be done with the negro, is a question that has seemingly been troubling the minds of a great number of the American people. It seems, however, plainly evident that he is a citizen of this country and should be treated as such. This, in my mind, is the only solution to the supposedly knotty problem. Less than thirty years ago he was given his freedom, and turned loose to the cold charities of the world without a dollar or an acre of land. Turned loose as he was is there any nation of people who has made such rapid progress as the Negro has made? No. Search all history and we find them not. During all these years in a said-to-be Christian and civilized country, notwithstanding the rapid strides he has made, he has been looked down upon by both the church and party politics, both of which should have been his best friends. Being poor and used to it he had to obey the divine injunction, viz.: To earn his bread by the sweat of his brow. In so doing we find him a great competitor with the American white labor. It is at this period that we find that the labor organizations or rather some of them, did that which no other organization had done, the church not even excepted, threw open their doors and admitted him as a full member with the same rights and privileges as his white brother. This, in our opinion, was the first or initiative step toward the equality of mankind, and we are sorry to say that until the present day the labor organizations are the only ones that recognize the Negro as an equal and as a man. Recognizing this to be true it is also true that some of our people have not gained enough confidence in his white brother as to trust him very far. And yet, is this very strange? When we notice the fact that right in our midst we have some as bitter enemies as anywhere else.

While we admit that our labor organizations are our best friends, it would be well to teach some of our white brothers that a man is a man no matter what the color of his skin may be. We have nothing but the best of words to say for labor organizations, and hope they may continue in the same line of actions, and we are confident that they will not only better the conditions of the working classes, but will also wipe out all class and race distinctions, and in the meantime the Negro will be found as loyal to labor organization as his white brother. It has been said that the Negro as a union man was a failure, but we are inclined to think that those words were uttered more from a prejudiced mind than as a truthful statement. Let us hope for better days for organized labor with the Negro in the ranks doing his share in the way of emancipating labor.

Confidence in each other is the thing lacking. This we can readily gain if we will but try. Believing as we do that all the reform needed must and will come through the medium of organized labor, it should be our proudest aim to do all that we can for the upholding of our organizations. Let us make them grand and perfect, and in so doing we will have accomplished a noble work, and by following this line of action we will solve the race problem, better the condition of the toiling millions and also make our country what it should be, a government of the people, for the people and by the people.

R. L. Davis.

9 Whitecapping and the Market

The sporadic instances of racial violence that have so frequently plagued black people remain difficult to understand because the immediate catalyst (let alone its connection to larger social forces) is so often obscure. Exactly what it is that brings about such flare-ups and brutalizations of racial enmity naturally varies from one incident to another, but some clue to the complexity and even internal contradictions that characterize these incidents can be gleaned from a rash of threats, intimidations, and violence directed against blacks in some parts of Mississippi in the first years of the twentieth century. In these "whitecapping" incidents it became common for black farmers to be warned that they should move away from their homes to another area and that if they failed to do so coercion or death would be the result. Some moved. Others remained and became victims of night-riders. While blacks themselves resisted this pressure the effective element in securing a response from the government appears to have been those individuals in the community who saw in this a threat to the labor system. Governor James K. Vardaman hired an investigator from Pinkerton's National Detective Agency to probe the organizational apparatus behind the whitecapping so that it could then be successfully ended. The following documents generated by that investigator reveal forces at work that are more responsible for the violence than simple racial prejudice, which, after all, was neither new nor always violent in its manifestations. The violence was directed at two groups of blacks: one group included those who farmed property owned by merchants, and the other was a catch-all for "obnoxious" blacks who stepped out of their place. Increasingly, it became evident that two directly opposite forces were at work and that both victimized the black. That blacks on property owned by merchants should be singled out is only too clear an indication that the merchant, or perhaps more precisely, the crop-lien system that gave the merchant his power, was the target. A traditional society that prided itself on its paternalism, however much of an illusion or charade that may have been, was being undermined by the market system—the spirit of the New South. The chief beneficiary in the transformation was the merchant. Likewise the black man who got out of his place provided evidence that the older system of inherited status, position, and caste was giving way to a more individualistic system. Indeed, it could well be that such a social change heightened the sensitivity of whites to any action, however innocent, that could be construed to be a departure from rigorous standards of submission and genuflection. Part of the whitecapping appears, then, to have had its origins in this resistance to the change under way in the institutions and relations of the country as a whole and especially in the South at this time. Yet the investigation also produced evidence of a directly contrary motivation guiding the intimidation. While some resisted the market through whitecapping, others promoted, or enforced, the attractions of the market. When enticement failed to lure blacks away from their homes to places where purported advantages and better lives lay waiting, labor agents turned to other methods. That they would be able to recruit black people to join their ranks as whitecappers themselves may indicate the ambivalence of blacks on the issue or even the absence of any racial solidarity; more likely it represents the circumstances of despair, or of having only very limited choices available. One thing is clear: when the forces of change and resistance came into conflict an explosive potential resulted. And in that conflict blacks could only lose and be burned in the explosion.

Source: Operative A.J.H. report to Pinkerton agency, in a letter from Pinkerton agency to Governor Vardaman, July 16, 1904; Operative A.J.H. report to Pinkerton agency, in a letter from Pinkerton agency to Governor Vardaman, April 13, 1904; statement of Sam Jones, April 20, 1904; statement of L. W. Jones as taken by A. J. Hoyt, July 1, 1904; all located in volume 286 of the Governor's Records (RG27), State of Mississippi Department of Archives and History. I would like to thank William F. Holmes for helping me locate this material.

During the evening my informant arrived and called at my room and appeared to be very nervous. He commenced his information by saying "I believe I know why you sent for me and if you will promise to protect me I am going to tell all I know". "I never was in favor of the organization and was fooled into it by the statements of others that it was not against law and order, but upheld it, and while I never attended but one meeting in Franklin County and one in Lincoln County I know all about the whole thing". He informed me that he joined the order some time in Oct. or Nov., 1902 at a meeting at Rock Spring on McCalls Creek at which there were 25 present, but he afterwards learned they had a membership of 27, two being absent. This particular club had this membership. He informed me th[a]t he and Dr. Cane were taken into the meeting being duly obligated and given the signs and pass words. It was similar to the manner of initiating a member into any other order except the meeting was held in the woods. He states that those present were:

Thos. Lofton,	Wm. Martin,	Jeff Catton,	W. P. Adams,
Dr. Cane,	Gus Catton,	Floyd Pickens,	Doc Rawlins,
Asia Catton,	Baily Balin,	John Nettles,	Tom Nettles,
Kager Nettles,	Nat Westbrook,	Buster Rushing,	Tom Gice,
			———Rushing,

He could not recall who the others were. He was assigned his regular number which was #29 and Dr. Cane was given #28. He informs me that he cannot exactly remember the wording of the obligation, which was read by John Nettles, but it was about as follows. "With right hand upheld I solemnly swear to keep and never reveal any of the secrets of the organization, and do solemnly swear to live and abide by any of its rules as they now are or may be hereinafter revised; that if ever called to sit upon any Grand Jury or other Jury to hold out forever against any bill or verdict directed against a member of the organization; also that I will assist in every way directed by the organization to compel the negroes to vacate any an[d] all property owned by merchants and to assist to put out of the way any an[d] all obnoxious negroes in the jurisdiction of this club; and that I fully understand that the penalty shall be death to any or all members revealing any of the secrets or workings of this order. After taking the oath Doc Rawlins gave me the signs and pass words. The pass word for entering and to be given the sentry was:

Sentry: - "Who comes there"?

Member: - "A friend".

Sentry: - "A friend of whom"?

Member: - "A friend of Free America".

The recognition sign word to be used in learning whether or not the person addressed in a casual conversation was or was not a friend was: "be cautious", and the recognition sign was to pass the right hand across the heart then up to the left chee[k] as though brushing something from it. The answer was for the other person to use the left hand in the same manner. The grip was to shake hands in the ordinary way but to press the end of the thumb against the third knuckle of the person with whom you were shaking hands. He also stated that from time to time they changed the pass word and at one time the word was "Napolian" and the answer "Wellington".

He agreed to appear before the Federal Grand Jury but stated that he would be killed outright should it be found out that he was giving information, but he agreed to do all he could to bring the law breakers to justice by giving me the information and agreed to go before the Executive Committee and make his statement which I thought a good idea and arranged for such a meeting after consulting with Mr. Brady as to the advisability of such a plan. He stated that if we would arrest himself, Tom and Henry Lofton and Perry Smith and take them to Jackson that he could induce them to talk and [corroborate] every word he stated by telling them that he was going to turn the whole business up to save himself and that the others would do the same if promised protection. This seemed a very good plan as Henry Lofton was in the List Killing according to the informant and Tom Lofton, and with the crowd who posted the notices and made the raid through Franklin County and western Lincoln County. I had him to agree to meet the Committee in the morning, gave him $2.00 for hotel and livery expenses and discontinued.

Brookhaven, Miss., Friday, April 8, 1904.
I could not go to Cold Springs or Bogue Chitto on account of the bad condition of the roads.

I first visited Dr. Nelson who has had some of his Negroes driven away and he is endeavoring to run to earth the guilty parties; also, he informs me that he will drive with me sometime next week and take me to a man who claims to have heard the conspiracy against the life of Eli Hilson. He also said he would furnish me with other valuable data at the same time.

I then visited Sheriff Applewhite, who has some information which leads him to believe that Louis Jones will be in town tomorrow night. He informed me that he had a reliable colored fellow by the name of John Smith whom he always used to locate negroes and he would send him out with me and his deputies and himself would make a thorough search for Jones, as he too was of the opinion that Jones was in the vicinity of Brookhaven.

I then visited an informant at the Post Office who informed me that the letter fro[m] Louis Jones was still at the office and that his clerks were all acting under his instructions to keep an eye on him until the sheriff could be notified if he should call for the mail and if some one else called to learn who it was.

I then visited Dan bryne (white) who said he knew Louis Jones well and claimed that he saw him at a house opposite his on Friday, one week ago, and that the negro lady was his friend and he would find out for me if Jones was there or coming there. He called upon her and informed me that Jones was expected there on Saturday night, as he had some clothes at her place.

I then called again on the Sheriff and he and I went to Pearl Haven and through the Negro settlement in that vicinity and one of his men and Tom Smith went to the vicinity of the Negro village where Jones used to preach about four miles from Brookhaven. We were all unsuccessful, found no trace of him whatever. The same search will be made and a constant watch kept for him in places where he frequents to-morrow night.

I continued my investigation by driving to Cold Springs and interviewing Mr. Broome who stated he had seen Green Hughs and that he was a badly frightened Negro and he believed if he knew anything that he would be able to get it from him.

I then drove to Aron Carter's place to find out if he had heard anything from Louis Jones. He informed me that he had watched the house each night since I had last seen him and that Louis Jones had not been home.

I then drove to Sebe Spurlock's place and he had secured three typewritten notices from Al Smith (colored) who was driven off his place (one of the best farms in the county) by white caps the first of the year. The Notices read as follows:

The typewritten portion reads:

NOTICE

"Negro, you must leave this place or else suffer the penalty of death."
On the back was written:
"You and your hol Faml must not be cout back in Miss. Take your boys to and you mus not stop ounder 600 miles."

To All Smith.

Then on the 5Th day of December, 1903, he received one which read— typewritten:

"Negro you must leave this place at once or else suffer the penalty of death."

Written on back:

"Dec. 5, 1903
Negro we give you a notice last Wednesday night and I understand that you did not get it."

The written part of this notice greatly differs from the writing upon the other notices and seems to have been written by some one who could write a very good hand and endeavored to disguise it, while the first one was evidently written by one who could write but little and spelled poorly.

The other notice was received a short time after Al Smith's son was shot and read: Typewritten:

NOTICE

"You must leave this place at once or else suffer the penalty of death."

Written in the same hand writing as the first one herein quoted:

"You must cross the Mississippi River or will kill you and burning you and your hole family.
We are only watin for your boy, We think WE think he can go now, you mus all go wher we sed for yo to go or dy and burn shor".

There are a few other words not eligible. After he received the last notice he at once left his place and moved to Cold Springs upon a rented place.

I then returned to Brookhaven and together with Sheriff Applewhite, his brother and John Smith, made a thorough search for Louis Jones, but could not locate him.

Brookhaven, Miss., Sunday, April 10, 1904.

I continued my investigation by accompanying John Smith to the Negro Churches at Brookhaven and in the vicinity, looking for Louis Jones. We first went to Arlington Church, four miles west of Brookhaven, but could get no trace of him: We then drove to the "Good hope" Church, three miles South East of Brookhaven, with the same result. Jones has preached at both places and I was in hopes to locate him on Sunday at one of these places.

I then returned to Brookhaven and was at the Colored church just south of town when it burned to the ground but could not locate Jones.

Brookhaven, Miss., April 11, 1904.

I drove to Cold Springs, then west to Al Smith's place and interviewed him. He stated that the White-caps began sending him notices early in the fall of 1903, shortly after he had made extensive improvements upon his house and out buildings. Smith informed me that he owned 120 acres of land as good as there is in the County and that for ten years he and his family had worked hard to get 88 acres cleared and under cultivation and had just succeeded in having his land free from stumps and roots when Reuben Pasey who lives near proposed to buy the place. Smith did not want to sell it and so informed him: Two weeks later he informed me he received the first notice which read as all the others following did.

Typewritten:

"Negro you must leave this place at once or else suffer the penalty of death."

He paid no attention to the first few which came regularly every two or three weeks. They scared him badly, but he remained and during this time Reuben Pasey made him offers several times for his place and finally Smith offered to sell it to him for $1500.00 which Smith claims was $500.00 less than it was worth. Pasey then offered him $600.00 for it and he refused and the Pasey boys began picking trouble and misusing his children. Then he received another notice warning him to leave or be killed or burned. Shortly after this Smith's sons, Levi and Elijah were sitting beside the road a short distance from the Pasey farm when Ben Franklin and Sam Pasey drove along and said some mean things to the Smith boys and Ben Franklin struck at Elijah Smith with the butt end of his pistol when Levi Smith caught Franklin's arm and held it firmly to prevent him from killing his brother, Elijah, which he threatened to do. Elijah saw the trouble that was coming and ran away leaving Levi and Franklin scuffling for possession of the pistol. When Sam Pasey saw that Levi Smith was holding Franklin firmly he called out to Levi. Let loose that gun damn you or I will kill you: Levi was afraid to let loose; Sam Pasey jumped out of the rig and deliberately shot Levi Smith through the left thigh, the ball breaking the bone of the leg. Levi fell to the ground and Pasey again drew the gun upon him: this time pointing it at his head; when Franklin caught hold of Sam Pasey and said, you have broken his leg that is enough for now. They walked away a few steps, when Sam Pasey took from his pocket a Jack knife and opened it, threw it upon the ground, then picked it up and said to Levi Smith, What are you doing with that knife, you S. of a B? Levi stated that he had no knife and told Pasey that it was his knife. The two then left Levi lying on the ground and drove away. Presently Reuben Pasey came to where Levi lay and remained some time. Elijah Smith ran to Eli Hilson's place and endeavored to get him to come and help him get his brother home, but Eli Hilson would not come, as he was afraid of the two boys, Sam Pasey and Ben Franklin, as he had suspicioned that they were the ones who had threatened to kill him if he did not leave in notices which he had previously received. Elijah then went to Levi Putman and he came with his wagon and they took Levi Smith home.

The following morning Al Smith claims he rode to Brookhaven with Eli Hilson whose house had been riddled with bullets three weeks before. Smith informed me that Eli Hilson usually carried his Winchester rifle with him after he had received the notice and especially since receiving the bombarding of shot and bullets at his home. Hilson informed Smith that he believed he recognized Reuben Pasey's voice the night his house was shot into. Smith further stated that he heard Oscar Franklin say that if Eli Hilson had done his mother as he did Mrs. Pasey, he would kill the S. of a B. (Reuben Pasey accused Hilson of shooting in the vicinity of the Pasey home when Mrs. Pasey was confined to her bed by illness) Eli Hilson was killed the following Saturday night after Levi Smith was shot by Sam Pasey.

Smith also informed me that when the last notice was posted at his place he was in the house and saw the rig drive up to his gate; in the rig were two men, who he could not identify, but he could the horse, which was a small Grey poney and he believes was the property of Louis Jones. At this time I am informed by Dr. Martin, Mayor of Cold Springs that Louis Jones owned a small Grey pony which he afterwards mortgaged to him and then sold without paying the mortgage and for which he has since sworn out a warrant for his arrest, but unable to locate him.

Smith also informed me that the man who is suspected of having furnished the type-written notices is a brother-in-law of Reuben Pasey and employed at a printing office in Brookhaven. I then returned to Brookhaven and went to the Post Office and learned a letter signed D. Steward 319 Washington St., Vicksburg, Miss, postmarked newton Landing, Miss., reading "Now F. Steward." had been received for Louis Jones. In my opinion this letter is from Louis Jones intended for Louis Jones' wife so she may know his address.

STATEMENT
of
Sam Jones.   April 20, 1904

Statement of Sam Jones, given voluntarily.

I hereby declare that the information following is true to the best of my personal knowledge.

Mr. Daily came to the county farm and paid my fine which he said was $28.00 and I came back to Brookhaven with him. He told me not to let anyone see me and that papa (Louis Jones) would meet me at Chas. Thompson's. I went there and met papa, changed my clothes. Papa said he was going home but was going by the church first. I walked on and overtook him just below Elder Burtons. He was then with Green Hughes, Mr. S. G. Buchanan, Will Markin, Sam Campbell and three other, two white and one colored whom I did not know, but would recognize one white man and the negro at sight. They had about six quarts of whiskey. Buchanan and the white man I did not know were in a buggy and had a regular arsenal, which they distributed. Will Martin had his own shot gun, and Sam Campbell had a winchester rifle. Mr. Buchanan stopped me and wanted to know where I was going. Papa said "thats only Sam". Buchanan said that they were going out to scare Aunt Sally Bullock and Gwynn Rogers, so that they would go to the Delta, but that if I told any body about it if one of them did not kill me the other would. They all took several drinks, Will Martin and Papa then started for the house about three hundred yards from where we were standing. Either Martin or Papa fired one shot as a signal for us to come up, which we did marching like soldiers. When within about one hundred feet of the house all that had guns commenced shooting into the house. It seems to me they shot fifty times. Harris Rawls also joined the crowd when they were drinking, before the shooting was done, and joined in the shooting. They all returned to the buggy and the crowd scattered after taking a few drinks. Buchanan collected his guns and told me he would meet me next day in Brookhaven. Papa, Green Hughes and I came back within about a mile from town. Green Hughes stayed with us until nearly morning, when he left. Papa and I stayed in the woods all night, and drove to Brookhaven next morning and joined Mr. Dailey. He did not give me any money, but bought our tickets to Minter City and accompanied us there on the night train. We went to work on Mr. Chas. Townes farm.

Signed:
Sam Jones.

A. J. Hoyt.
L. B. Killough.

[Statement of L. W. Jones, July 1, 1904.]

Q. When was the first time that you knew that White-cap notices were being used by labor agents, Crawford and Buchanan, to secure families for the north?

A. About December 15th. [1903]

Q. Who was the first to receive a notice that came from or through Crawford or Buchanan?

A. Aaron Carter and Greene Hughes were the first ones that I knew about.

Q. Do you know who wrote or delivered these notices?

A. Yes sir. Buchanan wrote the notices on paper taken from his day book and Tom Crawford addressed the envelopes, which he gave me to mail. I mailed them at the Brookhaven Post Office. There were other notices mailed at the same [t]ime, but I cannnot remember who they were to, but, I could pick them out if I could see them, no matter where I saw them.

Q. See if you can find any of these notices among this pile of papers, that you mailed on any occasion? (After looking, finds one and answered, "Here is one".

Q. To whom is it addressed?

A. Aaron Carter.

Q. Can you swear positively that you mailed this particular notice?

A. Yes sir.

Q. And who wrote it?

A. S. G. Buchanan.

Q. Who addressed the envelope?

A. Tom Crawford.

Q. Who stamped the envelope?

A. It was already stamped when Crawford addressed it.

* * *

Q. Did you not know, positively, that you were mailing white-cap notices and violating the United States postal laws when you dropped those letters in the post office?

A. I knew they were labor agent notices, but did not know that they were considered the same as white-cap notices.

Q. How did you know that they were labor agent notices?

A. Because I saw them writing them, heard what they said about them, and, afterward, mailed them myself.

Q. What did they say about them?

A. They said they did not want to hurt any one but simply to scare them negroes nearly to death so that it would be easy to persuade them to go to the plantations in the Delta?

Q. Who said this?

A. Mr. Buchanan.

Q. What did Crawford say with reference to the hurting of negroes?

A. He said the same as Buchanan, laughed, and remarked that he guessed these would do the work.

Q. What did you say?

A. I laughed too, and thought it a good joke to scare a man away from his own home and get $25.00 for scaring him, which they had agreed to pay me as soon as the man and his family were at the depot.

* * *

Q. What did Crawford ever say to you about the Delta, or about going there, or securing families for the Delta?

A. He told me to get all the families that I could and that I would certainly get well paid for it- that it was a nice man that they were going up there to work for and that they could make plenty of money, and that all the negroes that did not go were Dam fools- for he knew what he was talking about and, if I did not believe it, he said that they would gladly take me up to this country and let me see it, that my influence might be greater in securing families on my return, and that the trip would not cost me a cent.

Q. Did you go?

A. Yes sir.

Q. What did you think of the country?

A. A fine country, but I did not like the way they were treating the families up there.

* * *

Q. Now, what do you know about the shooting into the different negroes' homes?

A. I do not know anything about the shooting, except the shooting into Elder Burton's home.

Q. What do you know about that?

A. Well, I know all about it.

Q. How do you know all about it?

A. I was there with the crowd.

Q. When was this?

A. Sometime in January.

Q. Explain in your own words the full account of this affair.

A. I left home in the evening and road my gray horse to Brookhaven and then to Charlie Thompson's place, where I remained most of the evening I was called from there on two occasions by Mr. Dailey and we went through the alley to the rear of the place with Mr. Dailey and he asked me to get all the negroe families I could between this time and the next night, as he, Dailey, was going up to the Delta the next night on the first train. I told him that I would do all I could and, then, between 5:00 and 6:00 P. M., Tom Crawford and S. G. Buchanan came to Thompson's and called me. We all went to Hartman's back lot and Crawford asked me which way I was going when I went home. I informed him that I had not decided- he then said, "I want you to come and go around by Pink Harrington's place and show me how to get to Elder Burton's house"., I asked him how long it would be before he would be ready to go and he said, as soon as we can get things ready, and, for me to meet them around on the street below the Masonic hall. This I did and, after waiting for them about an hour, Crawford and Buchanan drove up with a team and surrey, or sort of a hack, from Curls Stable and I followed along behind the team on my Gray horse until they reached a road that turned out of the big road towards Elder Burton's place. When they come to the Tram-road, they turned out of the big road and stopped- Crawford and Buchanan took a drink and asked me to drink with them, but, I would not do so, having had all I could stand while with Mr. Dailey. Mr. Crawford then asked me the nearest way to Burton's house, I directed them and they drove on, and I followed behind. When they got within half a mile of the house, one of the men fired one shot from a breach loading shot gun, as a signal for the crowd to come up. This shot was answered by two shots, one from the south-easterly direction and one from the west. We remained at this place for sometime, it was quite dark and probably between 8:00 and 9:00 o'clock. While here, I noticed that Crawford and Buchanan, who were seated in the front seat of the surrey had several double barrel, breach loading shot guns and some bottle of whiskey in the back part of the rig. We remained here, until the crowd came up from the west, and I recognized, in this crowd, Dan Bolin, John, Ira, Jabe and Tom Red, besides two that I did not know. All this crowd were armed and they all took a few drinks, which Mr. Crawford gave to them from the buggy, and then started toward Elder Burton's house. Just before they arrived at the house, at a little road running east and west across the road that we were on, we met another crowd of eight or nine and they were not all armed. They stopped and had a drink and Buchanan called me to come and join them, but I informed them that I had had enough. This was probably a hundred yards from Burton's house, where they tied their horses and were all standing around the buggy, when Crawford gave orders, like a Major general, "Boys get ready"., Crawford passed out some guns to those who were not armed and called to me, and told me to take a gun but I refused, on the ground that Elder Burton was a very close friend of mine, and I had rather not shoot.

Buchanan then said, "Form a line", which they did and marched in a line toward the house. I followed probably seventy-five or a hundred feet in the rear. Just before they arrived at the house, they were joined by the third crowd, which made a total of twenty or thirty men. The only person that I recognized in the last two crowds was Al Martin, who passed within six feet of me and spoke, and I spoke to him. When the crowd reached a point about a hundred feet from the house, they all fired a volley at the command of Mr. Buchanan. They, then fired another volley and were given the order, by Mr. Buchanan, to scatter. I am not positive who was in the crowd who joined in the little road near the house, except Al Martin, but, I think there was a man and his son, who had recently moved in the vicinity and who had endeavored to buy Elder Burton's place. This answers the description of Chas. Avery. I, also, think that Harris Rawls was with this crowd but I cannot swear positively who they were in the last two crowds as I said except-Al Martin, it being too dark to distinguish them, and from the fact that I was too far in the rear when the shooting took place.

Q. When did you next see Buchanan and Crawford?

A. I saw Crawford and Buchanan on Saturday following.

Q. What did they say with reference to the shooting?

A. Simply laughed about it and remarked that they guessed that that would do the work, refering to the shooting, and Crawford then began to endeavor to get me to leave as he said I was suspected of being in the crowd that did the shooting.

Q. What did Buchanan say to you with reference to this matter?

A. He said the same as Crawford, and that I must leave at once.

Q. When did you see these men again?

A. On the following Monday.

Q. What did they say to you?

A. They both told me to get away as quick as I could for "You are suspected".

Q. What did you say?

A. I told them I would leave Wednesday night.

Q. What did they say?

A. Crawford said that it would be alright.

Q. Well, what happened next?

A. On Tuesday evening I came to town with my horse and buggy and met Tom Crawford in front of the Commercial Bank of Brookhaven and he told me that he wanted to see me in Hartman's back lot right away. I went around to the lot and met him, Buchanan, and Dailey, and they told me, "You leave here tonight". I insisted that I would like to see my folks first, when Crawford said that he would see to it that my wife followed me up to Minter City.

Q. When was this?

A. February 16th, 1904.

Q. What did you tell them after they had told you to leave.

A. I told them I would go that night.

Q. What did they say further in this matter?

A. Crawford said, "By God, you'd better leave tonight", I said, "Alright I will go", and asked Mr. Dailey about my boy, Sam.

Q. What did Mr. Dailey tell you?

A. He said he would go at once to the County farm, pay my boy's fine, and that I could take him with me, which he did.

Q. Why did they want you to leave on this particular night?

A. Crawford said, "The reason we want you to go to-night is because we are going to raise hell tonight and we don't want you in it". They scared me badly and I agreed to leave and did leave with Samie, my boy, Howard Nelson, his wife and mother, and Mr. Dailey, who paid all our expenses to Minter City, Mississippi.

Q. Did Mr. Dailey go with you?

A. Yes sir. He rode in the same coach with us until we were nearly to Jackson, when he went to the white coach.

Q. Did Mr. Dailey stay with you all night?

A. No sir. We met him the next morning at 4:00 o'clock and he took us to Minter City.

Q. What happened after you arrived at Minter City?

A. A wagon met us at the train and took us to the plantation. Mr. Dailey then returned to Brookhaven where he remained for about four days, and when he came back, he came to see me and laughed about the Elder Burton shooting affair, and Dailey told me that they were playing the devil with the negroes down there now, and that they might as well leave there first as last, for they would have to leave any how. I saw Mr. Townsend and he told me that he would furnish me all the money I needed if I would go and get him hands, and pay all my and their expenses, and, for each family that I secured, he would give me $25.00 and that the money was already on deposit in the Commercial Bank of Brookhaven waiting for me. I agreed to do this, and came to Jackson and then took on the Gulf and Ship Island road to Hattiesburg, and have been dodging the labor agents and detectives, who, I knew, were after me until I was captured in New Orleans by Mr. Hoyt.

Q. What did you learn while you were at Minter, relative to the treatment of the negro, the money they earn, the settlements they secure, etc.?

A. I learned that fifty families from Brookhaven had been scared from their homes near Brookhaven and taken to Ex-Governor Longino's plantation by labor agents, but I do not know who these agents were. These families were brought there three days after I arrived at Minter City. A negro living upon Mr. Townsend's place told me he had made $500., paid to him by Mr. Townsend since Christmas, or in less than two months, that he had secured families from Texas, Alabama, Louisiana, and Mississippi, and that he had been driven out of nearly all these states by the authorities for scaring hands and inducing them to go to this particular plantation. He said that Mr. Townsend was endeavoring to get him to go back to Louisiana but he was afraid. Mr. Dailey is Mr. Townsends regular agent and he hired Buchanan and Crawford and others to do the out-side work while he, Dailey, would remain in town and persuade the negroes to leave the county after Crawford and Buchanan had frightened them from their homes. A negro by the name of Nelson Sharpe informed me that he had been trying to get away from the Townsend plantation for ten years and had been unable to steal away or get away, under any pretense, and that, the negroe stood no chance, whatever, of getting away after once landing upon a plantation. When the negroe's crops are gathered in the fall they are not settled with in full unless they agree to remain another year and then a portion of their earnings is withheld until the following March. In this way they are seldom in possession of money enough to get away on. He also told me that Mr. Townsend had men at Glendora and Minter City watching every out-going train to see that no negroes were running away, and that, if one was caught in the act of running away he was taken back to the plantation, and whipped then placed on the County farm. The over-seer rides on horseback with a pistol in his belt and a whip in his hand and the negroes say, that he beats a negro at the slightest provocation, and I was advised, by this Nelson Sharpe, that if I could get away for "God's sake do so, because if I waited until I had a crop started, I would never get away.

Q. What else can you tell me about this labor agent business prior to your going to the Delta country?

A. Mr. McRae tried to get me to get hands for him.

Q. Did you do so?

A. No sir. I informed him that I was working for two men but had not secured any hands yet.

Q. What other men tried to induce you to secure hands for them?

A. There was a big fat man from Widow Richardson's place tried to persuade me and to hire me to secure families for him. He brought a negro with him by the name of Irving Love to assist him, and I am sure that he posted notices for this big fat man. This was no doubt Hill.

Q. What do you know about Charles Christman with reference to writing notices?

A. Nothing, except what I have heard and that was that he was caught with a grip full of typewritten notices while out in Franklin County.

Q. Who told you, and who do you believe could give me the facts relative to these notices?

A. I believe that Jeff Jones, who lives in Franklin County, could tell all about it, if arrested as I am sure he knows. He is known to have been mixed up with these agents on several occasions, in fact, has been with the lawless element every since the Bulldozing of years ago, and Mr. Coon Bird, of Franklin County, who used to work with me at Martin and Holms mills, told me one day that Jeff Jones was a S of a B. and that he was with him when a crowd hung a negro boy, and that Jeff Jones was with the crowd that whipped several negroes in Franklin County and that there is no doubt that he could tell all about the Christman notices.

[P. F. Williams' wife, a colored school teacher, told Andrew Gill and Louis Jones that Jeff Jones was reported to have had a grip full of typewritten notices sometime ago and the colored people generally believe that he is responsible for nearly all of the notices that have been posted in Franklin and Lincoln Counties].

10 The Darkness and the Horror of the Present Situation

Whitecapping was one thing. The epidemic of lynchings was something else. Whether conceived as a frontier system of justice to take the place of established authority or the outgrowth of "mob-psychology," the lynching of blacks left a mark on the South. The meaning of that mark, beyond the gory trail of blood, however, is difficult to establish. Clearly, as the following account suggests, justice—in the sense of punishment (not to mention rehabilitation) of the offender—was not a major consideration. For here, even when the crowd knew that it had the wrong persons it went ahead with its deadly plan. The crowd even knew that the real culprit would go unidentified and unpunished because of its determination for immediate blood. The retribution was simply an action that emphasized caste and race more than individual merits or deserts. Indeed, throughout the discussion and subsequent course of events individual distinctions mattered little. The division over the fate of the victims, whether to let the processes of the law take their course or to let the crowd have its way immediately, appears to have been based on social and political prominence, with those identified with the establishment favoring the legal routes. This crowd seems to have consisted mainly of more reckless young farmers, with only a few of the "maturer and more conservative" citizens among their number. The lack of an individualistic set of perceptions can be seen also in the justification developed by even the critics of lynching; when the allegation involved an affront to or rape of a white woman lynching appears to have been nearly universally approved. No matter which woman, no matter which black, no matter what the circumstances or evidence, a black would have to die. To do otherwise would have the white women of the South, they said, "at the mercy of the lustful brutes." As it was, the women would be only at the mercy of the white men, whether conceived as protection or subjugation. It may be that in all this the real basis and origin of lynching can be detected. As Levell indicated, "Lynching is resorted to not merely to wreak vengeance but to terrorize the Negro." It was first and foremost an important and powerful element of a system of social control. The target of the lynching was not the unfortunate victim of the crowd but all blacks. They were put on warning that their race made them vulnerable to serious reprisal at the whim of the white community. So too was it a warning to whites that their friendly actions or gestures toward blacks could spell doom for the blacks, all the more so for white women. Thus lynching served to generate fear among blacks and unity among whites. But two other points made by Levell suggest that it also generated unity among blacks in a counterproductive way. Criminality among blacks, he noted, made individuals heroes in the black community; and the black man pursued, regardless of his offense, could find sanctuary among others of his race, "even the best of them." It was not, then, simply that the system of laws and established justice did not work; it worked, rather, to the opposite ends: individualizing the situation when popular attitudes focused upon caste and collectivity, and allowing the possibility of freedom for an innocent black man (or, as in this case, for a black woman and her daughter and son). That possibility could not be permitted to surface without completely undermining social attitudes and structures built up over long generations. Indeed, it is entirely possible that lynching emerged, with these characteristics, precisely in response to the forces of market, law, and polity which were undermining that caste society where white men and white women and black men and women occupied distinctive and separate realms by virtue of their genes alone.

Source: William Hayne Levell, "On Lynching in the South," *The Outlook*, 69 (November 16, 1901): 731-33.

Last summer I happened to be spending my vacation at "Cotesworth," the old country home of the late United States Senator George, about two miles from the town of Carrollton, Miss. During the time I was there I heard one day that on the night previous two defenseless old people had been done to death in a most foul and brutal fashion, and that because of it the people of the county were coming into town, and there was like to be a lynching of several negroes who were suspected of the crime. Never before having been in the immediate neighborhood of a lynching, and wishing to learn something of the character of these repeated outbreaks, I rode into town to study the situation close at hand, hoping that something might occur which would make it possible to prevent any violence. I found that three negroes, a mother with her son and daughter, tenants of the murdered couple, had been arrested on suspicion of having committed the murder or having guilty knowledge of the facts, and were at that time confined in the county jail. I found present on the streets of the town many young farmers from the county who were carrying rifles, shotguns, or pistols, and mixed with them a few of the maturer and more conservative citizens of the county, to whom the young fellows seemed to look for direction. All of them had a serious and determined look upon their faces.

I found also that a committee of prominent men, among them the State Senator from that district, the District Attorney, and a lawyer who had several times represented the county in the Legislature, had been formed and at the hour of my arrival were at the jail examining the negroes. The committee was earnestly solicitous to prevent a lynching. It satisfied itself that those three negroes did not personally commit the crime, but knew who did, and were as yet not willing to reveal their guilty secret. Several times, both individually and as a committee, these gentlemen addressed the mob, trying to dissuade it from violence, and pleading, in the name of humanity and for the good name of the county, to let the law take its course, the more particularly because the only apparent hope of learning who were the real murderers was involved in keeping these three negroes alive. The mob was not to be dissuaded. As the authorities offered practically no resistance, the mob took the negroes, hanged them just outside of town, and riddled their bodies with bullets.

Realizing that it would be regarded as an impertinent intrusion for me to offer any suggestion, since I was an outsider, and knowing that there was no chance for me to do what well-known gentlemen who had the confidence of their neighbors there failed to do, I rode away home some time before the lynching took place.

From what I learned of the whole matter, of the circumstances leading up to the crime, it seemed to be a case particularly demanding that the law should be permitted to take its course. It was not a question of the rape of a white woman by a negro brute. It was the assassination of the aged parents of a young white man who had previously shot to death the son of the negro mother for attempted poison. The young man was out on bail awaiting the action of the Grand Jury. But there was only one way to prevent that lynching. That way was by superior force, and the constituted authorities did not offer it.

In connection with my experience and observation on the day of the lynching, I took care afterwards to discuss the case itself and the whole matter of lynching, as it obtains in the South, with some of the best and maturer and more conservative citizens of that part of the State of Mississippi, to learn whether and how far they approved of lynching for crime. Of course I found some extreme men, who are good citizens in their way, who are yet very nervous over the whole question of the negro and his preponderance in their part of the State, and who assert that for any considerable crime, of whatever nature, committed against a white person by a negro, they would take the law in their own hands and shoot him down as they would a dog. These are extremists.

The greater part of the educated, conservative, thoughtful, and, in ordinary situations, more influential citizens approve of lynching for the rape of a white woman, but deplore the seeming necessity for it, and are groping helplessly in the dark for some way to make lynching unnecessary. They see that it is gradually undermining their civilization, destroying all respect for law, and, with reference to all sorts of offenses, is substituting mob law for the ancient forms which have safeguarded the liberties of the English-speaking peoples for centuries. They contemplate the future with something akin to terror, and confess themselves tied hand and foot to a situation from which it seems impossible to break away without hastening the very thing they fear. They believe that to turn over to the law a black fiend who has raped a defenseless white woman and made over her whole life into a living hell would inevitably tend to multiply rapes and practically put all our women at the mercy of the lustful brutes.

Their explanation of the situation as it is now found in the South may not be entirely satisfactory to the denizens of the cities and the dwellers amidst a predominant white population, but I will try to give it as it was given to me by some of the most conservative, most thoughtful, and most wise citizens of the South.

1. The natural barbarism of our human nature, whose first impulse is to wreak vengeance for an outrage, is to be always considered, for, as a matter of fact, neither individuals nor communities ever get far away from nature—and that is human nature.

2. From the earliest times in the South seduction has always resulted in either what is known as a "military wedding" or a homicide. The community has always supported the family of the seduced woman for killing the seducer if he would not redeem the situation as far as possible by marriage. If that was the result where there was "consent," how much more certainly would homicide be the result where there was force used to accomplish the ruin of a woman—where there was rape? A white man would no more escape than a negro. If the white man must pay with his life for rape, how much more certainly a negro for the rape of a white woman, where in addition the revolt of all the instincts of race was involved?

3. In many if not most rural communities in the South the white population is very small compared with the negro population. The whites are really at the mercy of the blacks, if the latter but once should get the notion that there is a reasonable hope of escape. For there are always enough vicious negroes in every community ready to commit the crimes of lust if they can do so and yet escape justice or vengeance. Lynching is resorted to not merely to wreak vengeance but to terrorize the negro.

4. Every one who handles large bodies of negro laborers—every one with whom I talked—believes that the average negro fears nothing so much as force. The whites believe that the moment the negro ceases to fear the power of the white man crimes will rapidly increase—crimes of the most revolting character. Among the negroes, criminals, when the crime is committed against a white man, attain to a certain heroic character, and are the objects of a certain sort of admiration which they crave and rejoice in. The conviction is general that terror is the only restraining influence with the average negro.

5. The negroes, even the best of them, will ordinarily conceal a fleeing negro, assist him in his flight, and whenever practicable, protect him; and this without regard to the requirements of justice or the character of his offense.

6. The famously slow processes of the law and the frequent miscarriages of justice. In New Orleans a few months ago a negro insulted a refined white woman, was arrested and put upon his trial. The woman put aside her modesty

and went on the witness-stand and testified to the facts. The facts were outrageous and cruel. The lawyer for the defense succeeded in deferring the case some months upon a technicality, and later the brute upon conviction got only a three months' sentence. One such case as that does away with the confidence in the law engendered by a hundred cases where justice is accomplished, and the mind of the people turns to lynching as the only certain remedy.

If you call their attention to the fact that lynching does not stop rape, their answer is, No, but it prevents it more than any other process would do.

The thinking men of the South realize the horror of their situation; they see that mob law is coming to be the law for all sorts of crimes, that it is beginning to be used even in private quarrels and against the whites themselves. They think it is a cruelty to serve them with condemnation, when they need the sympathy and assistance of that portion of our people who live securely amid a predominant white population. It is easy to prescribe practically impossible premises, but you can by such means get no satisfactory or adequate result.

It will need the best wisdom and the best conscience and the best heart of our whole people, of the North and of the South, to lead us out of the darkness and the horror of the present situation.

11 A Savage Ritual

The course of an individual lynching provides some insight into the forces shaping race relations in a given situation. The collective pattern of lynchings also suggests ways of understanding race relations. In either form of inquiry several components are especially revealing.

First, the frequency of lynchings in itself indicates beyond doubt that the killing of black people was neither isolated nor occasional. Those murders, instead, were systematic and common. Even excluding consideration of the gross homicide evident in actual race riots in major cities in the period, more than 2,500 black people were murdered by groups of white people between 1889 and 1918. Between 1891 and 1895 an average of 127 black people were killed each year, or an average of one homicide or more at least every third day for five years. In 1892 alone 155 black people were put to death, a lynching occurring almost every other day. This was indeed an environment of terror, not just occasional, individualized cases.

Second, while as previously noted even the detractors of lynching would support the practice when it involved an affront to white women, and while that oft-assumed justification in many circles provided the pretense of legitimacy to the practice, it appears to have been a carefully constructed myth. Less than a third of the *allegations* (not proven charges) involved either raping or insulting a white woman. In a congressional report inquiring into a proposed anti-lynching bill in 1920, the following charges resulting in lynchings in 1919 alone added up to more than the number of deaths resulting from assault on a white woman: member of Non-Partisan League; talking of Chicago riot; not turning out of road for white boy in auto; leader among Negroes; circulating incendiary literature; misleading mob; intimacy with a white woman; expressing himself too freely re lynching of Negro; causes unknown; and abetting riot. The lynchings were not massive efforts to protect white womanhood.

Indeed, in many of the instances the "crime" appears to have been extremely obscure, or something as highly subjective as appearing to a white man to have neglected the required standards of obsequious behavior and deference, or simply being black.

Third, it is again worthy of note that in most instances offenses were simply charged and not proven. Moreover, the system of justice prevalent in the South makes even "convictions" suspect regarding fair trial and sufficient evidence. The notorious lack of indictments and prosecutions of whites involved in lynchings only confirms the heavy bias in the system of justice. Again, that the victim of the lynching was patently innocent of a crime mattered little in numerous instances. In the following accounts a number of blacks lost their lives not in the name of any kind of "justice" but in a frenzy of blood-lust directed at any available black.

It is this savagery that marks the fourth element of the pattern of lynchings. Often revealed below, in accounts selected from a large number compiled by the NAACP, is a level of brutality and sadism that compounds the seriousness of the practice by giving it a pathological character. The burnings of live people attracted a crowd not noted for its solemnity but one marked by a holiday spirit that was even accompanied by dancing and singing on occasion. Such a grisly scene should make it clear that this is not exclusively a subject for analysis in the framework of due process. The ceremonies were more than vaguely reminiscent of witch burnings of previous centuries. Indeed, the functions may have been remarkably similar. The burning of the witch had served not only justice, in the eyes of the perpetrators, but was the only effective redress against a problem which they were powerless to counter otherwise. Or, in a slightly different vein, Kai Erikson's analysis of the Salem witch prosecutions two centuries earlier indicated that they served to set the behavioral and spiritual limits of the community at a time when older notions of purpose were being undermined by major social changes. Both of these understandings appear relevant to the understanding of lynchings as ceremonies that took on an almost ritualistic complexion. They would normally start with a supposed or believed infraction— the violation by a black of some sacrosanct part of the code of caste obligations—and then move to the quest for a person to be sacrificed, an offering, to redress the grievance. Often the ceremony would become that much more virulent if some force or individual happened to frustrate, even slightly or temporarily, the search for a sacrifice. The frustration might come in the form of the law, or the successful escape of the assumed culprit, or even the mistake of the crowd itself.

That the "crime" was the violation of the unwritten code of caste suggests further the appropriateness of a larger social analysis. In the years in which lynching was most frequent the pressures upon the social structure of the South were enormous. Whether in the concrete forms of social changes generated by the spread of markets and new relationships generated by the growth of "the New South," or in the more threatening but less tangible promises of people like Lewis Harvie Blair who saw in market relations the possible rise of blacks in a competitive society, the strains on an older pre-market system intensified. It would not be misleading, moreover, to find some of the most intensive pressures exactly within those years 1891-1895 when lynchings were most abundant. In 1892 the white power structure based on a single-party South received a significant challenge from a third political party that caused a number of whites, though embittered by an unresponsive government, to recoil at the implications of such a move in racial terms and to support the government of their economic oppressors. Moreover, in those years the severity of the structural changes in society were accentuated by a nation-wide depression of unprecedented magnitude. The problem, then, was the transformation of society by overwhelming forces; the solution, all too often, was not to fight those forces of change (which may even have required an acceptance of some of their elements) but to intensify efforts to hold on to or actively revive the caste system with a deepening of commitments as exhibited in what almost amounted to a contest for barbarity resulting in the sacrifice of blacks. Such unforgettable experiences could not help but be reminders to blacks of their limits; but they were even stronger symbols to the crowds of white witnesses of the omnipotence of the whites. The irony, however, is that such incidents arose out of their very lack of omnipotence. Rather they were victims of social change and market expansion and a colonial system within that market. The South and its farmers—and its poor farmers most of all—were in a colonial situation where their power had vanished or was fading in an industrial society and their way of life was being altered to conform to the habits and disciplines of modern society. J. Glenn Gray speaks of this phenomenon in his essay, "Understanding Violence Philosophically," when he observes that the frustration of the power of the individual, and possibly the collective entity as well, to act in a meaningful way, and indeed the existence of a situation where he can only be acted upon and rendered unfree, gives violence a special appeal. In a much different but equally relevant context, Frantz Fanon, in *The Wretched of the Earth*, argues that in a colonial situation tribal feuds (of which this may be an example) serve an important function: "by throwing himself with all his force into the vendetta, the [colonialized] native tries to persuade himself that colonialism does not exist, that everything is going on as before, that history continues." In other instances Fanon notes that "at the level of individuals, violence is a cleansing force. It frees the native from his inferiority complex and from his despair and inaction; it makes him fearless and restores his self-respect." As Fanon wrote in defense of black revolution against white power, the logic used to understand lynchings should not be mistaken for a defense of them. The lynchings were frequent and brutal. The allegations were often objectively trivial. Many victims were never proven guilty. The tragedy was, however, that even when the crowd lynched a person who may have been guilty of a crime, the attack was misdirected; they killed the wrong person—not the one who generated social problems, but the one who was convenient.

Source: National Association for the Advancement of Colored People, *Thirty Years of Lynching in the United States, 1889-1918* (New York, 1919), pp. 12-16, 18-24, 26-27.

Georgia, 1899

Sam Hose, a Negro farm laborer, was accused of murdering his employer in a quarrel over wages. He escaped. Several days later, while he was being hunted unsuccessfully, the charge was added that he raped his employer's wife. He confessed the murder, but refused, even under duress, to confess the other crime.

The following account of the lynching is taken from the New York *Tribune* for April 24, 1899:

"In the presence of nearly 2,000 people, who sent aloft yells of defiance and shouts of joy, Sam Hose (a Negro who committed two of the basest acts known to crime) was burned at the stake in a public road, one and a half miles from here. Before the torch was applied to the pyre, the Negro was deprived of his ears, fingers and other portions of his body with surprising fortitude. Before the body was cool, it was cut to pieces, the bones were crushed into small bits and even the tree upon which the wretch met his fate was torn up and disposed of as souvenirs.

"The Negro's heart was cut in several pieces, as was also his liver. Those unable to obtain the ghastly relics directly, paid more fortunate possessors extravagant sums for them. Small pieces of bone went for 25 cents and a bit of the liver, crisply cooked, for 10 cents."

No indictments were ever found against any of the lynchers.

* * *

Louisiana, 1899

A peculiarly horrible affair occurred two days ago at Lindsay, near Jackson, La. Mitchell Curry, hearing that someone was in his cornfield, took two Negroes and went to drive away the intruder. There had been an attempted assault on a white woman by a Negro, Val Bages, and by some unexplained course of reasoning, Mitchell Curry, on seeing a large Negro in the field, became convinced that the man was the criminal.

The fellow took fright, was followed, and finally climbed a magnolia tree. The tree was surrounded and the Negro ordered to remain where he was while one of the pursuers was sent for rope to hang him. Presently, however, the man deliberately slid down out of the tree, and halfway down he was shot to death. On examination of the body the man's clothing marked No. 43, was found to be that worn at the State Insane Asylum in the neighboring town of Jackson. On investigation it was learned that the insane occupant had escaped a few days before and the helpless fellow, wandering at large, had suffered death for a crime he had not committed.

* * *

Tennessee, 1901

Ballie Crutchfield, a colored woman, was lynched by a mob at Rome, Tennessee, because her brother stole a purse.

The mob took Crutchfield from the custody of the sheriff, and started with him for the place of execution, when he broke from them and escaped.

"This," says the despatch, "so enraged the mob, that they suspected Crutchfield's sister of being implicated in the theft and last night's work was the culmination of that suspicion."

The Coroner's jury found the usual verdict that the woman came to her death at the hands of parties unknown.

* * *

Louisiana, 1901

Louis Thomas, at Girard, La., a Negro, broke into a local store and stole six bottles of soda-pop. He was later found by a white man named Brown, disposing of its contents, and on being accused of theft, struck his accuser. Brown procured a rifle and shot the Negro twice through the body, but as neither wound proved fatal, a mob of white men took the Negro from the house where he lay wounded and strung him up.

* * *

Georgia, 1904

For the brutal murder of a white family (the Hodges family) at Statesboro', Georgia, two Negroes, Paul Reed and Will Cato, were burned alive in the presence of a large crowd. They had been duly convicted and sentenced, when the mob broke into the courtroom and carried them away, in spite of the plea of a brother of the murdered man, who was present in the court, that the law be allowed to take its course. None of the lynchers were ever indicted.

* * *

Georgia, 1904

Because of the race prejudice growing out of the Hodges murder by Reed and Cato and their lynching, Albert Roger and his son were lynched at Statesboro', Ga., August 17, for being Negroes. A number of other Negroes were whipped for no other offense.

* * *

Georgia, 1904

On account of the race riots which grew out of the above murder (Hodges) and lynching, McBride, a respectable Negro of Portal, Ga., was beaten, kicked and shot to death for trying to defend his wife, who was confined with a baby, three days old, from a whipping at the hands of a crowd of white men.

* * *

West Virginia, 1912

In Bluefield, W. Va., September 4, 1912, Robert Johnson was lynched for attempted rape. When he was accused he gave an alibi and proved every statement that he made. He was taken before the girl who had been attacked and she failed to identify him. She had previously described very minutely the clothes her assailant wore. When she failed to identify Johnson in the clothes he had, the Bluefield police dressed him to fit the description and again took him before her. This time she screamed on seeing him, "That's the man." Her father had also failed to identify him but now he declared himself positive that he recognized Johnson as the guilty man. Thereupon Johnson was dragged out by a mob, protesting his innocence, and after being severely abused, was hung to a telegraph pole. Later his innocence was conclusively established.

* * *

Texas, 1912

Dan Davis, a Negro, was burned at the stake at Tyler, Texas, for the crime of attempted rape, May 25, 1912.

There was some disappointment in the crowd and criticism of those who had bossed the arrangements, because the fire was so slow in reaching the Negro. It was really only ten minutes after the fire was started that smoking shoe soles and twitching of the Negro's feet indicated that his lower extremities were burning, but the time seemed much longer. The spectators had waited so long to see him tortured that they begrudged the ten minutes before his suffering really began.

The Negro had uttered but few words. When he was led to where he was to be burned he said quite calmly, "I wish some of you gentlemen would be Christian enough to cut my throat," but nobody responded. When the fire started, he screamed "Lord, have mercy on my soul," and that was the last word he spoke, though he was conscious for fully twenty minutes after that. His exhibition of nerve aroused the admiration even of his torturers.

A slight hitch in the proceedings occurred when the Negro was about half burned. His clothing had been stripped off and burned to ashes by the flames and his black body hung nude in the gray dawn light. The flesh had been burned from his legs as high as the knees when it was seen that the wood supply was running short. None of the men or boys were willing to miss an incident of the torture. All feared something of more than usual interest might happen, and it would be embarrassing to admit later on not having seen it on account of being absent after more wood.

Something had to be done, however, and a few men from the edge of the crowd, ran after more dry-goods boxes, and by reason of this "public service" gained standing room in the inner circle after having delivered the fuel. Meanwhile the crowd jeered the dying man and uttered shocking comments suggestive of a cannibalistic spirit. Some danced and sang to testify to their enjoyment of the occasion.

* * *

Oklahoma, 1914

Marie Scott of Wagoner County, a seventeen-year-old Negro girl, was lynched by a mob of white men because her brother killed one of two white men who had assaulted her. She was alone in the house when the men entered, but her screams brought her brother to the rescue. In the fight that ensued one of the white men was killed. The next day the mob came to lynch her brother, but as he had escaped, lynched the girl instead. No one has ever been indicted for this crime.

12 The Urban Side of Racial Violence

It should not be thought that vulnerability to racial violence was felt by blacks only in the rural South. As the following testimonies indicate, those blacks who moved from the farm in the South to the cities of the North knew similar experiences. In August 1900 a riot erupted in the Tenderloin district of New York City that pitted blacks against whites. As additional police arrived at the scene they joined the melee, using their clubs indiscriminately on blacks. There is probably no adequate count of the casualties but it is clear that what some called a "nigger chase" was the most searing event in the streets of New York since the Civil War. The origins of this violent episode, however remote in appearance from those violent incidents in the countryside, could be found in similar social pressures. Tensions had been growing in this part of the city since blacks began to move into the working class neighborhood. Of course that move to the North and to the city had been spawned by the very forces reshaping life in the rural South. The clash of cultures and the sensitivity of whites to the inroads made in their neighborhood by blacks, as well as a frequent presumption that blacks belonged properly in the South, made for a volatile situation which would take little to ignite. That the trend of migration from the South was not abating but growing with each year no doubt heightened apprehensions by the whites. They too, like white Southerners, felt their society was being undermined. They too lashed out at what they saw to be the most visible manifestation of their problems.

Source: Frank Moss, *Story of the Riot* (New York, 1900), pp. 11-19, 40-41, 61-63.

City and County of New York, ss.:
Richard C. Creech, being duly sworn, deposes and says that he resides at No.

137 West 53rd Street. That on Wednesday morning, August 15th, 1900, he had been to visit a friend at No. 312 West 45th Street, and left there at about 10:45 P. M. and walked to 8th Avenue, and had reached the corner of 8th Avenue and 45th street, when he was set upon by a gang of rioters, and assaulted by them. That he shouted "Police!" and seeing two officers on the east side of the avenue, corner of 45th Street, he ran towards them when he saw them coming towards him and slackened his pace, thinking that they were coming to his assistance. When they came up to him, without saying a word, they commenced clubbing him, and knocked him unconscious on the sidewalk. He lay there unconscious for some time, he does not know exactly how long, but when he came to he found one of the policeman standing over him, and when he scrambled to his feet the policeman said, "Well, you black son of a b——, I guess you will be good now, won't you? Get out of here as quick as you can!" He then went towards Broadway, and on Broadway between 45th and 46th Streets engaged a cab to take him home, and when he arrived home found that his pocketbook, containing thirty-six dollars in money and a pawnticket for a watch, was gone. He also lost his hat and an umbrella. He sent for his physician, Dr. Robert L. Cooper, 156 West 53rd Street, who took three stitches in his scalp and dressed other wounds on his arm and hand, the result of the clubbing.

RICHARD C. CREECH

Sworn to before me this 1st day of September, 1900.
Geo. P. Hammond, Jr., Notary Public (164), N. Y. County.

City and County of New York, ss.:
Chester Smith, being duly sworn, deposes and says:

I reside at No. 320 West 37th Street. I am employed in Flannery's drug store, at No. 103 West 42nd Street, and have been so employed for the last ten months. On August 15th, 1900, at about ten o'clock P. M., while going to my home, walking on the west side of 8th Avenue between 38th and 39th Streets, I saw a crowd of people, composed mostly of police officers and children. Some one in the crowd said, "There is a nigger!" pointing at me. One of the policemen ran towards me, and seeing that I was in physical danger I ran away from the place, going north to 39th Street on 8th Avenue. Somebody threw a brick at me, which struck me in the back, and then one of the policemen came up to me and struck me in the left eye with his club. My eye and my forehead are still lacerated and discolored. I then ran into the saloon at the southeast corner of 39th Street and 8th Avenue. One of the policemen ran in after me, and told me to go outside and run towards Broadway; that the mob had dispersed. I started toward the door, and as I reached it I saw that they were still waiting outside. I said to the officer as I started back into the saloon, "No, sir, I can't go out there; they'll kill me." The policeman then lifted me from the ground and threw me through the swinging door into the street. The glass in the door was broken, and I fell on my hands and knees. The policemen and the mob then began beating me, the policemen beating me with their clubs. They did not disperse the crowd or protect me from it. I then started to run towards Broadway; another policeman ran after me and struck me in the back with his club. I staggered, made one or two jumps, and fell in front of No. 236 West

39th Street. The lady of the house, a white woman, came out, and I was taken into the house by some one, I don't know whom. Two or three days after she told me that the officers soon left the house, but that the mob tried to break in, and that she told them that if they would not leave she would kill them. The lady rang for a messenger boy and sent word to my employer to call. He came and brought some bandages, etc., and bandaged my head. He then called two police officers and asked them to take me to the station house. They refused. He insisted, and they finally yielded and took me to the station house. I was treated there by a police surgeon. My employer remained with me until three o'clock the next morning. I did not work for three days after this. I saw one man treated very harshly at the station house, being clubbed by police officers, and I believe he would have been treated still worse if it had not been for the presence of reporters. I did nothing whatever to justify this brutal treatment on the part of the police officers. I believe that had it not been for the presence of my employer I would have been beaten still more. There were over twenty-five policemen in the crowd. I was unconscious part of the time. I have never been arrested in my life.

CHESTER SMITH.

Sworn to before me this 5th day of September, 1900.
Geo. P. Hammond, Jr., Notary Public (164), N. Y. County.

City and County of New York, ss.:
John L. Newman, being duly sworn, deposes and says:

I reside at No. 351 West 37th Street, in the rear house. On August 15th, 1900, I went to the restaurant which is in the front building, for supper. This was about 10:30 P. M. After I had been there a few minutes some one told me that the mob was coming. I had seen them beat colored people during the evening, without any cause, so I walked out of the restaurant into my apartments, which are in the rear, only a few steps away; I live in the basement floor. I did this so as to avoid any trouble. As I reached the front door and walked in I closed it, and proceeded to go into my apartments. Four officers immediately came, and one of them said, "Stop!" and kicked open the door. Then one of them grabbed me and said,"Here is a d——d nigger; kill him!" The four officers then beat me with their clubs until I became unconscious. They then carried me to the station house. I was unconscious during all this time, but my friends tell me that the police were beating me all the way to the station house. It is located one block west from where I live. At the station house I recovered my consciousness. I was arraigned before the sergeant, and the officer who struck me first made the complaint against me. At the sergeant's desk I felt very weak, bleeding from my head and eye, and I held on to the railing for support. One of the officers struck me in the ribs with a night stick, and said, "God d——n you, stand up there!" I fell forward on the sergeant's desk, and I said, "For God's sake, take a gun and blow out my brains! If you have got to take a life, take mine, and don't murder me this way!" The sergeant then said very gruffly to the officer, "Take him away!" While all this was going on Chief of Police Devery was in the station house standing about ten feet away, talking to somebody whom I did not know. He saw all this, but did not interfere, conversing with the man all the time, as if nothing unusual was going on. I have known Chief Devery for three or four years, and have spoken with him in a friendly way many times. When I was brought into the muster room, in the rear of the station house, I saw several colored people being treated for their wounds. I was bleeding from my head and eye, and could not see well, and I sat down in the wrong chair. Two policemen then came over to me, pulled me out of the chair, and were raising their clubs to strike me when some one said, "Don't hit this man any more," and they obeyed. My wounds were then dressed, and I was taken to a cell. About twelve o'clock, when the officer who was making the prison rounds came to my cell, I asked him for permission to see the sergeant. He asked why, and I told him that my house was unlocked, and that I wished he would send an officer to lock it. He said he would speak to the sergeant about it. In a few minutes he returned and said, "The sergeant said, 'D——n him,' and that 'he had not business with the house,'" and he did not send anyone to lock it and protect my property. While I was in the station house I saw a colored man, John Haines, struck by several officers with their clubs. He was naked, only wearing a little undershirt. The officers were striking all the colored men in the station house, and without any interference. In court, the next morning, I was arraigned before Judge Cornell. The officer swore that I was causing a riot in the street. I denied this. I did not have any witnesses in court, because I did not have any opportunity to produce them. The Judge did not ask me whether I wanted an examination or not, and expressed his doubts as to my guilt, and said the case was "very curious." But the officers were persistent in their false statements, aforesaid, and the magistrate put me under $100 bonds to keep the peace. Not being able to furnish this, I was sent to the Penitentiary, where I was for thirty days. I was treated at the Penitentiary by Dr. Thomas Higgins, who told me that my head would never be right as long as I lived. I have been sick ever since. Dr. Higgins told me that he would testify for me in any proceeding which I might institute. I am employed by the Metropolitan Street Railway Company as a rockman, but am unable to work at present. I have lived in New York City for over forty-three years, and have never been arrested before in my life. I did not participate in the riots, was not on the street, and did nothing whatever to justify this conduct on the part of the police. I can recognize the officer who made the charge against me; he was the first to strike me.

JOHN L. NEWMAN.

Sworn to before me this 19th day of September, 1900.
John F. Maccolgan, Notary Public (4), N. Y. County.
(The officer in the case was Holland.)

City and County of New York, ss.:
Mrs. Martha A. Brown, being duly sworn, deposes and says:
I reside at No. 351 West 37th Street. On Wednesday, August 15th, 1900, about 10:15 P. M., while on my way upstairs I saw John Newman, who lives in the rear house at the above number, come in the front door and close it; he had almost reached the rear of the hall when the front door was opened by a policeman who had his club raised, and who ran up to the said Newman, struck him over the head with his club, felling him to the floor; he then dragged Newman to

the street, clubbing him meanwhile, and at the front door he was joined by four other officers, who assisted him to drag Newman out into the street, where they threw him into the midst of a mob which had congregated outside, and some of whom jumped on Newman, stamping on his stomach with their feet. Newman was then again taken by the officers and dragged to the station house on the next block. Deponent states further that Newman did not appear to be trying to get away from anyone, when he entered the front door, and further when he was struck first he was struck from behind.

MARTHA A. BROWN.

Sworn to before me this 24th day of September, 1900.
Geo. P. Hammond, Jr., Notary Public (164), N. Y.

13 That Old Black Magic

The persistence of various beliefs and assumptions concerning the supernatural has not only served to mark black people with a peculiar component in stereotypes but can also serve to reveal something about black culture itself. Toward the end of the nineteenth century a fascination with black beliefs in magic, conjurers, spirits, and the like resulted in the frequent reporting of the contents and forms of such beliefs. In the following accounts some of the representative fears and hopes generated by this supernatural structure can be seen. Two points should be noted concerning this phenomenon. One is that while many of the beliefs show an obvious African source, they have often been merged with, or coexist with, Christian religious habits. As such they demonstrate not only the persistence of African culture and separateness in blacks but also ways of making the cultural forms to which they were exposed in this country more palatable. Second, such beliefs have often made their holders vulnerable to charges of irrationality. It should not be forgotten, however, that "rationality" itself is a cultural attribute associated with modernity which includes a certain calculating proclivity and a system of logic based upon the concrete as evidence that renders the material world the prime source of reference in understanding. Such magic, more than a secularized religion which places a premium on man as agent in the world, thus served not only to exalt the spiritual in the face of materialistic pressures that reached painful intensities, but to provide a continuing sense of identity that integrated the individual into the traditions of his people. Indeed, the problems of that supernatural world, and the hopes and promises too, remained deeply personal in an increasingly impersonal world. Holding on to the spiritual beliefs of the past may have marked many blacks as irrational but it did so by allowing a dignity and power that transcended the pressures of contemporary society.

Source: "Concerning Negro Sorcery in the United States," *The Journal of American Folk-Lore*, 3 (October-December 1890): 281-87.

There are in Atlanta perhaps a hundred old men and women who practice voudooism. They tell fortunes, point out the whereabouts of lost and stolen goods, furnish love philters, and cast spells upon people and cattle. The patrons of these professors of the black art belong to all ranks and classes of negroes. It is by no means uncommon to find an intelligent house servant, a church member in good standing, and a leader in the "Society of the Holy Order of the Sisters of Senegambia," thoroughly under the influence of some withered old mummy of a voudoo doctor, who keeps her in a state of abject fear, and extorts a large portion of her monthly wages. Good, clever negroes frequently lose their health and spirits without any known cause, and in some instances they admit to white friends, in whom they have confidence, that they have been conjured or voudooed. An endless number of instances could be mentioned. At the present writing, there is in the city a respectable negro who believes that he is under a spell and must die. His offense consisted in dismissing his voudoo doctor. In revenge, the old fraud turned upon his patient, and with a menacing look and gesture said, "For this your vitals shall burn, and burn, and burn!" The victim of the curse firmly believes that his vitals are burning up, and, if he fails to bribe his persecutor to let him alone, he will probably lie down and die. [1885]

* * *

From daylight until dark, and from dark until daylight again, the woman lies upon her bed, an immovable and almost lifeless body. Her eyes are always open, and fixed with a steady gaze upon the ceiling. Occasionally her hands go up to her forehead, and as they do she moans as though enduring the greatest pain. She positively refuses to talk, if talk she can. Since the day she was seized with the strange illness, she has not closed her eyes one moment. But the strangest part of the story is her total abstinence from food. Not one mouthful of food has passed her lips for nearly a month, and yet she does not seem to have fallen away one ounce. The woman's neighbors all declare that she has been "conjured" by the old woman, who bears the reputation of being the only successful "conjurer" in Atlanta. The "spell," as they call it, was occasioned by the bottle, in which there was water and a half dozen hairs. These hairs constitute the power of the charm, and are supposed to have been pulled from the right hind leg of a cat, which the "conjurer" turned loose as soon as she secured what she wanted. The only cure for the "spell" is the capture of that cat, and as the particular cat is known to only the "conjurer," its capture seems almost impossible. The husband of the afflicted woman has offered the "conjurer" fifty dollars for the cat, or to have the "spell" removed, but with a peculiar persistency she avows she has had no hand in the affair. This declaration none of her acquaintances credit. They all declare she never admits anything of the kind. In vain hopes of getting the right cat, about fifty members of the feline tribe have been butchered in that part of the city recently, but the death of none has removed the spell. [1883]

* * *

In Charleston, S. C., less than two years ago, a negro girl of about eighteen or nineteen years, a domestic, became hysterical very suddenly, and seemed to show symptoms of insanity. This occurrence followed close upon the girl's refusal of a persistent suitor. The employers of the girl at once called a competent physician, who was unable to account for her condition and recommended that she be removed to the city hospital, which was done. Here, after treatment proved unavailing, she was pronounced insane, and the physicians in charge urged that she be sent to an insane asylum. As the sister of the patient refused to allow this to be done, the girl's former employers were much perplexed to know what to do with her, after her removal from the hospital, but at this juncture a woman "voudoo doctor," who plied her calling surreptitiously among the negroes of the city and vicinity, offered, through a third person, to take off the spell for twenty dollars. The family with whom the sick girl had lived finally paid the money, the voudoo doctor treated the patient for about a week, gave her medicine, and cured her. It was generally believed by the girl's colored friends that her insanity was caused by a "spell" laid on her by the rejected lover, and removed by the voudoo doctor. My informant in regards to this case is a man of ample education and much culture, of marked scientific tastes, and personally acquainted with most of the parties concerned. He saw the girl while in the hospital, and had the account of her case from the attending physician, as well as from her employers.

* * *

We have before us something of a curiosity in the shape of a voudoo or conjure bag. Negroes in this section, even in their most enlightened circles, have never gotten rid of that lowest order of superstition common to the race since the birth of their most ancient forefathers, which is a firm belief in and practice of what has been called voudooism. The little bag we have before us was picked up on Broad Street, in front of the Selma Furniture Store, a few days since. It contains a rabbit's foot, a piece of dried coon-root (a bulbous plant that grows spontaneously in Southern forests), also some other herbs and roots dug from the woods, and some small particles of parched tobacco. The rabbit's foot, perhaps, possesses more powers of sorcery than any other instrument in use among the black magicians of the South. Numbers of negroes in the South carry a rabbit's foot in their pockets, or concealed about their persons, as constantly as the plowboy carries his knife. There is not one negro out of every hundred who will allow another person, white or black, to approach them with the enchanted foot. They will almost go into spasms of terror, and will fight as for dear life, rather than come in contact with a rabbit foot in the hand of another person. What there is about the foot of an ordinary rabbit, or more properly speaking hare, that sways such a powerful influence for the negro juggler, is something we can't understand, but that it does is a settled fact. There is an old negro at labor for the city now who was arrested and tried for vagrancy several days since. He claims to be a voudoo doctor, and many negroes in town actually fear him as they would a rattlesnake. Perhaps the bundle of trash before us is the property of this same old superstitious negro, and if so, according to the doctrine of voudooism, its magical powers are all lost. [Selma, Alabama, 1884]

14 The Song of the Black Man

The separateness of black culture never ceased to amaze the curious and cosmopolitan at the end of the century. So too did they seldom understand that culture. One of the most salient qualities, visible to all to some degree, was black music. While some attributed that music to the "natural rhythm" and inherent musical abilities of the blacks, it was pre-eminently an important form of cultural expression. It would often have its own syncopated rhythm and be unrestrained by the more gentle or delicate lyrics of white music. And it owed much to long generations of growth in a separate culture. In the following account of experiences on the eastern shore of Chesapeake Bay some of the elements of that music were noted at a time when the music, and black culture, showed signs of a transition. Note the impression made by "the abandonment" with which the blacks moved their bodies with the music. This, of course, to the author, fit the image of the natural rhythm of the race. More reasonably it testified to the lack of acculturation in a tightly disciplined society where restraint was rewarded more than was "abandonment." Thus, also, perhaps, the attraction it held for whites. It is significant too that the man sent to sing solo to the author did so with the greatest reluctance. The African archetype, away from which black music had strayed little, was instead group oriented with the greatest variation being in the leader call-group response form. This was evident in church and in work. As is clear from this description the same "spirituals" which were voiced in religious services accompanied blacks into the field. So ardent were these commitments to spiritual songs that the faithful would sing no others. Among many blacks secular song was still suppressed vigorously. In time the legitimacy of the solo singer and the secular song would emerge and bring with it new forms of, again, distinctly black music. As of this point, however, the necessary individualism and this-worldliness of

American social pressure were resisted. Indeed, even when those elements could surface in black music they did so in ways which would turn topsy-turvy the notions of individualism and materialism. Note also the connection made by the author with this form of musical expression and other elements of black culture—namely the prevalence of beliefs in the supernatural.

Source: Mrs. Fanny D. Bergen, "On the Eastern Shore," *The Journal of American Folklore*, 2 (October-December 1889): 296-98.

I was not a little surprised to find how far back in the history of civilization one turns on entering into the state of mind of the country negro. The disorderly host of ghosts and spirits, the witchcraft, charms, spells, and conjuring against which Reginald Scot brought to bear the whole arsenal of his learning, in England in the sixteenth century, finds its counterpart here within a half-day's ride of one of our foremost American universities. I shall here insert a few examples taken somewhat at random from the collection of folk medicine, animal lore, songs, divinations, folk tales, ghost stories, and tales of witchcraft, numbering some two hundred items in all, gathered in less than a fortnight of available collecting-time.

My little son observed that nearly every colored man employed on the farm wore a narrow leather strap or thong fastened about one wrist or forearm, usually the right. I asked a boy of perhaps fifteen what was the object of these straps. He grinned in a very sober fashion, watching intently his bare feet, one great toe all the time scraping the floor of the piazza, and insisted that he knew nothing of the practice, though I am fully persuaded that at the very time he wore under his ragged shirtsleeve such a strap on his own arm.

Further inquiry in other quarters, however, informed me that these leather straps are believed to give one strength, and are also efficacious in relieving rheumatism or a sprained wrist. Another common custom in Chestertown is wearing a leather string about the neck to prevent taking the whooping-cough when that epidemic is prevalent. The whites also to some extent use this prophylactic.

The most pleasing thing in our intercourse with the colored people was their singing. We were fortunate enough to be on the farm at the time of the wheat-threshing, and were greatly entertained by the singing of the hands after supper, as they gathered in the roomy kitchen or on the benches out-of-doors. It was most interesting to see the abandonment with which they swayed the whole body back and forth, sometimes keeping time also with feet and hands as they sang. One of the men was at another time sent in to sing to me, when I had much difficulty in getting him to vocalize at all. He had a cold, was going to town in a few minutes, and so on. Evidently the surroundings were not favorable, and it was hard for him to sing away from his fellow-workmen and the familiar atmosphere of the kitchen. At length, however, he managed to get through with one characteristic selection, but when I suggested another, a favorite song among the men, he declined, saying that that was a song, and the churchmembers could not sing songs. "But wouldn't it be all right for you to sing it to me, Will?"

"No, ma'am; it might be all right for anybody out in de fiel' [a person not a follower of the faith], but ef you is tryin' to serve de Lord, ef you is in de fold, then you mus' only sing hymns, or what they call the sperichul songs." And this distinction between worldly songs and those that church-members might rightly sing I found to be carefully observed by the latter.

* * *

To show how indefinable was the quality which distinguishes the "sperichul songs" from the secular ones, I insert two fragments, the former overheard at a negro camp-meeting by a white minister of the Methodist denomination who had gone to the meeting with the hope of lending some assistance in the exercises,—a hope which the character of the proceedings soon dispelled. The latter selection was the only bit which I could secure of a song which all church-members refused to sing on account of its worldly character.

> Jesus died for you an' me,
> Hang yo' bonnet on a tree;
> Ef you want to save yo' soul,
> Get yo' bonnet with a pole.
>
> Way down yander to de sunrise,
> The Devil thought he'd torture me;
> He burnt down my ole apple tree,
> Way down yander to de sunrise.

15 Ragged Music

The division between spiritual music and the more worldly songs was sometimes most subtle. Those secular forms of music were nonetheless popular in parts of the black community—and in some parts of white society as well. In the late 1890s one form, ragtime, emerged with a flair. Partly because of its origins in the red-light district and partly because of its structure, which was a fusion of syncopated rhythms characteristic of black music with a more classical metered rhythm, this musical form was controversial. To some it was a jubilant and creative fulfillment. To others it threatened all that was sacred. Some of the appeal that it had as well as some of the atmosphere surrounding it can be seen in the reminiscence of Willie the Lion Smith. His last sentence conveys what many found attractive about ragtime—a fusion of the mind and the soul.

Source: Willie the Lion Smith with George Hoefer, *Music on My Mind: The Memoirs of an American Pianist* (New York: Doubleday & Company, 1964), pp. 25-26.

Back in those early days churchgoing Negro people would not stand for ragtime playing; they considered it to be sinful. Part of that feeling was due to the fact that the popular songs you heard played around in the saloons had bawdy lyrics and when you played in a raggy style, folks would right away think of the bad words and all the hell-raising they heard, or had heard about, in the red-light district.

Yeah, in the front parlor, where the neighbors could hear your playing, you had to sing the proper religious words and keep that lilting tempo down!

I kept telling my mother I was tired of playing the same old melodies the same old ways. In my wanderings around town in the saloons, dance halls, and theaters, I picked up on such tunes as the "Maple Leaf Rag" by Scott Joplin, the "Cannonball Rag" by Joe Northup, and the "Black and White Rag" by George

Botsford. But in those days I didn't know the names of the rags, or who they were written by, because I had learned them by listening to other piano players. One of my favorites was the famous "Don't Hit that Lady Dressed in Green." Man, the lyrics to this song were a sex education, especially for a twelve-year-old boy.

Musically, I was beginning to get the mind and soul talking, and from then on it was to be music on my mind, all the time.

16 A Black Migration

The circumstances of black life in America were clearly changing early in the twentieth century as the system of market relations intruded further and deeper into the entire nation, and indeed the world. At its narrowest and most literal that market could even be seen in the migration of large groups of landless people in search of independence or survival, whether from one part of the world to another as market systems replaced feudal or seigneurial relationships in southern Europe, or from one part of the country to another as the exodus from the farm to the city evident at least since the end of the Civil War. But many of the changes involved in this transformation were muted in those same years by a desire to retain blacks on the land as a cheap and servile labor force. The depopulation of the black countryside had been threatened previously, as with the Exodusters in the 1870s, but it was not until the years surrounding World War I that the process gained momentum—irreversibly. In those years black wishes to escape oppressive restraints merged with powerful market forces like those that had previously pulled and pushed others from the land to the factory. The floods, boll weevils, and unremitting discrimination provided the push; the possibility of new jobs due to wartime production efforts and a possible labor shortage provided the pull. This is not to say that the promised land lay waiting in the cities of the North any more than it had to a previous generation in Kansas. But the power of the market in reshaping the conditions of life, even to the point of bringing masses of people to chance it all and move into another kind of life, was unmistakable. The following letters illustrate the despair, the hope, the faith, the sincerity and the belief in hard work shared by many of those who migrated.

Source: Emmett J. Scott, ed., "Letters of Negro Migrants of 1916-1918," *Journal of Negro History*, 4 (July 1919): 291-94, 296-99, 319-20, 325-26.

DALLAS, TEX.,
April 23, 1917.

Dear Sir:

Having been informed through the Chicago Defender paper that I can secure information from you. I am a constant reader of the Defender and am contemplating on leaving here for some point north. Having your city in view I thought to inquire of you about conditions for work, housing, wages and everything necessary. I am now employed as a laborer in a structural shop, have worked for the firm five years.

I stored cars for Armour packing co. 3 years, I also claims to know something about candy making, am handy at most anything for an honest living. I am 31 yrs. old have a very industrious wife, no children. If chances are available for work of any kind let me know. Any information you can give me will be highly appreciated.

JACKSONVILLE, FLA., 4-25-17.

Dear Sir:

in reading a copy of the Chicago defender note that if i get in touch with you you would assist me in getting imployment. i am now imployed in Florida East coast R R service road way department any thing in working line myself and friends would be very glad to get in touch with as labors. We would be more than glad to do so and would highly appreciate it the very best we can advise where we can get work to do, fairly good wages also is it possible that we could get transportation to the destination. We are working men with familys. Please answer at once. i am your of esteem. We are not particular about the electric lights and all i want is fairly good wages and steady work.

MARCEL, MISS., 10/4/17.

Dear Sir:

Although I am a stranger to you but I am a man of the so called colored race and can give you the very best or reference as to my character and ability by prominent citizens of my community by both white and colored people that knows me although am native of Ohio whiles I am a northern desent were reared in this state of Mississippi. Now I am a reader of your paper the Chicago Defender. After reading your writing ever wek I am compell & persuade to say that I know you are a real man of my color you have I know heard of the south land & I need not tell you any thing about it. I am going to ask you a favor and at the same time beg you for your kind and best advice. I wants to come to Chicago to live. I am a man of a family wife and 1 child I can do just any kind of work in the line of common labor & I have for the present sufficient means to support us till I can obtain a position. Now should I come to your town, would you please to assist me in getting a position I am willing to pay whatever you charge I dont want you to loan me not 1 cent but help me to find an occupation there in your town now I has a present position that will keep me employed till the first of Dec. 1917. now please give me your best advice on this subject. I enclose stamp for reply.

17 The Price of a Corrupt System

In the first two decades of the twentieth century racial violence erupted time and again in the major urban areas of the nation. The source for that racial enmity is often obscure but in at least one case the roots were obvious. After the riots in East St. Louis in 1917 Congress appointed a special committee to undertake an investigation. The committee's inquiry uncovered a variety of developments which contributed directly and indirectly to the explosive situation. They included the rapid influx of more than ten thousand black people seeking work (often after glittering promises of rewards had been tendered) in the single year of 1917 (indeed most likely in the half year preceding the riots), the discharge of white workers in favor of blacks who would work for less, the rise of dramatic unemployment and poverty among the blacks, the use of blacks as strike-breakers, and in fact the emergence of an entire underworld racket thriving on the needs and vulnerabilities of this community. As that criminal activity needed the protection of the law, it had, over the years, merged with the political establishment and erected a complex system of rewards and obligations in the management of the city which responded least of all to public needs and most of all to entrenched power. The city was plundered, corporations diverted public money and resources to their own use, and criminals were protected by the law enforcement machinery and system of justice. It was in this context that blacks were saddled with the blame and responsibility for urban problems. A statement by one of the bosses at the end of the section that "something had to be done to the 'niggers' or they would have taken over the town" indicates just how clearly the most vulnerable and powerless group in the city had been used as a scapegoat or a red herring to divert attention from their own sins. The only action possibly more deliberate in its viciousness was that of Alexander Flannigan, a noted attorney in the city who, according to the committee, "ha[d] long been a menace to decency and order in East St. Louis," and who delivered a speech to the workingmen of East St. Louis. This incendiary address gave the rioters specific advice about what they ought to be doing. According to the committee, "They followed his advice, and the scenes of murder and arson that ensued were the logical result of his utterances." Thus this selection of the committee's report is significant not just for its description of the racial violence, which amounted to a pogrom similar to those that had occurred in other cities, from the riot in Memphis at the end of the Civil War well into the twentieth century, but because it lays out openly the systematic nature of the oppression of blacks and whites by powerful men and corporations, and the neat transfer by those same men and corporations of the responsibility for all that was wrong to the blacks they had encouraged to come, and had exploited once they arrived. The brutal suffering inflicted in the riots was but an additional price shoved onto blacks by that system.

Source: *East St. Louis Riots*. Report of the Special Committee Authorized by Congress to Investigate the East St. Louis Riots, 65th Congress, 2d Session, House of Representatives, Document No. 1231 (Washington, D.C., 1918), pp. 1-11.

Your committee appointed under House resolution No. 128 for the purpose of making investigation of the East St. Louis riots which occurred on May 28 and July 2, 1917, reports that as a result of unlawful conditions existing at that place, interstate commerce was not only openly and violently interrupted but was virtually suspended for a week or 10 days during and following the riot of last July. For months after the July riot interstate commerce was interfered with and hindered, not, however, by open acts of violence, but by a subtle and effective intimidation of colored men who had been employed by the railroads to handle freight consigned from one State to another. So many of these men were driven out of East St. Louis as the result of the July riot that the railroads could not secure necessary help. After the worst effects of the riot had passed this class of labor remained so frightened and intimidated that it would not live in East St. Louis. Some of them took up their residences across the river in St. Louis, and would go over to East St. Louis in the morning to work and would return to that place before nightfall. In order to get out of East St. Louis and back to St. Louis before night came on the length of the day's work was reduced. The fright of these laborers went to such an extent—and it was fully justified by existing conditions—that special means of transportation had to be provided for them back and forth between St. Louis and East St. Louis in order to get them to work at all. Besides the killing of a number of these negro laborers, a very large number, indeed, fled from the work and never returned to it. In addition to this 44 freight cars were burned and serious damage done to the railroad tracks, all of which will be referred to further along in this report.

Your committee made an earnest, nonpartisan effort to determine the basic cause of the riot. We endeavored to pursue every avenue of information to its source, searched the hearts and consciences of all witnesses, and sought the opinions of men in every walk of life. The officers of the mills and factories placed the blame at the door of organized labor; but the overwhelming weight of testimony, to which is added the convictions of the committee, ascribes the mob spirit and its murderous manifestations to the bitter race feeling that had grown up between the whites and blacks.

The natural racial aversion, which finds expression in mob violence in the North as in the South, was augmented in East St. Louis by hundreds of petty conflicts between the whites and the blacks. During the year 1917 between 10,000 and 12,000 negroes came from the Southern States to seek work at promised high wages in the industries of St. Clair County. They swarmed into the railroad stations on every train, to be met by their friends who formed reception committees and welcomed them to the financial, political and social liberty which they had been led to believe Illinois guaranteed. They seldom had more than enough money to exactly defray their transportation, and they arrived dirty and hungry. They stood around the street corners in homesick huddles, seeking shelter and hunting work.

How to deal with them soon became a municipal problem. Morning found them gathered at the gates of the manufactories, where often they were chosen in preference to the white men who also sought employment. But as rapidly as employment was found for those already there fresh swarms arrived from the South, until the great number without employment menaced the prosperity and safety of the community.

The Aluminum Ore Co. brought hundreds and hundreds of them to the city as strike breakers, to defeat organized labor, a precedent which aroused intense hatred and antagonism and caused countless tragedies as its aftermath. The feeling of resentment grew with each succeeding day. White men walked the streets in idleness, their families suffering for food and warmth and clothes, while their places as laborers were taken by strange negroes who were compelled to live in hovels and who were used to keep down wages.

It was proven conclusively that the various industries in St. Clair County were directly responsible for the importation of these negroes from the South. Advertisements were printed in various Southern newspapers urging the negroes to come to East St. Louis and promising them big wages. In many instances agents were sent through the South to urge the negroes to abandon profitable employment there and come to East St. Louis, where work was said to be plentiful and wages high.

One of the local railroads sent an agent to the Southern States, and on some trips he brought back with him as many as 30 or 40 negro men, all of them employed at their southern homes, making from $2 to $2.50 a day. A number of these men testified before the committee that they were promised $2.40 a day "and board" if they would come to East St. Louis; but when they did come they were paid only $1.40 a day, with an allowance of 60 cents a day for board, and were fed on coffee, bread and "lasses" and made to sleep on sacks in box cars, where they suffered keenly from the cold.

Responsibility for this influx of 10,000 or more negroes into East St. Louis rests on the railroads and the manufacturing establishments, and they must bear their share of the responsibility for the ensuing arson and murder that followed this unfortunate invasion.

It is a lamentable fact that the employers of labor paid too little heed to the comfort or welfare of their men. They saw them crowded into wretched cabins, without water or any of the conveniences of life; their wives and children condemned to live in the disreputable quarters of the town, and made no effort to lift them out of the mire.

The negroes gravitated to the unsanitary sections, existed in the squalor of filthy cabins, and made no complaint; but the white workmen had a higher outlook, and the failure to provide them with better homes added to their bitter dissatisfaction with the burdens placed upon them by having to compete with black labor. This resentment spread until it included thousands who did not have to work with their hands.

Ten thousand and more strange negroes added to the already large colored population soon made East St. Louis a center of lawlessness. Within less than a year before the riot over 800 "holdups" were committed in the city. More than 80 per cent of the murders were committed by negroes. Highway robberies were nightly occurrences; rape was frequent; while a host of petty offenses kept the law-abiding citizens in a state of terror.

White women were afraid to walk the streets at night; negroes sat in their laps on street cars; black women crowded them from their seats; they were openly insulted by drunken negroes. The low saloons and gambling houses were crowded with idle vagabonds; the dance halls in the negro sections were filled with prostitutes, half clad, in some instances naked, performing lewd dances.

Negroes were induced to buy homes in white districts by unscrupulous real estate agents; and, as a consequence, the white people sold their homes at a sacrifice and moved elsewhere.

Owners of cheap property preferred negroes as tenants, charging them $15 a month rent for houses for which white workmen had paid only $10.

Corrupt politicians found the negro vote fitted to their foul purpose, and not only bought them on election day, but in the interval protected them in their dens of vice, their low saloons and barrel houses. They had immunity in the courts; crooked lawyers kept them out of jail; and a disorganized, grafting police force saw to it that they were not molested.

East St. Louis wallowed in a mire of lawlessness and unshamed corruption. Criminals from every quarter of the country gathered there, unmolested and safe from detection.

This was the condition of affairs on the night of July 1, 1917, when an automobile—some witnesses say there were two—went through a negro section of the city and fired promiscuously into their homes. No one was injured, but the act aroused a fierce spirit in the breasts of the negroes.

The ringing of a church bell at midnight, which was a prearranged signal, drew a crowd of negroes from that immediate section armed with guns and pistols. They marched through the streets ready to avenge the attack on their homes. They had not gone far until an automobile containing several policemen and a newspaper reporter crossed their path, having been notified by telephone that there was danger of an outbreak. The negroes cursed them and told them to drive on, although one of the detectives flashed his police badge and assured them that they had come to protect them.

For answer the negro mob fired a volley into the machine which, at the first shot, drove rapidly away. The negroes continued to empty their guns and pistols, with the result that one of the officers was instantly killed and another so badly wounded that he died later.

The police automobile, riddled with bullets, stood in front of police headquarters next morning and thousands viewed it. The early editions of the papers gave full details of the tragedy of the night before. And, on July 2, East St. Louis awoke to a realization of the awful fact that the dread which had knocked at every heart for months could no longer be denied. Years of lawlessness had at last borne bloody fruit. As the day wore on negro mobs killed other white men, and shot at men and women who were offering them no wrong.

Dr. McQuillan, a well-known physician, and his wife were dragged from their machine and shamefully abused. The doctor was shot, his ribs were broken, and both he and his wife were badly beaten. One of his assailants remarked, "Boys, this is Dr. McQuillan, the Aluminum Ore Co. doctor," and pleaded for his life. The would-be murderers, some of whom must have been employed by the Ore Co., helped the doctor and his wife into their machine and, cranking it for them, sent them on their way.

The news of these murders and fresh outrages spread rapidly, and the streets soon filled with excited people. Men and boys, girls and women of the town began to attack every negro in sight. All fared alike, young and old, women and children; none was spared. The crowd soon grew to riotous proportions, and for hours the man hunt continued, stabbing, clubbing and shooting, not the guilty but unoffending negroes. One was hanged from a telephone pole and another had a rope tied around his neck and was dragged through the streets, the maddened crowd kicking and beating him as he lay prostrate and helpless.

The negroes were pursued into their homes, and the torch completed the work of destruction. As they fled from the flames they were shot down, although many of them came out with uplifted hands, pleading to be spared.

It was a day and night given over to arson and murder. Scenes of horror that would have shocked a savage were viewed with placid unconcern by hundreds, whose hearts knew no pity, and who seemed to revel in the feast of blood and cruelty.

It is not possible to give accurately the number of dead. At least 39 negroes and 8 white people were killed outright, and hundreds of negroes were wounded and maimed. "The bodies of the dead negroes," testified an eyewitness, "were thrown into a morgue like so many dead hogs."

* * *

East St. Louis for many years has been a plague spot; within its borders and throughout its environs every offense in the calendar of crime and every lapse in morals and public decency has been openly committed, each day increasing the terrors of the law-abiding. No terms of condemnation, applied to the men who were responsible for the appalling conditions revealed before your committee, can be too severe. No punishment that outraged justice may visit upon them will be adequate. In many cases they deserve the extreme penalty; in every case they merit the execration of a despoiled and disgraced community.

The purpose of the politicians of both political parties, who found East St. Louis respected and prosperous and in a few years robbed its treasury, gave away valuable franchises, sank it in the mire of pollution, and brought upon it national censure and disgrace, was deliberate. They united to elect men to high office who would further their schemes of spoilation even when they feared to share their plunder. It was a conspiracy as shameless as it was confident. They left nothing to chance. It took account of the executive; it provided for an unscrupulous legislative board; it made certain of police commissioners who would take orders and deliver the goods; it embraced the courts high and low; it went into partnership with every vile business; it protected every lawless saloon; it encouraged houses of prostitution in the very shadow of the city hall; it gave protection to gamblers, immunity to thieves and murderers.

The gang that took possession of East St. Louis harbored the off-scourings of the earth. The vag, the safe blower and the "stick-up man" flocked to its sheltering arms, safe from arrest or disturbance.

The good people of this sorely afflicted community were powerless. The chamber of commerce, which should have had the courage to rally the law-abiding and drive out the lawless, was ineffective. They actually "laid upon the table" a resolution of inquiry to investigate the conditions that made property unsafe and life perilous.

The owners of the great corporations whose plants were in and about East St. Louis lived in other cities. They pocketed their dividends without concern for the municipal dishonesty that wasted the taxes, and without a thought for the thousands of their own workmen, black and white, who lived in hovels, the victims of poverty and disease, of long hours and incessant labor.

The greed that made crooks of politicians made money grabbers of the manufacturers, who pitted white labor against black, drove organized labor from their plants, brought thousands of inefficient negroes from the South, crowding the white men from their positions. All this stirred the fires of race hatred until it finally culminated in bloody, pitiless riot, arson and wanton murder.

Mayor Mollman surrounded himself with advisers who were familiar with the game of politics. They were not interested in securing an honest and economical administration. Their business first was to elect a man who would be subservient; one who possibly might not put his own hand into the public treasury, but would look the other way if a friend were so engaged. They needed a man who would stand between them and the indignant taxpayer; a fair promiser but a poor performer; personally honest, maybe but so weak, so feeble, and so easily influenced that the conspirators were able to dictate his policies, and in the shadow of his stupidity loot the municipality. This was not the result of corruption in only one political party. It was brought about by a combination between the leaders of the worst elements in both parties. They pooled issues in the city election and declared regular dividends on their investment at the expense of honest people.

In the history of corrupt politics in this country there never has been a more shameless debauchery of the electorate nor a more vicious alliance between the agencies and beneficiaries of crime than for years existed in East St. Louis. It is a disgraceful chapter. It puts an ineffaceable brand on every man engaged in the conspiracy. Its contamination, spreading from a reservoir of corruption in the city hall, filtered through carefully laid conduits into every street and alley; into the hotels where girls, mere children of 15 years of age, were violated; into the low dance halls where schoolgirls listened to lewd songs and engaged in lascivious dances, and in the interval retired to assignation rooms with the drunken brutes who frequented these resorts; into the gambling houses where poorly paid workmen were robbed of their daily earnings; into the 350 saloons which kept open on Sunday, many of them running without license; into the barrel houses, where the vilest of whisky was sold in bottles, the resort of vagrants and drunkards, rendezvous of criminals and schools of crime.

This corruption palsied the hands of prominent officials whose duty it was to enforce the law. Lawyers became protectors of criminals; the courts were shields for the highwayman, the prostitute, the gambler, the sneak thief and the murderer. The higher courts were not free from this baneful influence, which invaded all ranks and brought them to its low level.

Local judges were found who would take straw bonds that the worst criminals might escape; exacting only costs, two-thirds going into the pockets of the judge and one-third into the waiting palm of the chief of police.

A police force is never better than the police commissioners; and the police commissioners, in turn, reflect the character and wishes of the mayor. If a city has a mayor of courage and ability, who is not the weak and willing prey of political crooks and grafters, he is certain to appoint a board of police commissioners who will name policemen intelligent enough to know the law and brave and honest enough to enforce it.

East St. Louis was doubly unfortunate. In the person of Mayor Mollman it had an executive who obeyed orders from a gang of conscienceless politicians of both political parties, who were exploiting the city for their own aggrandizement, careless alike of its good name, its security or its prosperity. They were harpies who closed their eyes to the corruption that saturated every department of the public service and fattened on its festering carcass. Without conscience and without shame they led the mayor into devious paths, tempted him with assurances of political support for his future ambitions, packed the police force with men whose incompetency was only surpassed by their venality, and so circumscribed him with flattery and encouraged his cupidity that they were able to take the reins of government from his feeble hands and guide it to suit their own foul and selfish purposes.

The great majority of the police force appointed by Mayor Mollman's board of police commissioners had served an apprenticeship as connivers at corrupt elections; as protectors of lawless saloons, and hotels run openly as assignation houses. They turned criminals loose at the dictation of politicians, and divided with grafting justices of the peace the fines that should have gone into the treasury.

This was the general character of the police force of the city of East St. Louis on July 1, 1917, when the spirit of lawlessness, long smoldering, burst into flame.

When acts of violence were frequent on the night of May 28, after a largely attended public meeting in the city hall, at which Attorney Alexander Flannigan, by unmistakable implication, suggested mob violence, the police department failed to cope with the incipient mob.

When the lawlessness began to assume serious proportions on July 2, the police instantly could have quelled and dispersed the crowds, then made up of small groups; but they either fled into the safety of a cowardly seclusion, or listlessly watched the depredations of the mob, passively and in many instances actively sharing in its work.

The testimony of every witness who was free to tell the truth agreed in condemnation of the police for failure to even halfway do their duty. They fled the scene where murder and arson held full sway. They deserted the station house and could not be found when calls for help came from every quarter of the city. The organization broke down completely; and so great was the indifference of the few policemen who remained on duty that the conclusion is inevitable that they shared the lust of the mob for negro blood, and encouraged the rioters by their conduct, which was sympathetic when it was not cowardly.

Some specific instances will be given in proof of the above conclusions:

After a number of rioters had been taken to the jail by the soldiers under Col. Clayton, the police deliberately turned hundreds of them loose without bond, failing to secure their names or to make any effort to identify them.

In one instance the mob jammed policemen against a building and held them there while other members of the gang were assaulting unoffending negroes. The police made no effort to free themselves, and seemed to regard the performance as highly humorous.

The police shot into a crowd of negroes who were huddled together, making no resistance. It was a particularly cowardly exhibition of savagery.

When the newspaper reporters were taking pictures of the mob, policemen charged them with their billies, broke their machines, destroyed the negatives, and threatened them with arrest if any further attempt was made to photograph the rioters who were making the streets run red with innocent blood, applying the torch to reach their victims who were cowering in their wretched homes.

* * *

Many . . . cases of police complicity in the riots could be cited. Instead of being guardians of the peace they became a part of the mob by countenancing the assaulting and shooting down of defenseless negroes and adding to the terrifying scenes of rapine and slaughter.

Their disgraceful conduct was the logical fruit of the notorious alliance between the City Hall and the criminal elements, aided by saloons, gambling houses and houses of prostitution. The city administration owed its election to their support and rewarded them for their fealty by permitting them to debauch the innocent, rob drunken victims, make assignation houses of the hotels, protect the gambler and the thief, and commit any act by which they might profit.

Mayor Mollman appointed the police commissioners. He was responsible for their failure to divorce the police from its partnership with crooked lawyers, corrupt justices of the peace and notorious criminals. He knew full well what the conditions in the police department were. Prominent citizens had warned him repeatedly and had supplied convincing proof of their charges against the department. He paid no attention to their warnings and appeals. By his failure to remove the police commissioners he acquiesced in their misfeasance, and equally is responsible with them for the heartless crimes committed by an unrestrained mob, and for the lawlessness that was encouraged and fostered by his failure to enforce the law and to hold his subordinates responsible for the proper conduct of the police department.

Much of the energy, some of the brains, and nearly all of the audacity of the gang that in recent years has held East St. Louis in its merciless grasp were centered in Locke Tarlton, president of the East Side Levee Board. It was his cunning mind that helped devise the schemes by which he and his associates were enriched. It was his practiced hand that carried them out. He made Mayor Mollman believe he was his creator; that he had elevated him to high station; and that his blind obedience to orders would mean rich political rewards in the future.

As president of the levee board, Tarlton deposited millions in a local bank and exacted no interest from it. The taxpayers suffered, while the bank lent the money and pocketed the proceeds. In further proof of the close relationship that existed between the levee board and the bank, Thomas Gillespie, brother of the bank's president, was elected attorney for the levee board.

Locke Tarlton knew how to handle the negro vote. He had an unanswerable argument to use with "floaters." He told them for whom he wanted them to vote, agreed on the price they were to get for casting their ballots, or rather having them marked for them by corrupt election officers, and always paid them promptly. Locke Tarlton was a man of honor when dealing with crooked voters. He always kept his word; he was sure pay. One of the picturesque sights in East St. Louis was to see Locke Tarlton with a stack of $5 bills in his hands publicly paying the negroes who helped him win an election.

When the levee board needed a right of way over certain land that was owned by a widow, Dr. R. X. McCracken, the health commissioner appointed by Mayor Mollman, bought the land from the widow for $5,000 and sold it a few weeks later to his friends, the levee board, for $20,000. The widow did not know when she sold the land that the levee board wanted it. McCracken's wife also sold land in the same locality to the levee board for $600 an acre, while adjoining land was purchased for $300 an acre.

When an organized effort was made to close the houses of prostitution the mayor would not give a definite answer until he had sent for Tarlton, who rented property in which the low saloon with assignation and dance-hall attachments were featured. In the presence of Rev. George W. Allison, who was conducting this crusade, Tarlton was purposely profane and vulgar; betrayed his interest by his anxiety; showed no sympathy with the movement; said in the presence of the mayor that the "town was full of jail-birds and crooks and always would be."

Whenever profitable vice was imperiled Tarlton was always found ready to defend. The criminal element believed, as publicly expressed by them, "that he owned the mayor body and breeches;" and they looked to Tarlton to save them from interference by the police and from prosecution by the courts. He kept his compact faithfully. They never called for help in vain; and on election days the ranks of crime and its immediate beneficiaries, the saloon, the gambling den and the house of prostitution, paid him back with compound interest.

Locke Tarlton was aided in his work by Tom Canavan, superintendent of public improvements. They were partners in many enterprises. Their desires ran along the same lines; their minds met in countless devious plans for personal gain and political advantage. Canavan was not as bold an operator as Tarlton, but he was more subtle. Possibly he lacked the resistless energy that carried Tarlton over obstacles that would have deterred a more cautious man; but he was shrewd and resourceful, and found ways and means to accomplish his ends, and one of his principal agencies was Locke Tarlton. The mayor was another.

Tarlton and Canavan were "the men higher up." They knew how far to go without taking a personal risk. They knew, too, who could be depended upon to put things over; and the courts and the police force were so organized that no real friend of the "gang" ever suffered.

After the riots Canavan is reported to have said: "Something had to be done to the 'niggers,' or they would have taken the town."

18 1919: A Readiness, Willingness, and Eagerness

Another in the series of riots besetting America's cities was that which engulfed Chicago in the summer of 1919. Since at least 1917, when masses of blacks had poured into Chicago to seek employment, racial friction had steadily grown. The systematic problems encountered by blacks in Chicago resembled those in East St. Louis, though the government was much less patently corrupt. As tensions mounted, an incident in July between black and white swimmers who were supposed to be using separate parts of the lakeshore provided a catalyst for the week-long riot. As whites and blacks confronted each other in this period local officials proved powerless to subdue the violent spirit manifest in both communities. More than thirty people, black and white, were killed, and hundreds more injured. One quality in this riot stands out as especially important. While the mayor waited and waited before seeking state assistance in suppressing the violence, blacks refused to wait with him and proceeded to take measures themselves to quell the attacks being made upon their homes and persons. They fought back. The taking up of arms, whether bricks or machine guns, symbolized a huge repudiation of the paternalist stance that would increasingly pose a barrier to blacks: working within the system of law and order and placing reliance on the professional elite to handle threats and problems. To have done this in the summer of 1919 in Chicago would have been suicidal. To respond to the attack in the same spirit may possibly have meant, as the black lawyer interviewed in the following selection from *The Messenger* indicates, that those whites who were not friendly toward blacks would "at least have a decent respect for us based on fear."

Source: "A Report on the Chicago Riot by an Eye-Witness," *The Messenger*, 2 (September 1919): 11-12.

1.—How many persons were killed of each race?

Unable to state exact number. One newspaper reported 16 white and 16 colored killed. The coroner puts the total number of casualties at 36—19 whites and 17 colored. There is a widespread belief, however, that the authorities have deliberately suppressed the truth about this matter. One white insurance adjuster, whose company insures 10,000 people, says that with his company alone 27 death claims, resulting from riot, were filed. John Dill Robertson, City Health Commissioner, however, denies that there has been any effort to conceal the facts.

2. What is the actual Negro population of Chicago?

It has been variously estimated anywhere between 100,000 and 225,000. The figure generally quoted is 125,000.

* * *

8. What weapons were used by Negroes? Where is it supposed that the Negroes got the weapons from?

Everything from a knife to a machine gun. A white alderman stated in the City Council that he had been reliably informed that the Negroes had 1000 army rifles and enough ammunition to last for years if used in guerilla warfare. It is known that a few Negroes broke into the Cadet School at Wendell Phillips and secured in the neighborhood of 100 rifles. They broke into the 8th Regiment Armory too, but did not find anything. Most of the discharged soldiers have guns obtained while in service. Pawnshops were looted and quite a bit of ammunition was procured from Gary, Ind.

* * *

12. Why was the Mayor so reluctant to ask for the use of the troops?

Evidently considered it a reflection upon his administration not to be able to cope with the situation. Did not want martial law, but when the situation grew serious was compelled to effect a compromise by asking the Governor to send troops to "assist" police force. We have never had martial law and soldiers have been recalled. Perhaps you have heard of the differences between Mayor Thompson and Gov. Lowden. I am not prepared to say, however, that that had anything to do with the Mayor's failure to ask for the troops sooner. Ed Wright, Assistant Corporation Counsel, told me that he advised the Mayor against calling for the troops, because he felt that they would line up with the lawless whites, as they did in East St. Louis. Thompson excuses himself for not being able to handle the situation because he has always maintained that our police force was inadequate. As a consequence, provision has been made for a thousand more officers.

13. Did the delayed use of the troops benefit or injure the Negro cause? Explain why, if your answer is yes or no.

Benefited it. While the delayed use of troops caused the loss of many innocent lives, colored as well as white, it afforded an opportunity for the Negroes to impress upon the whites their readiness, willingness, and eagerness to fight the thing through.

* * *

18. Your opinion as to how the riot will affect future relations between the races.

The riot will make the future relations between the races decidedly better. It will bring about "a meeting of the minds" to the effect that the colored man must not be kicked about like a dumb brute. Our white friends, seeing the danger that besets the nation, will become more active in our cause, and the other whites will at least have a decent respect for us based on fear.

19 1919: A New Liberation

Another racial riot in Washington, D.C., in 1919 provided a similar example of the same phenomenon—blacks fighting back when they were attacked. The meaning of the effort was eloquently put in the observations of a black woman who remembered her response to the riot.

Source: Francis Grimke, *The Race Problem* (Washington, D.C., 1919), quoted in Arthur Barbeau and Florette Henri, *The Unknown Soldiers* (Philadelphia, 1974), p. 182.

The Washington riots gave me the thrill that comes once in a lifetime. I was alone when I read between the lines of the morning paper that at last our men had stood like men, struck back, were no longer dumb, driven cattle. When I could no longer read for my streaming tears, I stood up, alone in my room, held both hands high over my head and exclaimed, "Oh, I thank God, thank God!" When I remember anything after this, I was prone on my bed, beating the pillow with both fists, laughing and crying, whimpering like a whipped child, for sheer gladness and madness. The pent-up humiliation, grief and horror of a lifetime—half a century—was being stripped from me.

20   1919: Fighting the System

To return fire and to do violence unto your enemies and oppressors may have had, as Frantz Fanon argued and as the black woman's response to the Washington riot exemplifies, a cleansing and liberating effect. It does not, however, provide an immediate solution to the systematic problems facing the oppressed. The fact remained that the origins of the problems confronting the black population, in the city or in the country, lay in the system of power. In 1919 a small but symbolically significant effort by black people to alter the political and economic system emerged among sharecroppers in part of Arkansas. Their efforts received national public attention partly because of the larger instances of racial violence already witnessed in that year, and partly because local whites were charging these blacks with organizing for the purpose of launching an insurrection and massacre. Two points are evident in this. One is that whites were obviously hypersensitive to resistance and challenge by blacks in the wake of the confrontations in Chicago and Washington, D.C. Whites everywhere knew that blacks were fighting back. Second, a modest effort to challenge systematic exploitation appeared to these planters and their retinue as nothing less than insurrection. There is another point that deserves mention too: in this area blacks appeared to have taken heart from the black responses to white violence in the big city as they prepared for possible attack by whites; this seems to have happened at the church battle near Hoop Spur. In all of this, of course, whether in Washington, St. Louis, Chicago, or Hoop Spur, blacks consistently came out the losers. But the question for the rest of the twentieth century was being posed: Would blacks be able to secure, for themselves, equality and self-respect?

Source: Walter F. White, "'Massacring Whites' in Arkansas," *The Nation*, 109 (December 6, 1919): 715-16.

Early in October the report was spread broadcast in this country that Negroes in Phillips County, Arkansas, had organized to massacre the whites. A group of Negro farmers, members of the Progressive Farmers and Household Union of America, were charged with having plotted insurrection, with "night riding," with the intention to take over the land of the white men after the owners had been massacred. Investigation has thrown a searching light upon these stories and has revealed that the Negro farmers had organized not to massacre, but to protest by peaceful and legal means against vicious exploitation by unscrupulous landowners and their agents.

On October 1, W. D. Adkins, a special agent of the Missouri Pacific Railroad, in company with Charles Pratt, a deputy sheriff, and a Negro trusty were driving past a Negro church near Hoop Spur, a small community in Phillips County. According to Pratt, persons in the church fired without cause on the party, killing Adkins and wounding Pratt. According to testimony of persons in the church, however, Adkins and Pratt fired into the church, apparently to frighten the Negroes gathered. The fire was returned with the casualties noted. Whatever the facts may be, this incident started four days of rioting. Negroes were disarmed and arrested, while their arms were given to whites who hastened to the community from Mississippi, Arkansas, and Tennessee; Federal troops were called from Camp Pike; Negroes who had taken refuge in the canebrakes were hunted down and killed; and the final death roll showed five whites and twenty-five Negroes killed, although some place the Negro fatalities as high as one hundred.

According to the facts gathered on the scene, the purpose and plan of the organization was as follows: The Progressive Farmers and Household Union of America came into being in order to combat a system of exploitation known as "share-cropping," which has served for half a century as a convenient means of gaining wealth by many whites without the inconvenient necessity of working. This system will be described later. Organized at Winchester, Drew County, the articles of incorporation were drawn by Williamson and Williamson of Monticello, white men and ex-slaveholders. These articles were filed in due legal form with the county clerk at Winchester, the county seat. Branches or lodges were to be formed in other communities, and it was hoped that the movement would spread to all parts of the South, as the economic exploitation pictured below existed in all of them. The Farmers Union was in the form of a fraternal organization or secret order because the State tax for such an organization is much lower than for any other and because the veil of secrecy with passwords and grips and insignia appealed to the untutored minds of most of the members. Each male member was to pay $1.50 and each female fifty cents. The money thus collected was to go into a common fund to be used to employ a lawyer to make a test in court of cases where Negroes were unable to secure settlements.

A careful examination of the literature of the organization does not reveal the "dastardly" plot which has been charged. The organization was declared to be for the purpose of "advancing the intellectual, material, moral, spiritual, and financial interests of the Negro race." Applicants for membership had to answer under oath such questions as "Do you believe in God?" "Do you attend church?" "Do you believe in courts?" and "Will you defend this Government and her Constitution at all times?" There is nothing in any of the literature seen or published which indicates any other motive than that of aspiring towards the securing of relief from exploitation.

A "Committee of Seven" composed of white citizens of Helena held hearings for the purpose of determining the facts in the case. At least two members of that committee are plantation owners themselves. According to two sources of information, when suspects were brought before this committee they were seated in a chair charged with electricity. If the Negroes did not talk as freely as the Committee wished, the current was turned on until they did so. This committee has declared that it secured many confessions from Negro suspects, but so far as could be learned none of the details of these confessions has been published.

The cause of the Phillips County trouble, according to Governor Charles H. Brough, was the circulation of what he considers incendiary Negro publications like *The Crisis*, the official organ of the National Association for the Advancement of Colored People. Having been a professor of economics for seventeen years before becoming Governor, it is incredible that he is ignorant of the exploitation of Negroes in his State. It is also reasonable to believe that Governor Brough should know that no publication would have much chance of creating unrest and discontent among contented, justly treated people. A further fact for consideration is that 78.6 per cent. of the population of Phillips County is Negro—the actual figures being: white, 7,176; colored, 26,354. With the whites outnumbered almost four to one, it appears that the fatalities would have been differently proportioned if a well-planned murder plot had existed among the Negroes.

* * *

On November 2, the Negroes arrested were brought to trial in Helena, the county seat of Phillips County, where, because of the intense feeling, there was practically no chance of an unbiased and fair trial. According to the press dispatches, counsel for the defense was assigned by the court; no change of venue was asked; no Negroes were impanelled for jury duty (although Negroes outnumber whites four to one in Phillips County); no witnesses were called to testify for the defense. The first five defendants, charged with murder in the first degree, were jointly tried, the jury returning a verdict of guilty in exactly seven minutes after retiring, and the defendants were jointly sentenced to electrocution on December 27. In five days a total of twelve men were sentenced to death and eighty others were sentenced to prison terms ranging from one to twenty-one years. Gov. Brough on November 28 announced that he would postpone the executions to allow appeals to be filed in behalf of the condemned men. Unless the result of these appeals is a removal of the death penalty twelve Negroes will meet death, additional victims of America's denial of rudimentary justice to 12,000,000 of its citizens because of their color.

II

A Modernizing Society

21 A Stranger in His Land

When the offices of the Klan identified the organization's purpose and origins, they naturally adopted a defensive and conservative posture. And, unlike the namesake organization of the Reconstruction years, the rhetoric of the Klan found its elemental cause not in an explicit yearning for the days of slavery but in an analysis of the problems besetting the nation. With such an approach many who were not notable for the virulence of their racism could find a home and companionship in the Klan. The changes of the past decades had left a mark on many who, at the very minimum, as the statement of principles declared, found themselves uncomfortable in the 1920s.

The rise of interest group liberalism as a system that rewarded the organized power of producers at the expense of others in an inflationary ritual; the emergence of powerful systems of controlling the economy whether by government or by monopoly and oligopoly; the centralization of power in the hands of big business and the federal government; the catastrophic and disillusioning experience of Wilson's efforts to reshape the world in his own image; and the depersonalization and automation of relationships bespoke the ravages of a modernizing society on the lives of many people who felt their power to control events and their own lives slipping away, their traditional sense of morality being replaced with a laissez-faire system of moral behavior, and their own identities and values, as passed on by tradition through the generations, challenged by a system that appeared increasingly to be dominated by materialistic priorities and power relations. No doubt it was that defensiveness or effort to hold onto the past, even if embellished and romanticized, that motivated many to put on the white sheet and to move toward what they considered the proper kind of society under the cover of darkness.

Source: Hiram Wesley Evans, "The Klan's Fight for Americanism," *North American Review*, 223 (March-April-May 1926): 38-39.

. . . These Nordic Americans for the last generation have found themselves increasingly uncomfortable, and finally deeply distressed. There appeared first confusion in thought and opinion, a groping and hesitancy about national affairs and private life alike, in sharp contrast to the clear, straightforward purposes of our earlier years. There was futility in religion, too, which was in many ways even more distressing. Presently we began to find that we were dealing with strange ideas; policies that always sounded well, but somehow always made us still more uncomfortable.

Finally came the moral breakdown that has been going on for two decades. One by one all our traditional moral standards went by the boards, or were so disregarded that they ceased to be binding. The sacredness of our Sabbath, of our homes, of chastity, and finally even of our right to teach our own children in our own schools fundamental facts and truths were torn away from us. Those who maintained the old standards did so only in the face of constant ridicule.

Along with this went economic distress. The assurance for the future of our children dwindled. We found our great cities and the control of much of our industry and commerce taken over by strangers, who stacked the cards of success and prosperity against us. Shortly they came to dominate our government. The bloc system by which this was done is now familiar to all. Every kind of inhabitant except the Americans gathered in groups which operated as units in politics, under orders of corrupt, self-seeking and un-American leaders, who both by purchase and threat enforced their demands on politicians. Thus it came about that the interests of Americans were always the last to be considered by either national or city governments, and that the native Americans were constantly discriminated against, in business, in legislation and in administrative government.

So the Nordic American today is a stranger in large parts of the land his fathers gave him. Moreover, he is a most unwelcome stranger, one much spit upon, and one to whom even the right to have his own opinions and to work for his own interests is now denied with jeers and revilings. "We must Americanize the Americans," a distinguished immigrant said recently. Can anything more clearly show the state to which the real American has fallen in this country which was once his own?

22 Like a New Religion

The new music of jazz lay at the core of a distinctive way of life that symbolized much of the cultural renaissance among blacks in the 1920s. It was, as Eddie Condon describes it in the following discussion of his new friends' regard for jazz, "as if a new religion just come from Jerusalem." Condon himself likened the magical effects of the undisciplined sounds to hypnosis. And in fact this jazz sound was far removed from the restrained and tightly patterned rhythms and scales of white music, which had been "sacrificed to civilization." Musical improvisation at its best formed a large part of jazz and the improvisation itself seemed keyed to the cultural qualities nurtured by blacks for generations.

Source: Eddie Condon, *We Called It Music* (Westport, Conn., 1947, 1970), pp. 107-8. Reprinted with the permission of Greenwood Press and McIntosh & Otis, Inc.

Between sets we gabbed and I discovered that [Jimmy] MacPartland and [Bud] Freeman were from the west side. They were about my age; they had been in Austin High School together and with some other students had formed a band. They talked about jazz as if it were a new religion just come from Jerusalem. When MacPartland mentioned King Oliver smoke came out of his eyes. "He's playing a fraternity dance at the Chez Paree tonight," Freeman said. "Let's go down there after we finish."

We arrived in time for the last set; the musicians were reassembling as we pushed our way to the stand. "That's Oliver," MacPartland said, pointing to a big, amiable looking Negro with a scar over one eye who stood in front of the band holding a cornet. Near him was a slightly smaller and much younger man, also holding a cornet. "That's Louis Armstrong," MacPartland said. He pointed to the others: Johnny Dodds on clarinet and his brother Baby on drums, Honoré Dutray at the trombone, Johnnie St. Cyr playing banjo, and Lillian Hardin at the piano. Oliver lifted his horn and the first blast of Canal Street Blues hit me. It was hypnosis at first hearing. Everyone was playing what he wanted to play and it was all mixed together as if someone had planned it with a set of micrometer calipers; notes I had never heard were peeling off the edges and dropping through the middle; there was a tone from the trumpets like warm rain on a cold day. Freeman and MacPartland and I were immobilized; the music poured into us like daylight running down a dark hole. The choruses rolled on like high tide, getting wilder and more wonderful. Armstrong seemed able to hear what Oliver was improvising and reproduce it himself at the same time. It seemed impossible, so I dismissed it; but it was true. Then the two wove around each other like suspicious women talking about the same man. When they finally finished MacPartland said, "How do you like it?" There was only one thing to say: "It doesn't bother me."

We listened until the last note; Armstrong was reaching, showing his high shoes and his white socks; Oliver was looking at him with a fatherly smile. We hit the cold air outside and Freeman said, "Let's go down to Friar's Inn." It was a late place, open until the customers stopped buying or went home. I spotted a few changes when I got to the bandstand; Schoebel wasn't at the piano and Ben Pollack was playing drums. Rappolo, Mares, Brunies, Pettis, and the others, including Lew Black, were still setting fire to Shimmy Shawabble, Angry, Sobbin' Blues, Sugarfoot Stomp, and Everybody Loves Somebody Blues. What was left of our capacity for enjoyment we turned over to Rappolo. He played clarinet the way Shakespeare played English. It was afternoon when I got back to Chicago Heights.

23 The Mecca of the New Negro

The impulse to move north remained a powerful one for many blacks into the 1920s and the main focus of that impulse became Harlem. What had been not long before a district of New York City with a large German population was by 1920 indisputably a separate black center. By the middle of the decade of the 1920s it held possibly a half-million black people. Increasingly black people around the nation identified Harlem as a unique cultural center where black creativity and distinctiveness could flourish and grow. This artistic and literary bent as well as the commercial success surrounding it provided the environment for what was often called "the new Negro." As Langston Hughes expressed it, "Harlem was like a great magnet for the Negro intellectual, pulling him from everywhere." The attractiveness of Harlem greatly transcended the crude market in labor that brought many from the croppers' huts in search of jobs; it brought blacks in search of blacks and in search of black culture. A variety of cultures thus flourished, including a strident race consciousness, a hope for acceptance into white society, competing religions, and of course various combinations of these. To put it differently, this Mecca for blacks often had a cultural appeal that overpowered the material drives. In 1924 Konrad Bercovici offered a lengthy assessment of the emergent black metropolis within New York City in which he found a new sense of fulfillment for blacks and also new kinds of problems. In this selection part of the new spirit of the black community can be seen.

Source: Konrad Bercovici, "The Black Blocks of Manhattan," *Harper's Magazine*, 149 (October 1924): 622-23.

In general, what one feels very distinctly in Harlem is that it is composed practically of two elements: those whose ambition it is to "cross the line" or have their offspring cross the line to live with the whites as whites; and another, much better element who refuse to live with whites under false pretenses, who want to live as negroes, race conscious, who hope by their achievements to compel the white people surrounding them to recognize them as their equals. And they insist that their best men have been full-blooded negroes. To them the great numbers of their kind invading Harlem and New York is very agreeable. They have them all together. They can hold meetings with larger crowds. They can lecture to them. They can make them race conscious and with their help agitate for such legislation as is favorable to the negro.

People like Mary Burroughs and the crowd of the Association for the Advancement of Colored People are laboring for the education of the negro by making his life more complete, by pointing out to him values in literature, by making him conscious of a poetry all his own, a theater all his own, encouraging sculpture and painting and higher education; building a new edifice on an old foundation by pointing out the great arts that have flourished at all times in Africa, in olden times and down to the time when their ancestors were ravished from the coasts of Africa and brought here as slaves. Native music and dance are almost entirely of negro origin. A visit to musical comedies such as "Shuffle Along" and "Runnin' Wild," which have been tremendous hits on Broadway and in most of the principal cities of the country, proves their contention. These comedies have been written, staged, and executed from first to last by negroes, and have a quality all their own. The tunes and dances are both intoxicating and infectious. Not one risqué or obscene joke. And yet the woman dancers have been forced into tights by our censors, while the white dancers in revues and follies romp bare-limbed in other theaters. And when a man like H. O. Tanner, the painter, becomes famous, the negroes get angry because he is referred to as an American painter, and not mentioned as a negro, which he is.

24 The Whole Game . . .

Harlem, its bold opportunities for the literati notwithstanding, also harbored a more sinister side where lived those black people who found themselves vulnerable, often powerless, and frequently hoping for the main chance that always lay just out of reach. Extortionate rents, uncaring and unscrupulous physicians and pharmacists, and virtually every opportunity for profiteering abounded. The Mecca of the New Negro had its traps. In the following description of the numbers racket the victimization of blacks by other blacks is only part of the story. The main theme is unspoken: the enormous despair that combines with a huge faith in fortune's hand to produce the numbers racket betokens a lack of confidence in the system of work and wages as a path to success, and a certain feeling of helplessness that continues to generate the blues and the quest for satisfaction in other ways that also reject the promises of the work ethic.

Source: Winthrop D. Lane, "Ambushed in the City: The Grim Side of Harlem," *The Survey*, 53 (March 1, 1925): 692.

An unkempt woman, with hair graying, shoulders rounded and eyes rimmed with thick glasses, reads a newspaper on a subway car in New York City. She is colored. Her skirt is in rags, one toe shows through a shoe, an elbow pushes the lining of her sleeve into sight; perhaps she has just left her mop and pail in some downtown office building. Turning the pages hastily, she seems to be hunting for a particular place. At last she stops. Her forefinger runs up and down the columns. She is looking at the financial page. Finding an item, she gazes closely at it for a moment, and then throws the paper onto the seat beside her. She has a dejected look. Apparently she is through with the paper.

She has been lookin for "the numbers." The numbers she wanted were the day's totals of bank exchange and bank balances—announced each day by the

Clearing House and published by the newspapers. On these she has been gambling. Suppose the exchanges were $793,482,450 and the balances $86,453,624. She is then interested in the number 936, because that is made up of the seventh and eighth digits, reading from the right, of the first, and the seventh digit of the second. She and many others are playing this game—a species of policy. If she had put her money, which may be only a few pennies, on 936 that day, she wins. Each day she looks forward to discovering what this combination is. It is the bright spot for her.

The stakes are high if she wins. She reaps 600 times what she wagers. If she wagers a nickel she wins thirty dollars; if she wagers a quarter, she wins $150; a deposit of fifty cents will bring her $300. These stakes have lure; they are a king's stake. They will make her rich for the moment. She does not consider the chances against her. She does not consider that she has never won and that only once did she ever hear of anybody winning. The bare possibility of capturing so much money makes her heart beat faster.

Since there are 999 numbers of three digits, or 1000 if we include 000, she seems to have about one chance in a thousand of winning. By the law of averages, she might play the same number daily for three years without a strike. The banker pays 600 times the sum wagered. He, therefore, seems to have a sure thing; barring lucky wins by large gamblers, he can't lose in the long run. That does not interest her, either.

All Harlem is ablaze with "the numbers." People play it everywhere, in tenements, on street corners, in the backs of shops. "Bankers" organize it, promote it, encourage it. They send their runners into flats and stores. You give the runner the money you are betting, write your number on a slip of paper, and wait. If the number you chose is the one that wins next day, you get your money. Runners round up new business, stake off territory and canvass all the people they can reach. A person living in an apartment house may be the agent for that house. The names of these bankers are known in the neighborhood. One rides around in a $12,000 limousine and has a liveried chauffeur. Minor bankers abound; men and women, getting $200 capital, start in the "numbers" business. Recently, it is said, white men have been trying to wrest control of the game from blacks; a Jew who formerly used his talents in the hooch business is spoken of as the leader of this effort.

"Always out first with the bank clearing numbers" reads a placard advertising the New York Sun in Harlem. Inspiration for lucky numbers is got from every source. People get their numbers from dream books; fifteen or twenty cents will buy a dream book, and a dream about any topic listed in it has an appropriate number. Or two people exchange street addresses. "Ah'm gonna play it! Ah'm gonna play it!" says one, as he takes down the address of the other. They get their numbers from the numbers of hymns given out in church, from subway cars, from telephone numbers, from dates, from baseball scores, from the prices they paid for purchase articles, from the license tags of passing automobiles. By combining or rearranging these, or using them unchanged, they tempt fortune.

One trouble is, of course, that they don't always get what they win. Many a banker, finding that large sums have been won from him, avoids payment; his victim has no recourse, since the whole transaction is outside the law. The streets of Harlem are being walked by people looking for those who owe them money won at "the numbers." The New York Age, a colored weekly, published a story about one banker who skipped to Cuba with $100,000 taken from the Negroes of Harlem; it is common to win $12, $18 and $30 and not get it. This is only an exasperation of the extortion. The whole game, as it is staged, smells of exploitation.

25 Harlem Discovered . . . and Transformed

Just as Harlem for a brief period offered seemingly limitless opportunities for the fullness of the expression of raw black culture, so too did the expressions and images released sometimes become institutionalized, then crystallized, then lifeless. The objective appeal of the creativity and artistry so evident in Harlem accounts for a large part of the process. It is, after all, not uncommon for anything, once discovered, to be smothered by its admirers. Yet there is more at work. Much of the attention drawn to the life of Harlem came not out of technical or cultural appreciation or even popular taste. Some came from the appeal of anything different—color, language, music, dress, or anything else—in a repressive society dominated by a materialistic drive that generated its own massive frustrations. But the prevalent slumming impulse indicates that often those frustrations were assumed rather than explicitly developed or addressed, for Harlem, so the image beckoned, was the place where white New Yorkers (and Americans) could go on a vacation from their morals as well as their music, or at a very minimum, could be entertained by peoples who were themselves casting aside the vestiges of "civilization." As a licensed culture Harlem provided a safe and respectable release from the tensions of modern society, but at the expense of the blacks who lived there. Gilbert Osofsky pointedly depicted the phenomenon: "Whatever seemed thrilling, itself worthy of exploitation, bizarre or sensuous about Harlem life became a part of the [white] community's image; whatever was sad or tragic about it, ignored." Then, of course, whites claimed for themselves what they found there, as Rudolph Fisher describes in the following section.

Source: Rudolph Fisher, "The Caucasian Storms Harlem," *The American Mercury*, 11 (August 1927): 393, 398.

It might not have been such a jolt had my five years' absence from Harlem been spent otherwise. But the study of medicine includes no courses in cabareting; and, anyway, the Negro cabarets in Washington, where I studied, are all uncompromisingly black. Accordingly I was entirely unprepared for what I found when I returned to Harlem recently.

I remembered one place especially where my own crowd used to hold forth; and, hoping to find some old-timers there still, I sought it out one midnight. The old, familiar plunkety-plunk welcomed me from below as I entered. I descended the same old narrow stairs, came into the same smoke-misty basement, and found myself a chair at one of the ancient white-porcelain, mirror-smooth tables. I drew a deep breath and looked about, seeking familiar faces. "What a lot of 'fays!'" I thought, as I noticed the number of white guests. Presently I grew puzzled and began to stare, then I gaped—and gasped. I found myself wondering if this was the right place—if, indeed, this was Harlem at all. I suddenly became aware that, except for the waiters and members of the orchestra, I was the only Negro in the place.

After a while I left it and wandered about in a daze from night-club to night-club. I tried the Nest, Small's, Connie's Inn, the Capitol, Happy's, the Cotton Club. There was no mistake; my discovery was real and was repeatedly confirmed. No wonder my old crowd was not to be found in any of them. The best of Harlem's black cabarets have changed their names and turned white.

* * *

What occasions the focusing of attention on this particular thing—rounds up and gathers these seasonal shims, and centers them about the Negro? Cabarets are peculiar, mind you. They're not like theatres and concert halls. You don't just go to a cabaret and sit back and wait to be entertained. You get out on the floor and join the pow-wow and help entertain yourself. Granted that white people have long enjoyed the Negro entertainment as a diversion, is it not something different, something more, when they bodily throw themselves into Negro entertainment in cabarets? "Now Negroes go to their own cabarets to see how the white people act."

And what do they see? Why, we see them actually playing Negro games. I watch them in that epidemic Negroism, the Charleston. I look on and envy them. They camel and fish-tail and turkey, they geche and black-bottom and scronch, they skate and buzzard and mess-around—and they do them all better than I! This interest in the Negro is an active and participating interest. It is almost as if a traveler from the North stood watching an African tribe-dance, then suddenly found himself swept wildly into it, caught in its tidal rhythm.

26 A Credit to the Race

It would be wrong to suggest that the division between black music and white music was universal. Indeed, just as many blacks sought acceptance into white society, so did many draw their standards of morality, music, and propriety from white cultural forms. While this often followed class lines in black society, so too did those norms and standards often have a class base in white society. The choices were never quite clear-cut, as Mahalia Jackson reveals in the passage from her autobiography printed below. As she confessed, "It was a battle within me to sing a song in a formal way." In her case, her view of race and class (a notable rejection of "high-class" music) led from feelings of being mixed up to a certain sense of pride.

Source: Mahalia Jackson with Evan McLeod Wylie, *Movin' on Up* (New York, 1966), pp. 58-59. Reprinted by permission of Hawthorn Books. All rights reserved.

People who heard me sing were always complimenting me on my voice and telling me I should be taking lessons. One night in 1932 when we each had made four dollars singing at a church, my girl friend and I took our money and went around to see Professor DuBois about some singing lessons. Professor DuBois was a great Negro tenor who had a music salon on the South Side. He was a tall, light-skinned Negro who had a very grand way about him. He was very proud of his career as a concert and operatic singer and it didn't take me long to find out that he didn't think much of my way of singing a song.

First off, he had me sing the spiritual "Standing in the Need of Prayer." I had such a rhythm inside of me that I kept picking up the beat and out of the corner of my eye I could see the Professor frowning. He held up his hand. "That's no way to sing that song," he said. "Slow down. Sing it like this."

He clasped his hands together and sang in a real sad and solemn kind of way. I tried again, but his way was too slow and mournful for me. I got going again with my rhythm, but the Professor shrugged his shoulders and broke me off in the middle.

"You try it," he told the girl who had come with me.

My friend had a nice voice and she sang the song sweet and slow just the way the Professor wanted it.

"Now that's singing!" he exclaimed. "You've got a fine voice and great possibilities."

Turning to me, he said, "And you've got to learn to stop hollering. It will take time to build up your voice. The way you sing is not a credit to the Negro race. You've got to learn to sing songs so that white people can understand them."

I felt all mixed up. How could I sing songs for white people to understand when I was colored myself? It didn't seem to make any sense. It was a battle within me to sing a song in a formal way. I felt it was too polished and I didn't feel good about it. I handed over my four dollars to the Professor and left.

"Wasn't he wonderful?" exclaimed my friend as we went down the stairs. "I'm going to take some lessons as soon as I can."

The numbness in me was wearing off and I felt hurt and angry. "Not me," I snapped back. "I don't want to sing none of his high-class music!"

It was a long time before I had another extra four dollars, but even when I did, I never went back to Professor DuBois's music salon. It turned out to be my one and only singing lesson. I haven't had one since.

27 The Persistent Code of Caste

Despite the social changes evident in the twentieth century, race relations into the 1930s in the countryside of the South remained essentially unchanged and blacks remained subordinate in an unwritten code of caste that served not only to restrict the activities and aspirations of blacks but to shape the images whites created of their black neighbors. That caste system also worked to create an enormous cultural distance between the two races that served the cause of subordination in a setting where whites were outnumbered by blacks and where physical contact between the races was constant. It could even justify the forced intimacy between white man and black woman when the opposite relationship was a mortal crime. One of the distinctive qualities it created, as revealed in the following item, was the myth that Southern whites "knew" and understood their blacks, unlike people who had less contact with blacks. In reality, the blacks were largely unknown by the people who lived near them and were understood least of all by those who professed to know them best. Blacks would be most reluctant to confide in whites or to open themselves up to whites. Thus when Rollin Chambliss began to work on his master's thesis at the University of Georgia, examining black newspapers' concern for social problems, he entered a new world, although one that should have been obvious to him. As he reflected on his youth he realized that the blacks he thought he had known had never mentioned their reading and writing or any of their own private concerns. Perhaps the only time a black had been bold enough to assert his own sense of morality—which his white antagonists had violated—the result was almost violence, a violence that apparently was averted only by the black turning away and accepting humiliation, for the time being, as his fate. But to understand blacks was not the object of the system; it was rather to keep them in their place.

Source: Rollin Chambliss, "What Negro Newspapers of Georgia Say About Some Social Problems, 1933," M.A. thesis, University of Georgia, 1934, pp. 4-8.

It was less than a year ago when I saw for the first time in my life a Negro newspaper. Before that time I had not known that Negroes had papers of their own. They were not to be seen in the places I frequented, though I often went as a boy into the homes of Negro tenants. I do not believe I ever heard one of the Negroes that I knew say, I read thus and so in the newspaper. If they read at all, it was not of their reading that they talked to white folks.

I was in college before I read a book written by a Negro. I had been to Negro churches and heard their preachers. Probably the first singing I ever heard was that of Negroes. But I had never associated them with writing, or very much with reading. Those were things, like our Boy Scout troop and school picnics, in which they had no part. I remember the surprise I felt at finding DuBois' *Soul of the Black Folk*, my first contact with Negro writing, not different in outward respects from other books I had read. I don't know what I expected Negro writing to look like; certainly I knew that it would not be white ink on black paper. But I did feel that there would be something physical to show that this was done by a Negro. The Negroes that I knew worked in the cotton fields. Around the towns they did all kinds of odd jobs, for small pay. The women washed and cooked and kept house for the white folks. None of them wrote anything that I knew of.

There must have been more Negroes in the little South Georgia community in which I grew up than whites, for though there were only three or four white boys in the group with which I used to play, there were a half dozen or more Negroes. We did chores together there on the farm, and went "possum huntin' " and to the swimming hole down on the creek and played ball and did all those things that boys do in rural Georgia.

We did them together, and yet the Negroes were always a little apart. If we were swimming, they kept downstream. If we were playing ball, they were in the outfield and we did the batting. If we were gathering plums, the Negroes always left us the best bushes. There was no ill feeling in this. Negroes were different. They knew it, and we knew it. In the fields we all drank from the same jug, but at the pump the Negroes cupped their hands and drank from them and would never have dared to use the cup hanging there. I never knew a Negro to come to the front door of my home, and I am sure that if one had done so, someone would have asked him if he minded stepping around to the back. At the age of ten I understood full well that the Negro had to be kept in his place, and I was resigned to my part in that general responsibility.

As we grew to adolescence, the relationship with Negro boys became less intimate. We began then to talk of things which the Negro could not understand— of what we were going to do in life, of our little love affairs, of school life, of our hopes for the future. In such things the Negro had no part, and gradually we played together less and less. We were more often with grown Negroes, and I think now that we were always closer to the men than we were to the boys of our own age. They knew where rabbits were, how to tell when a dog had treed, when the wind was too high for squirrels to stir, where it was best to set a trap. I don't know how Southern white boys on the farm would learn anything without Negroes. And they sang a lot too and strummed guitars and were almost always in good humor. They never talked very much about their own affairs, and they never told things on other Negroes. I have never known a Negro to lead a white boy into anything vicious. I knew some of these old Negroes well, after a fashion, and they were in their way good people. They were friends of mine, and still are; and when I go back into my home community, I always look up those whom I knew best. I call them by their first names, as I always have; and they call me "Mister," as they always have; and I know that they are glad to see me.

But they were not like white people. There was a difference that we all recognized. It was to be expected that a Negro would steal a little now and then, not anything of consequence, of course, but petty things: watermelons, sugar cane, fresh meat, and things like that, and now and then a little corn for his shoat. It was a common saying with us that a Negro who wouldn't steal had gold toe-nails. An old Negro cobbler in my home town once said to me: "That boy workin' for me just ain't no good. I treats him well and gives him a chance to steal a little, and he just don't do nothin' but trifle." I think all of us must have figured that a little stealing was a part of the wage. Eight dollars a month was considered a fair price for farm help, with a house and some food furnished. Good Negroes were those who knew what not to steal. Stealing food and stealing money may be the same crime in that great chart of the good and the bad, but I have known Negroes who would lift a gallon of syrup without a scruple, and yet they could be trusted implicitly in the house with money and personal effects lying around.

Their moral codes were different from ours. I don't know that it ever occurred to any of us that a Negro girl was capable of virtue. White men had no hesitation in approaching Negro women. I do not know how often they met with refusal, but I do know that an intimate relationship between white men and Negro women was not uncommon. It is my belief that practically no children and very little disease resulted from this relationship, owing to the general knowledge of preventives that has penetrated even into rural Georgia. The better whites were much opposed to this intimacy, though white boys talked freely with one another of their experiences. Those who did not discontinue the practice when they were older, and they were few, became more reticent. Many Negroes keenly resented this intercourse with whites. An old Negro man once offered this as an explanation of the Negroes leaving the farm in such numbers and going to the city. "Our women," he said, "have no protection against low-down white men in the country and in small towns."

I have always understood that a Negro who touches a white woman must die. It is something that we learn in the South without knowing how or when or where. I have heard the statement made by men in the community who were models of right living. Somewhere out of the past this idea came, born of pride in our own culture and possibly of an unrecognized fear that it might not persist. It was intensified by the chivalric ideal of womanhood which has been traditional in the South. In the aftermath of the Civil War the motto of those who rode with the Ku Klux Klan was the protection of Southern womanhood. Whatever might be the law, however courts might rule, whatever amendments might be added to the constitution, the Negro must be kept in his place. It might have been seen even then that most of those Negroes who were lynched were not charged with attempts to assault white women, and that many of those who were so charged were not clearly proved to be guilty. It might have been seen that what claimed to be a defense of white womanhood was more often than not merely a riot of race antagonism, brought into existence by rumors and swept along by a kind of fear. We used to talk a great deal of that race war which was coming, when black and yellows would unite and meet the scorn of whites with violence. It was one of our favorite topics of conversation. It may have been no more than boyish prattling, and now that I can see how foolish is the thought, I wonder that we talked of it at all. But we had it from our elders. They taught us early to keep the Negro in his place, whatever the cost might be.

I'll never forget one of my first lessons. It was on a very quiet Sunday afternoon, and a group of white boys were lying on the grass beside the road eating peaches. One of the boys was a good deal older that the rest of us, and we looked to him as a leader. I think it was he who made some suggestive remarks to a Negro girl who passed along the road, and certainly it was he who stood up to answer to a young Negro man who came to protest when the girl told him what had happened. I think the girl would have been more flattered than annoyed had the remarks been addressed to her privately, for she was a bad sort; but there on the road in the presence of us all, she resented it. The Negro man was mad, and he said more than I ever heard a Negro say in defense of his women, or for any other cause. We all knew him, and it was not the first time that he had shown a disposition to argue with white folks. Our leader said nothing for a few minutes, and then he walked slowly up to my house, which was not far away, and came back with a shotgun. The Negro went away, and as the white boy lay down beside us and began eating peaches again, he remarked, "You have to know how to handle Negroes." I knew then, on that quiet Sunday afternoon almost twenty years ago, and I know now, that he was ready to use that gun, if it were necessary, to keep a Negro in his place. Such incidents were not common, and few white boys would have done a thing like that. But still that was one way.

I am looking back to the things that I knew. In cities perhaps it was different. It may be a little different in the country now, though I don't think there has been much change. I have known Negroes who were happy, despite poverty and squalid surroundings. I have known whites who were miserable, despite wealth and culture of a kind. Old Negroes have told me, most any kind of Negro gets more out of life any day than a real, high-class white man; and I believe them. We say here in the South that we know the Negro. We believe that we have found for him a place in our culture. Education and the passing of years may change everything, but I know that there are in my community now many white people who will die perpetuating the order as they found it, the scheme of things to which they belong.

28 No Jim Crow in This Town

That hard times did not inevitably drive races into a competitive posture or a violent confrontation can be seen from the experience of the white and black veterans in the Bonus Expeditionary Force that marched on Washington in the summer of 1932 to push for the immediate distribution of the remainder of the bonus promised to veterans of World War I. Once the problem was defined in a political and economic sense, common cause seemed only natural. But there is another meaning, too, and that is touched on when Roy Wilkins, the author of the following essay, contrasts the experience of this rag-tag army with that of the United States Army, which enforced a rigid pattern of segregation on its own troops in the notion that integration simply would not work. By assuming important adversities in the relationship between whites and blacks the United States Army had the same level of understanding of race relationships as those people in southern Georgia described by Rollin Chambliss in Document 27 and served mainly to perpetuate the code of caste. What is curious is the distinct possibility that it was the established system, not the spontaneous desires of the people themselves, that promoted racial enmity and subordination. Of course, these people—unemployed, poor, victims themselves of Woodrow Wilson's War—black and white together found the established system unresponsive to the needs of the people. Separate or together the people of the United States were finding themselves powerless in the face of great need. It is a distinct possibility, too, as the LaFollette Committee and the Pecora Investigation charged, that such need was in fact created by the established system of concentrated political and economic power.

Source: Roy Wilkins, "The Bonuseers Ban Jim Crow," *The Crisis*, 39 (October 1932): 316-317, 332. Reprinted with the permission of the editor of *The Crisis*.

Floating clear on the slight breeze of a hot June night in Washington came a tinkling, mournful melody, a song known by now in every corner of the globe. Lilting piano notes carried the tune that set my foot patting, in spite of myself, on the trampled grass of the little hill. Then, as I was about to start humming the words, a voice took up the cadence and rode over the Anacostia Flats on the off-key notes—

> *"Feelin' tomorrow,*
> *"Lak I feel today—*
> *"Feelin' tomorrow,*
> *"Lak I feel today—*
> *"I'll pack my trunk and make my*
> *get a-way"*

Never, I thought, was there a more perfect setting for W. C. Handy's famous *St. Louis Blues*. No soft lights and swaying bodies here; no moaning trombone or piercing trumpet; no fantastic stage setting; no white shirt frants, impeccably tailored band master or waving baton. Instead, a black boy in a pair of ragged trousers and a torn, soiled shirt squatting on a box before a piano perched on a rude platform four or five feet off the ground. A single electric light bulb disclosed him in the surrounding gloom. Skillfully his fingers ran over the keys, bringing out all the Handy secrets of the song. Plaintively he sang the well-known words. A little of the entertainer was here, for there is a little of it hidden in most of us, but the plaintive note was largely the reflection of an actual condition, not the product of an entertainer.

On the ground about and below him were grouped white and colored men listening, smoking and quietly talking. From my elevation I could see camp fires flickering here and there and hear the murmur of talk over the flats. Here was the main camp of the Bonus Army, the Bonus Expeditionary Force, as it chose to call itself, and here, in my musical introduction to it, was struck the note which marked the ill-starred gathering as a significant one for Negro Americans.

For in this army which had gathered literally to "Sing the Blues" with economic phrases, there was one absentee: James Crow. It is not strictly true, as I shall explain a little later, to say that Mr. Crow was not present at all; it is an absolute fact that he was Absent With Leave a great part of the time.

He was brought along and trotted out occasionally by some of the Southern delegations and, strange to say, by some of the colored groups themselves.

The men of the B. E. F. were come together on serious business; they had no time for North, East, South, West, black and white divisions. The main problem was not to prove and maintain the superiority of a group, but to secure relief from the ills which beset them, black and white alike. In the season of despair it is foolhardy to expend energy in any direction except that likely to bring life and hope. At Washington, numbers and unity were the important factors, therefore recruits of any color were made welcome and Jim Crow got scant attention.

Here they were, then, the brown and black men who had fought (some with their tongues in their cheeks) to save the world for democracy. They were

scattered about in various state delegations or grouped in their own cluster of
rude shelters. A lonely brownskin in the delegation from North Platte, Nebr.;
one or two encamped with Seattle, Wash.; increasing numbers bivouacked with
California and the northern states east of the Mississippi River; and, of course,
the largest numbers with the states from below the Mason and Dixon line.

And at Anacostia, the main encampment, there was only one example of Jim
Crow among the 10,000 men there and that, oddly enough, was started and
maintained by colored bonuseers themselves, who hailed from New Orleans
and other towns in Louisiana. They had erected a section of shacks for themselves
and they insisted on their own mess kitchen.

A stroll down through the camp was an education in the simplified business
of living, living not complicated by a maze of social philosophy and tabus. It is
hard for one who has not actually seen the camp to imagine the crudity of the
self-constructed accommodations in which these men lived for eight weeks.

Fairly regular company streets stretched across the flats, lined on both sides
with shelters of every description. Here was a tent; here a piano box; there a
radio packing case; there three doors arranged with the ground as the fourth
side; here the smallest of "pup" tents; there a spacious canvas shelter housing
eight or ten men; here some tin nailed to a few boards; there some tar paper.

Bedding and flooring consisted of straw, old bed ticks stuffed with straw,
magazines and newspapers spread as evenly and as thickly as possible, discarded
mattresses and cardboard.

At Anacostia some Negroes had their own shacks and some slept in with
white boys. There was no residential segregation. A Negro "house" might be
next door to a white "house" or across the street, and no one thought of passing
an ordinance to "preserve property values." In the California contingent which
arrived shortly before I left there were several Negroes and they shared with
their white buddies the large tents which someone secured for them from a
government warehouse. The Chicago group had several hundred Negroes in it
and they worked, ate, slept and played with their white comrades. The Negroes
shared tasks with the whites from kitchen work to camp M.P. duty.

In gadding about I came across white toes and black toes sticking out from
tent flaps and boxes as their owners sought to sleep away the day. They were
far from the spouters of Nordic nonsense, addressing themselves to the business
of living together. They were in another world, although Jim Crow Washington,
D.C. was only a stone's throw from their doors.

All about were signs containing homely philosophy and sarcasm on the
treatment of veterans by the country, such as: "The Heroes of 1918 Are the
Bums of 1932." I believe many of the white campers were bitter and sarcastic.
They meant what they said on those signs. But disappointment and
disillusionment is an old story to Negroes. They were philosophic about this
bonus business. They had wished for so many things to which they were justly
entitled in this life and received so little that they could not get fighting mad
over what was generally considered among them as the government's ingratitude.
They had been told in 1917 that they were fighting for a better world, for true
democracy; that a new deal would come for them; that jobs would come to them

on merit, that lynching would be stopped; that they would have schools, homes, justice and the franchise. But these Negroes found out as long ago as 1919 that they had been fooled. Some of them could not even wear their uniforms back home. So, while the indifference of the government to the bonus agitation might be a bitter pill to the whites, it was nothing unusual to the Negroes. They addressed themselves to humorous take-offs in signs, to cards and to music, the latter two shared by whites.

Thus it was I came across such signs on Negro shacks as "Douglas Hotel, Chicago;" "Euclid Avenue;" "South Parkway;" and "St. Antoine St." A card game had reunited four buddies from San Francisco, Detroit and Indianapolis and they were swapping stories to the swish of the cards.

Over in one corner a white vet was playing a ukelele and singing what could have been the theme song of the camp: "In a Shanty in Old Shanty Town." On a Sunday afternoon the camp piano was played alternately by a brown lad with a New York accent and a red-necked white boy from Florida, while a few rods away Elder Micheaux's visiting choir was giving voice, in stoptime, to a hymn, "God's Tomorrow Will Be Brighter Than Today." Negroes and whites availed themselves of the free choice of patting their feet either outdoors to the piano or in the gospel tent to the choir.

Outside the main camp (there were four settlements) James Crow made brief and intermittent appearances, chiefly because the largest Southern delegations were not at Anacostia. But even in the Southern and border contingents there was no hard and fast color line. On Pennsylvania avenue, where the men had taken over a number of abandoned buildings in the process of being torn down, were camped the Carolina, Florida, Alabama and Texas delegations as well as a scattering from Virginia, Tennessee and West Virginia.

In a five story building a company of Negroes was assigned the fifth floor, but they all received treatment from the same medical center on the first floor. At first they all ate together, but there was so much confusion and so many men (not necessarily Negroes) were coming in on the tail end of the mess line, that a system whereby each floor took turns being first in the mess line was adopted. This was an equitable arrangement, but even here whites and Negroes lined up together and ate together; no absolute separation was possible, nor was it attempted.

In a mess kitchen which served only Southerners I saw Negroes and white mixed together in line and grouped together eating. I was told there had been a few personal fights and a few hard words passed, but the attitude of the die-hard, strictly Jim Crow whites had not been adopted officially. Such Southern whites as I met showed the greatest courtesy and mingled freely with the Negroes.

Captain A. B. Simmons, colored, who headed his company, hails from Houston, Tex. He and his men were loud in their declarations of the fair treatment they had received on the march to Washington. They were served meals in Southern towns by Southern white waitresses, in Main Street Southern restaurants along with their white companions. They rode freights and trucks and hiked together. Never a sign of Jim Crow through Northern Texas, Arkansas, Tennessee, or Virginia. Captain Simmons attended the regular company commanders' councils and helped with the problems of administration. His fellow officers, all white Southerners, accorded him the same consideration given others of his rank.

His story was corroborated by others. A long, hard-boiled Negro from West Virginia who had just stepped out of the mess line behind a white man from Florida said: "Shucks, they ain't got time for that stuff here and those that has, we gets 'em told personally." And said a cook in the North Carolina mess kitchen (helping whites peel potatoes): "No, sir things is different here than down home."

In general assemblies and in marches there were no special places "for Negroes." The black boys did not have to tag along at the end of the line of march; there was no "special" section reserved for them at assemblies. They were shot all through the B. E. F. In the rallies on the steps of the nation's capitol they were in front, in the middle and in the rear.

One of the many significant aspects of the bonuseers' banishment of Jim Crow is the lie it gives to United States army officials who have been diligently spreading the doctrine that whites and blacks could not function together in the army; that they could not use the same mess tents, mingle in the same companies, council together on military problems. The B. E. F. proved that Negroes and whites can do all these things together, that even Negroes and white Southerners can do them together.

How can the army higher-ups explain that? Why can't the United States army with its equipment and its discipline enlist Negroes and whites together in all branches of the service? It can, but it will not. The army is concerned with refined democracy, with tabus, with the maintenance of poses. The B. E. F. is concerned with raw democracy and with reality. But hereafter the army will have to hide behind its self-erected tradition, for the B. E. F. has demonstrated, right under the August army nose, that the thing can be done.

And right there was the tragedy of it all. I stood again on the little rise above the Anacostia Flats and looked out over the camp on my last night in town. Men and women can live, eat, play and work together be they black or white, just as the B. E. F. demonstrated. Countless thousands of people know it, but they go on pretending, building their paper fences and their cardboard arguments. Back home in Waycross, Miami, Pulaski, Waxahachie, Pine Bluff, Cairo, Petersburg, Kansas City and St. Louis they go on pretending, glaring, jabbing, insulting, fighting. In St. Louis, where I first saw daylight, they separate them in everything except street cars.

A dump of a shanty town below the majestic Washington monument and the imperious national capitol . . . Ragged torch bearers futilely striving to light the path for the blind overlords who will not see . . . . A blue camp, its cheerfulness undershot with tragedy . . . . A blue race problem, its surface gayety undershot with poignant sorrow . . . .

As I turned away, stumbling in the dark over a hose which brought water to the camp from a nearby fire hydrant, a soft Negro voice and the tinkling piano notes came faintly to me:

"I got the Saint Louis Blues
"Just as Blue as I can be . . . ."

29 The New Deal Meets the Black Man: The Factories

The true test of the New Deal's commitment and energy in helping those in the nation who genuinely needed government assistance may well be in its regard for the black population. The black community obviously lacked the political and economic clout of big business; it could not compare in its organizational and financial leverage with other special groups in society; blacks were often excluded as a routine matter even from the major labor unions. To respond to the needs of black America would be a response to need and not to power. And indeed the Roosevelt administration (or was it mainly Eleanor Roosevelt?) did address the problems of these people enough for most blacks to shift their political allegiance from the Republican Party to the Democrats. That this party offered more for blacks than the Republicans, however, says little. It is always easy, as did one commentator in the course of the meeting described below, to say that it could be worse.

In its large programs significant doubt emerges about the New Deal's program for black America. At the same time, something is revealed about the purpose and method of the new regime. One of the largest programs, that of the National Recovery Administration, was also Roosevelt's initial attack on the problem of the depression in industrial America. Based on a scheme devised by the president of General Electric, Gerard Swope, and supported by the head of the United States Chamber of Commerce, the NRA was designed to eliminate competition in industry so that profits and prices could go even higher; then it was hoped that the additional money would trickle down through the business to the worker. While in theory important problems plagued the idea, since it would boost prices at a time when people were unable to pay the existing prices, in practice it generated an even more pressing and urgent social distress. This was especially true regarding blacks, who as consumers would be forced to pay the higher prices yet had no way of chasing them with higher wages. Indeed, the NRA codes for the South included lower wage schedules than for the North. Black workers were understandably less than enthusiastic about the program. At a meeting of black workers in Harlem the Roosevelt administration attempted to explain the program to these people. The explanation was met by those workers with taunts, jeers, laughter, and penetrating questions and retorts. And the administration had a prime opportunity, whether it realized it or not, to learn from these workers. If this meeting was any indication of how the Roosevelt administration was doing, the administration failed the test. In its purpose and in its method the New Deal was promoting precisely the tendencies that had victimized blacks before; the political economy was being further fragmented into competing groups which would attempt to push higher prices and costs onto other groups. And in that system those groups with the most power benefited most. In the nature of things blacks were left behind or out.

Source: Suzanne La Follette, "A Message to Uncle Tom," *The Nation*, 139 (September 5, 1934): 265-66.

The night was fearfully hot, and for a time it looked as if the last session of the Labor Institute which the Brotherhood of Sleeping Car Porters was conducting at the 135th Street Library in Harlem would be poorly attended. That would have been unfortunate, for the full-dress speaker of the occasion was none other than Dr. Gustav Peck, executive director of the National Labor Advisory Board. The general subject under discussion at the four sessions of the institute was "Negro Labor and the National Recovery Program"; and it had got round that the Administration had decided the occasion was auspicious for making Dr. Peck's address its pronouncement to the Negro world, which was known to be restive under the New Deal. As the meeting got under way, the audience began to arrive and at least half of the late comers were in the rough garb of manual workers. The Administration was speaking to Negro labor, was it? Well, Negro labor would hear what it had to say.

If Dr. Peck had come expecting that "it might be worse" would prove a soothing argument, he was quickly undeceived. He was preceded by Professor Emmett E. Dorsey of Howard University, speaking on "The Future of the Negro and the Recovery Program." And Professor Dorsey keyed up the audience to quite a pitch of skepticism by maintaining that if the recovery program had a future, the Negro, under it, had not—and no more had the white worker. Why had the NRA become steadily more compliant with the demands of employers and more contemptuous of the demands of labor? Because government is necessarily responsive to pressures. The NRA was under constant pressure from the most highly organized, articulate, and powerful groups in the country—the owners and employers. Labor, white and black, was inarticulate and weak. The A. F. of L., which claimed to represent labor, was, because of its reactionary leadership and its antiquated craft unionism, unequal to the task of organizing or leading it.

Understanding how things were done in Washington, said Mr. Dorsey, we could also understand why the NRA had allowed Negro workers to be paid less than white workers under the codes. The differentials had been established by usage, but the Administration had given them the force of law. Why? Because Southern employers were articulate and influential. They went to Washington and argued that the cost of living was lower in the South. What they called a lower cost of living was really a lower standard, forced upon the workers by starvation wages. The employers had also argued that Negro workers were inefficient. Why wouldn't they be? They were persecuted, lynched, kept in ignorance, underpaid. Were they likely to become more efficient so long as the government recognized discrimination and sanctioned it in the codes?

The only hope Mr. Dorsey could see for the Negro was in organization—not Negro organization, but the organization of workers, black and white, to work shoulder to shoulder in defense of their rights. For labor need expect nothing from employers or from government that it was not prepared to fight for.

Warm applause for Mr. Dorsey. The chairman introduced the Administration. Warm applause for the Administration.

The apologist for the New Deal spoke easily. Being himself a union labor man, he knew better than to patronize his audience or to throw it too many sops of political hokum. Dr. Peck said he hadn't known until he saw the printed program that he was supposed to address the meeting on "The Philosophy Back of the NRA." He had expected to discuss the differentials. However, he would do a little of both.

His definition of the philosophy was significant, not because it was news to anyone present, but because its explicit statement by a spokesman for the Administration was news. There seemed, he said, to be a lot of confusion about the nature of the NIRA. A good many people seemed to be aggrieved because it wasn't socialism or communism. They should remember that this was a Democratic Administration. The NIRA was a "sweeping but capitalist and conservative measure of reform," designed not to change the existing capitalist order but to preserve it. If labor wasn't pleased with it, that was just too bad. The purpose of the minimum wages set in the codes was to increase buying power; providing a living wage for workers was no part of it. If the minimums set under the codes were in some cases insufficient to support the recipients, that was also too bad. The Administration had done the best it could. It was under tremendous pressure from the employers. We might laugh at Mr. Mellon and the other representatives of big business. The NRA officials couldn't; they were too powerful. That, I think, about sums up Mr. Peck's remarks on the philosophy of the NRA. When he spoke of it as "revolution," the audience roared.

Dr. Peck deplored the fact that the large majority of Negro workers were agricultural and therefore not eligible to enjoy the blessings of the NRA, and the further fact that most Negroes in industry were unskilled and therefore able to enjoy those blessings only in moderation. When it came to the differentials, he had opposed them at first, but he was beginning to doubt the wisdom of his stand. Southern employers had advanced convincing arguments—he did not mention that they were "organized, articulate, and powerful." They had said:

"We are in a primitive state of industrial development; we aren't as efficient as the North. We haven't the long industrial tradition of the North, and we haven't the skilled immigrant workers to draw on. We must be allowed to pay lower wages." (What about those "fair practices" provisions, Dr. Peck? If they could be used to protect Northern coal companies against competition from the product of low-paid Southern labor, why not use them to protect Southern industrialists in paying the Northern wage?)

Even the Negro community itself, he said, seemed to be divided on this question of differentials. Certain Negro investigators had actually recommended them (murmurs of "lickspittles," "kept Negro economists," from the audience). Without the differentials wouldn't Negro workers be worse off? The Southern employers might close their shops, and where would the workers be then? He thought it likely that even under the present codes the position of Negro workers had improved. And he called attention to the service the Labor Advisory Board had performed in keeping the word "Negro" out of the codes. As they stood they applied to all Southern workers. Certain employers had tried to get authority to pay less than minimum wages to "subnormal" workers, meaning Negroes; but the NRA had nobly refused to stand for it. So things might have been worse. There was a lot of criticism from arm-chair authorities living below Fourteenth Street and writing for the liberal magazines. Let critics at least ascertain the facts; let them go into Southern communities, talk to Negro preachers (laughter so loud and long that it drowned the rest of the sentence).

At last Dr. Peck said he'd like to know how that audience felt about the differentials, and in general about the NRA. He really knew very little about how the Negroes were feeling. He hoped to be enlightened by the discussion.

He was. In the response of that Negro audience there was plenty of light but no sweetness. It happened that George Streeter was pinch-hitting for Frank R. Crosswaith as leader of the discussion; and Mr. Streeter was roiled. He remarked that Dr. Peck had made it quite clear that the NRA expected to save capital at the expense of labor; he pooh-poohed the pretense that the NIRA constituted anything revolutionary or that the New Deal meant anything more than the old deal for labor. He likewise invited the audience to bear in mind that Dr. Peck was a labor man who had put himself in the pay of the Administration and thereby acquired a vested interest in Administration propaganda. Mr. Streeter called to the platform John Davis, head of the Joint Board for National Recovery (not a government organization). Mr. Davis went, and when he stepped down he had brought out some interesting facts: that General Johnson has steadily refused to see representatives of Negro workers; that no statistical bureau of the government has allowed itself to be persuaded to investigate the effects of the NRA on Negro workers; that in his own investigations, which had taken him over some seven thousand miles of territory, he had found innumerable instances of chiseling on the part of employers, with the Administration doing nothing to protect even such rights as Negro labor had under the codes.

But the most telling criticism came from the manual workers in the audience. Here were no arm-chair critics; each worker, as he rose, gave his name, trade, and union affiliation. They were untutored, but they spoke remarkably well, with a fervor derived from their sense of wrong and with the simple directness of speakers unembarrassed by having to make a case. By the time the discussion period was over we had listened to story after story of discrimination against black workers by all the agencies of government having to do with labor. One union official told how he had been snubbed at the New York offices of the NRA until it was found that he was there representing white workers. Another told how the daily minimum in his trade, which used to be five dollars, had been reduced to four. Another brought out the fact that skilled Negro workers were ineligible for PWA jobs because they were black; another how Negroes were discriminated against in the granting of relief. They demolished the argument that Southern industry must be nursed along at the expense of labor by pointing out that Northern industrialists had moved South precisely because Southern labor was cheap. They asked why the government was allowing the burden of price-lifting to be placed squarely on the backs of the workers. They brought out that the differentials in the coal codes were obviously aimed at Negro labor. They hammered the whole labor policy of the NRA. And they repudiated the suggestion that labor support a scheme admittedly designed to benefit the exploiters of labor.

In rebuttal Dr. Peck said he wished he could persuade his hearers to give the NRA a chance. After all, it was only nine months old, and had within it great possibilities of usefulness. Already it had abolished child labor, established the forty-hour week (he didn't mention the 211 exceptions), and taught employers to think of labor as something more than a large item in the cost of production. It had also established the wonderful principle of settling disputes by conference (cries of "What about Toledo, Minneapolis, San Francisco?"). The audience might object to Section 7-a (cries, "We don't object to it; we object because the government hasn't enforced it"), but it was a great charter of rights for labor. And labor was taking advantage of it; *vide* the tremendous increase of labor-union membership. And if labor didn't like the deal it was getting under the codes, why didn't it take advantage of Section 7-a? Why didn't it organize? He was a labor man himself; he believed labor should organize and insist upon its rights instead of running to the government with complaints. If labor didn't give the NRA a chance it might get something much worse—"for you can't go back, you know" (cries, "We'll go forward, to a workers' society!").

It was very late and warmer than ever, but the audience was too excited to notice either the hour or the heat. Its members were filled with the exhilaration of the chase; they would have kept it up all night if the chairman had not called off the final impromptu speakers and adjourned the meeting. In their faces as they filed out was the glow of satisfaction that comes from work well done. The Administration had spoken to the Negro, and it had been taught that the Negro is not to be safely treated as a dumb and faithful Uncle Tom, devoted to the interests of his white master and conveniently meek about his own.

30 The New Deal Meets the Black Man: Agriculture

Agricultural reform resembled in important respects the New Deal's efforts to rejuvenate the industrial economy since it too stressed the need for increased prices and reduced competition in the marketplace. Through a series of measures including the Agricultural Adjustment Administration and the Bankhead Cotton Control Act the New Deal promoted the modernization of agriculture through a system of incentives (and enforcement devices) to cut the production of commodities and thereby to alleviate what appeared to be a glutted market. That move, however, intensified the problems already encountered by sharecroppers as landlords, who usually felt little desire to share allotments with croppers, reduced the acreage in production and gave notice to the croppers and tenants that their services would no longer be needed. Indeed, the additional income from the subsidy would often provide the additional capital necessary for investment in farm machinery, especially tractors, thereby making the services of even more of their croppers unnecesary. This depopulation of the countryside produced in some cases, as in the instance of the first letter reprinted below, simply the desire for government help for those forced from the land. (Indeed, in an earlier portion of that letter to Secretary of Agriculture Henry Wallace the writer expressed favorable views toward the Bankhead Act which had put him in this position.) In other cases the responses were filled with resistance to the practices of the landlords under the new laws. The second letter details some of the practices experienced by the croppers, again in eastern Arkansas. It is out of these experiences and frustrations that blacks and whites joined together in the Southern Tenant Farmers Union to change the laws and their administration, another striking example of the potential for class issues to transcend racial tension. As in the city, the New Deal in the countryside responded more to power than need. The poor blacks and poor whites thus remained even more in need.

Source: Letter from Henderson Bentley, Tyronza, Arkansas, to Secretary of Agriculture Henry A. Wallace, December 15, 1934, and unsigned statement, December 5, 1934, Gilmore, Arkansas, both in Records of the Office of the Secretary of Agriculture, Legal Division, AAA, Record Group 16, File 467, The National Archives.

Lots of us have got Notice to move By the 5th of this month and we have Ben going Ever sence we got the Notice to move on the 5th and haven got any place to go yet Both white and collord and Dear Secretary Notfide the government to give us Homeless Family tent to put our wives and children in and we will get Back in the woods some place offer the Landlord Land We have Family on this place ar suffer for the want of fire and all them that got Notice to move Mr H. N. Norcross wont let them have a team to Hall them a stick of wood with somthang. i Never Know a man to do tenant whoo made a crop with him Before the End of the year and we have hade some Hard Cold weather and the poor tenant he had give Notice to move suffer the ask him for a team to holl a little wood with and he fuse to let them have it and them have found some kind of place the way he is doing them he is given them 98¢ a acres for the par[i]ty payment Mr H N. Norcross is a outlower the way he is treated some Family white and Collord and Dear Secretary we Need some help and it dont do no good for us to See the County committee for he tole us if Mr Norcross says move to move for them was Mr Norcross Houses so Dear Secretary the Rented Land the government have it dont Look like he would Let the Big Land owner worke it and hole the poor farmer out of it and it Being Rented Land of the government that what makeing it hard with the labor the Land the government got Rented the ar handling that wright on and getting what the part out Rented Dear Secretary Look for the poor labor and help us out for the land lord ar gants us your truly

Henderson Bentley
Tyronza Ark

Secretary Wallace
Mr Norcross Rider ask me for the House a gane this morning and i haven got no place to go yet the Land owner cant give no place yet so they say and that given us whoo is on Mr Norcross place a Hard way to go so we Hope you wood see if the government will furnish us Homeless People a tent to Live in untell we can do Better for Mr. Norcross is pushen us out and have a 100 acres cleair up for to Be put in tenion [?] in 35 and we was tole it government Land

Our Landlord is Mr C. E Hughes

Dec 5 1934
Gilmore Ark

This is three of us Booker T. Lamberth and Frank James and Bill G[——] and we are stating the unfair Rule that we had to under go with ——the first thing We Work for 75¢ a day and the Landlord had us to plow our land up by the day and then charge us two Dollars a acer and enterus on that and the next is he had some kind of blank for us to sing and that said we as shear cropers was to give half of cotton and corn and the next is the landlord cut our crops and told us that we was loted so much but the amount we do not know for we have not receiv no lotment books at all and at cotton picking time he brought some blank sheet of paper for us to sing and told us we had to sing them or not sell cotton and the landlord force us to sell our cotton to him and he brought it at 12 1/2 and less and our perdie is missing we have not got it yet and we ar in crittenden county - gilmore ark

31 Straight Talk

It should not be surprising that many blacks came to identify their government with their landlords—or former landlords in the case of those forced off the land. In the following letter from a sharecropper to a union headquarters, in fact, the government appears mainly as an enforcer for the edicts to move issued by the owners. The government, he said, was "doing with us just like a man would do with a old poor dog." Possibly he reflected the thoughts of a number of blacks when he intimated that a price would be paid should the government expect sacrifices from blacks in a war again.

Source: *New Challenge*, 2 (Fall 1937): 92.

December 10, 1936.

Dear————:

They say that Gradnigo Island was a white settlement. The land belongs mostly to white but the tenants have always been colored. It wasn't till the big war that they put the road through and a few whites bought small farms. Before that the X family owned all this country and used just colored hands. There are very few grown white men born from............ on northwest from here for seven or eight miles. I know because I was born about a mile from here. My grandmother and grandfather were slaves on the old X plantation.

The government man was here yesterday and asked me a lot of questions about how much cotton I gathered and how many kids I got. He told me the organizer was going to get in trouble. He said "You got your notice yesterday from Mr. Y." I said yes but Mr. Z is my boss and he told me when I got my settlement that they was going to run it just like it had been and that they wasn't going to hurt none of us. He said "Yes, but you better move or the sheriff will come and take your stuff and load it up and throw it in the road." I said alright when they do it I said I'll go with it.

The only thing that made me sorry was when the world was in war before, they picked us up and registered us and sent us to war to fight for our country. Now the country is quieted down and steady and the government doing with us just like a man would do with a old poor dog. If they was going to fight again we would sit right here.

I talked pretty straight with him but a man in my fix can't talk crooked.

. . . .

Tenant on. . . . . .farm.

32 Slum-Clearance and the Progress of Modernization

One of the obvious calamities generated by the migration of blacks into the North where cities were unable or unwilling to respond to the vast needs of that new population growth was the ever present slum or ghetto. By the 1930s the federal government had even recognized the enormity of the combination of racial discrimination and poverty in the ghetto. Yet even as it moved to rectify the problem it intensified the pains and gave every reason for blacks and whites alike to believe that the government acted in collusion with their oppressors in the name of helping the powerless. As it would come to be time and again in the future, urban renewal or slum-clearance became more recognizable as Negro removal. As the government purchased property from the landlords the black tenants, like the croppers in the South, were moved off. The Relocation Office was designed to aid those people in finding new homes; it actually served to push them out as fast as possible. The Welfare Office obligingly cooperated in this effort with its chief positive action being that of getting the evicted families to double up.

The success of the clearance project could be found not in the destruction of the homes for the tenants who had lived in them, hovels though they might be, but in the adroit diffusion of the problem of poverty and race into narrower questions of zoning, planning, and city growth and in the diffusion of the solution into sharply severed areas of responsibility, with no single individual or agency that could be targeted for attack. The pattern of modernization was surging forward in the city as well as in the countryside. The pains of the process intensified with its accomplishments.

Source: Karen Dash, "Slum-Clearance Farce," *The Nation*, 142 (April 1, 1936): 410-12.

Since 1932 public-spirited people in Detroit have been manifesting sharp interest in slum conditions. Social workers have exposed painful facts concerning the misery and degradation of Negro families living in Detroit's East Side slum district. These Negroes are unemployed and destitute through no fault of their own. John F. Ballenger, Wayne County Relief Administrator, has placed the blame squarely where it belongs—on the shoulders of Detroit's big industrialists.

Public indignation has been further stirred by the statistics from city-wide social surveys which show the results of unsanitary and shameful housing conditions. The fifty-block area three blocks east of Woodward Avenue and about a mile from Detroit's City Hall, which was selected as the first site for a slum-clearance project, shows excessively high rates in disease and all social delinquencies. Crime is 7½ times the city average. Juvenile delinquency is 10¼ times, infant mortality is 1½ times, and pneumonia is 8 times higher than the average for the city as a whole. The tuberculosis death-rate for Site Number 1 is 15 times higher than in Site Number 30, a somewhat better section of Detroit. One-third of the families living in this fifty-block area are dependent on public welfare. The average monthly rent for a family is $8, and the average family income (1933) is $300 a year.

On September 9, 1935, ten thousand cheering persons, the majority of them Negroes, jammed the vicinity of 651 Benton Street, Detroit, as Mrs. Franklin D. Roosevelt formally opened work on the slum-clearance project. With a wave of her handkerchief she signaled to a group of workmen to pull down the first house. The building crashed in a cloud of dust, and the $6,680,000 project was under way. Mrs. Roosevelt then gave a short address.

The ceremony over, Mrs. Roosevelt returned to Washington, confident that all was well. But the Detroit program did not "go ahead" as she hoped. In the months that followed many old houses were torn down, a hundred Negro families were ruthlessly ousted from their homes, but not one new building is in process of construction. The East Side slum-clearance program, discussed for over two years, has resulted so far in exactly nothing.

Late last autumn I started on a house-to-house survey of the Negro slum district known as Site Number 1. Getting off the Charlevoix crosstown car at Eliot Street, near Saint Antoine, I stopped at the first house I saw which had a condemnation notice pasted to the door. It was a miserable shack in the last stages of decay; occupied as place of business and home by a Negro tailor and his family.

The man was at first afraid to talk. He said he had been handed two weeks' notice to get out. He was deeply worried about where he could find a place to run his shop and keep his family. The rental of this shanty was $10 a month, and the man declared that although he had been hunting around for some time he could not find another location as cheap. No information about the new houses to be constructed on the site had been offered him. He said he was very poor, and that he would have to borrow the money to pay moving expenses. He was very nervous while talking; he kept asking me not to quote him, or use his name, as he did not want to "get in wrong with the government."

The house next door, in similarly bad condition, was occupied by Mrs.

A——, an elderly Negro woman, and her son. The son, formerly employed by the Briggs Manufacturing Company, is now a "junker." He earns the family living by going around with a hand-cart collecting rags and old papers. The average income of these people is $6 every two weeks. The woman is almost totally blind.

Four days before, she said, a man brought the notice of eviction. He refused Mrs. A—— any definite information about when she must get out. "Right away!" he said. Mrs. A—— was panic-stricken. She had no idea where to move to, or where to turn for advice. She had never even heard of the Relocation Office, which is supposed to offer assistance to all the ousted families.

Thirteen persons, four adults and nine children, were living in an unheated five-room hovel over on Rowena Street, near Beaubien. A thin, tired-looking Negro woman came to the door, carrying a child in her arms. Inside the house, which was shabby and forlorn beyond all description, children were swarming everywhere. They were dressed in rags, and not one of them had shoes or stockings. The mother, Mrs. B——, apologized for their appearance. Five of the youngsters were her own; four were the children of her dead sister. The Welfare had promised them clothing and shoes so they could go to school, but hadn't got around yet actually to give the needed articles.

Mrs. B——'s husband was out looking for a job. He had worked for the Ford Motor Company from December, 1922, until July, 1926. He had then worked for the Western Waterproofing Company for two years, and for the City Garbage until 1931. He had been unable to find steady employment since that time.

Mrs. B—— said she didn't worry much about being evicted. "Things are so bad with us," she said simply, "they just couldn't be any worse."

This woman nurses her youngest child, a boy two and a half years old, at her breast. The Welfare is not giving out any more milk tickets, and Mrs. B—— finds she can supply milk herself by drinking cocoa made with water.

Albert C—— has a coal and wood store on St. Antoine Street. When I came to talk to him, he was hacking lumber into small pieces to sell for firewood. He said he was barely "getting by" in his present location, where the rent is $6 per month. He had built up a small neighborhood trade, and was worried sick by the sudden eviction notice. "I'm perfectly willing to move," he said, "but I know I won't be able to find another store at $6."

He had been several times to the Relocation Office but they had no help to offer. There are no vacant stores available in the neighborhood, and no stores which can be rented for $6 in any Negro section whatever. Albert C——'s average monthly income is $18.

The Relocation Office is in a vacant bank building at the corner of Erskine and Hastings streets, in the heart of the Negro district. The information clerk, a young white man, was surly and suspicious of me. "We are doing everything possible for these people," he said. "They are mostly junkers, anyway. We give them about two weeks to find a new place and get moved."

"What help do you offer?"

"Well, we keep a list of houses for rent. Better houses, mostly, than what they're used to. But they won't take them."

"Why not?"

He shrugged. "Oh, because they cost three or four dollars more a month!"

"What do you do about the families who haven't the money to move?" I asked.

"They must apply to the Welfare," he snapped. "We have nothing to do with that angle."

The District Office of the Welfare Department is at Alfred and Russell streets. A young man at the information desk told me that the slum-clearance project was bringing them more trouble than they knew how to handle. Since enough houses at low rentals could not possibly be found, the evicted families would simply have to "double up," he said, and share whatever hole or corner could be found for them. Miss Clara Kramer of the District Office confirmed this statement.

I asked Miss Kramer how much time was allowed the evicted families to find a new place and vacate their homes. "Legally," she replied, "they have thirty days. But we want to get them out quick, so we're telling them they've got to be out in anywhere from five days to two weeks."

I began to investigate the homes available for Negro tenants. Since an overwhelming majority of the families living in the condemned area are paying from $3 to $10 per month for rent, I made up my mind to look only at houses within this price range. I had to give up this plan because a full day's search proved to me that there were simply no houses to be had at less than $10. On the following day, therefore, I walked from nine in the morning until dusk, looking at the houses offered for rent at from $10 to $20 per month.

In Alfred Street I saw a house with a "For Rent" sign on it. It was a small, gray frame house, partitioned inside to serve for four families. The wooden steps leading to the front porch were completely rotted away. I groped my way through a dark hall to the vacant flat in the rear. There were three medium-sized rooms in each of which the filth and decay were indescribable. The rain beat in through the broken windows and trickled across the soggy wooden floors. The wallpaper hung in streamers. There was no stove to heat the flat, no gas, no electric lights. Window shades were completely missing, and in many places the plaster had fallen away, exposing the bare laths of wall and ceiling. I took a look at the kitchen. Rags were stuffed in the broken windows. There were no faucets in the rusty old sink, no covering on the floor, no cook stove, no icebox. In the bathroom a bathtub stood in one corner. Three of its legs were gone, and it was not connected with the water pipes. The toilet had obviously been out of order for months.

This flat was offered for rent by a Detroit real-estate company at $12 per month. I called up the office of this firm, commented on the bad condition of the house, and asked whether they would not make some essential repairs before a new tenant moved in. The girl who answered the telephone said that the owner had no intention of doing anything whatever to improve the flat. The prospective tenant could take it or leave it.

During the next two weeks I looked at many other houses and talked with various Negroes who run real-estate offices and rental agencies in the vicinity. Everywhere I heard the same story. There is a serious shortage of houses for Negro tenants, and the landlords are making hay while the sun shines. Even "shack" prices are from $12 to $20. The majority are without even a pretense of a bathroom, such as the Alfred Street house offered. Houses that the owners were glad to get $4 a month for a short time ago can now be rented within an hour for $15 and upward.

During the two months I spent making this survey of actual conditions among the Negro population of Detroit, I was also trying to arrange an interview with Mrs. Josephine Gomon, secretary of the Detroit Housing Commission. I finally got an appointment to meet Mrs. Gomon in her cheerful and pleasant offices in the new Water Board building. Mrs. Gomon spoke very hopefully about the Detroit Housing Commission's plans. She described the new housing soon to be erected in the Negro slum districts as modern, beautiful buildings with all sorts of conveniences, including play areas for the children and recreation facilities for adults. Rents, said Mrs. Gomon, would probably be from $16 to $25 per month.

I asked whether the evicted families were not having trouble finding homes at rents they could afford. Mrs. Gormon admitted this, but added that the one hundred families already evicted were managing somehow. "It's just a few dollars' increase," she said.

"What about the families on relief rolls?" I persisted. "How can they pay even a few dollars' increase when their allowance for rent is already so small?"

To this, Mrs. Gomon replied that the Welfare would increase relief checks to cover higher rentals. (This, unfortunately, is not true. John F. Ballenger, Wayne County Relief Administrator, has put into effect a 20 percent cut in all welfare aid, and this slash affects every family on the Detroit Welfare.)

On leaving I asked Mrs. Gomon whether the sum allowed for rent would be enough, in any case, to permit families on relief, evicted from condemned houses, to live in the new apartments when they were ready for occupancy. Mrs. Gomon replied very definitely that it would not. She went on to say that the new buildings were being put up for the benefit of industrious, low-income families—not necessarily for the people now living in the slum areas but for any family that could afford to pay the moderate rental of from $16 to $25 a month!

A week later I went back to the Relocation Office and asked to be given a list of the names and new addresses of the one hundred families, who according to Mrs. Gomon, had been successfully moved from their old homes and established in new locations. I said frankly that I wished to see how and where they were living, and whether their condition had been improved by the change. My request was met with an equally frank refusal. The clerk said he had been given definite instructions not to hand out such a list.

I spent the last week of my survey tramping the Negro section trying to find some of the relocated families. Many of the houses I had visited earlier had been razed. Their former occupants had disappeared without leaving an address. Eventually I found six families which had been "successfully relocated." Five had been unable to find decent homes within their means and were living "doubled up" with other families. Children were sleeping three and four in a bed or on the floor. One family—a grandmother, man and wife, and a sixteen-year-old daughter—had rented a five-room flat at $27.50 per month, and were taking in four men roomers, to help cover the cost of the rent. In no case was the condition of these people improved by the change. Instead, they were much worse off than before, especially those families which had been forced to "double up" with others.

These are facts, and further comment would be superfluous. It seems painfully clear that slum clearance is just another New Deal measure—a fake, a humbug, and a joke.

33 Still a Separate World

The powerful forces of change at work in American society in the 1930s drastically altered the circumstances of life for most people. The demographic changes were profound as more and more people lived in the city, worked in the factory, and had smaller families. Yet for some the changes may have intensified existing problems or altered the terms and appearance but not the substance of the conditions in which they existed. Those blacks who continued to live in the rural South could be counted in this group. Charles Johnson's perceptive analysis of black life in *Growing Up in the Black Belt: Negro Youth in the Rural South* presented a picture that was close to Du Bois' portrayal in 1900. Johnson's investigation came at the end of the 1930s and his report was published on the eve of the second world war. It was not, however, merely the objective circumstances that marked the life of these black rural people as different from that of the modern white society. The persistence of black traditions and cultural elements indicates the power and hold of tradition. Especially revealing is a core element of black culture—religion. The sermon recounted below seems to have a certain timeless quality to it, perhaps itself an indication of the lack of adaptation to a linear perception of time, as the preacher focuses once again on the lesson of Job and the perils of this world and the rewards of the next. The delivery, the style, and the points of reference in the presentation of the logic all mark it as firmly based in a black religious tradition. So too with the audience participation. But even as these people worshipped in an age old manner, the attractions it held for the youth seemed to fade. Just as they often thought in terms of leaving the farm to go to the city, a number of teenagers, while not completely skeptical, obviously were less committed to the religious forms than their elders. Some of their comments are presented below. The reason for this fading is not clear; it may even be that the process of socialization has not been completed yet and that they would come to hold convictions more closely resembling those of their parents before long. Or, just as likely, if the religion is based on social and economic experiences as well as cultural persistence, those experiences may be yet to come. This latter possibility in fact may well account for the blossoming of such religious practices in the inner cities of the major metropolitan areas. All the bracketed commentary in this item was provided in the original by Charles S. Johnson.

Source: Charles S. Johnson, *Growing Up in the Black Belt: Negro Youth in the Rural South* (Washington, D.C., 1941), pp. 137-40, 154-55.

Mount Pizgah Church in Johnston County, North Carolina, is a large, gray, single auditorium structure, with high ceiling and long horizontal iron bars overhead to brace the walls. The altar rests at the rear of a small, semicircular platform. There are four chairs directly in front of the platform which are usually occupied by the members of the deacon's board. Back of the altar is a large, frayed, and soiled red plush chair with a high back, in which the minister sits.

The church is filled with perspiring worshippers, both young and old, who are cooling themselves with fans provided by the undertaker. The women are dressed in organdy and voile, and the men in wash pants and shirts. A few wear coats.

After the opening hymn, the congregation is seated; a hard-faced, wiry, dark man remains standing. He is Deacon Eppse, and he prays thus:

Blessed Jesus, we thank you for life, the greatest blessing in the world, life. We thank you for the blood that circulates through our bodies. We thank you for the blood and the air so we can stand on our feet. We thank you for the loving hand of mercy bestowed upon us; that Thou are in our midst. Prepare us for our souls' journey through this unfriendly world, and when our life on this earth is ended receive us into Thy home which art in heaven.

The congregation sings, "We'll Understand It Better By and By." An elderly brown man of about 65 reads the scripture. There are groans and solemn exclamations from the four men in front of the altar, "Lord have mercy," "Amen." The reader interpolates:

We have to slip and straighten up the wick in the candle and lamp. We have to straighten up a car. Just like we have to straighten up a wick so the light will burn, and the car so it will run, we have to straighten up our lives so we can go the way our Lord wants us to go.

They sing:

Almighty God, Almighty God,
Hold me in the hollow of your hand,

I'll be your child, I'll be your child,
Hold me in the hollow of your hand.

The minister comes solemnly forward to the altar. He is a stout and pompous man who continuously rubs a large gold watch chain extended across a prominent waistline.

It's a privilege of mine and a blessing to be here, my friends. Since thirty days ago when we last met many things have been done. Some have gone to their judgment since that time. Gone to meet their Maker and stand in judgment before that stern judge. I'm glad God has spared me to be here. There're some who are sick today who desire this privilege we are enjoying. [Amens] Since we met last, death has reigned right here in our neighborhood. As sure as you see a man living, you see a man who is going to die. You look around you and look at some men and they look like the picture of health. The next thing you know they're dead. That makes us know we got to get on our traveling shoes so we can march right up to our heavenly glory. You know, I'm a lot old times. I'm one of them that don't go in for new fangled things. And one thing, I got that old time religion, that old time religion that works by faith, that purifies your heart. I ain't got no new religion, and I don't want no new religion. Why, don't you know, with all this new religion you can't tell how you got it, and you can't tell where you got it? How you going to tell you got religion at all? I got that same old religion, I can go back to where I got it and tell you all about it. I can tell you how I got it and where I got it any time you ask me. And I can go back to that same old spark and refresh myself and come out stronger in my old time religion. That's what I do all the time—go back to that same old spark. It lighted the way for my father and my mother, and it can light the way for me. [Shouts]

He turns attention to his double text: "If a man die shall he live again," and "I am the resurrection and the life," and discourses at length on the life and trials of Job. The sermon then gets down to everyday experience.

Now I've seen men in critical conditions, sometimes their fingernails decay and come off and disease is destroying their bodies. Sometimes we say sin cause disease. But it's not always so. Sin in the hearts of men causes diseases too. I'll make an example. Job was wrapped in sackcloth and ashes a'praying to God, and his wife said, "Look at old Job. He's no good to himself and nobody else. I'm tired of him being sick, and my children's all forsaken me." But Job heard her, and to Almighty God he said, "Lord, though you slay me yet shall I trust you." Job looked at his wife and his wife said, "Curse God and die!" But Job said to her, "Foolish woman, foolish woman. I brought nothing into the world with me and I'll take nothing out. All the time of my worriation has to be lived out somewhere. [The minister wipes his dripping face, and groans and gasps; the congregation groans and shouts.]
Job took his question to Daniel, and Daniel said, "I saw Him as a stone, hewn out of the mountain." But when Job asked him, "If a man die shall he live again?" Daniel said, "I don't know." Job kept on a'going till he come to Ezekiel, and Ezekiel said, "I saw Him as a wheel within a wheel. I saw Him in the haunts of women." But when Job asked him if a man die shall he rise again, Ezekiel said, "I don't know."
But here comes a man from a new country, a man called Jesus Christ. A man that said, "I am the Son of God, the friend of salvation. I am the lowly fisherman from Galilee. I've seen the face of God. I feed the leprosy cast out by yourself. I can cure the incurable disease. I can perform miracles such as the world has never known." And they brought out the leper, the man dying with that terrible disease, the man everybody shunned and

let alone to die. And the Nazarene cured him. [Shouts] Blessed be His name! [Shouts and shrieks]

The congregation is now fully stirred, and its fervent chorus of assent punctuates dramatically the minister's spaced phrases. He refers to the loved ones who have departed, and stresses the certainty of death for everyone.

It don't matter how much you know or how high you climb, you got to die. Mr. Roosevelt, the president of this country's got to die, just like you and I. He can run all these things and do all them big things that everybody talks about, but he's got to lay down and die just the same.

The audience becomes sobered, the preacher lowers his voice:

If we fail to live the life in this world, it'll be too late when we come to cross the River of Jordan. It'll be too late then to get ready. Just like you start dressing at home in your room. You got to get dressed at home before you come out in the street, 'cause if you don't when you get out in the street without no clothes, they'll arrest you and take you to jail. It's too late to get dressed up then. Children, let's dress up and get ready for heaven and glory now. Now's the time to get dressed. Don't wait 'til it's too late. Let's be like Paul was when he said, "I've fought a good fight, I've kept the faith, and now I'm ready for glory."

Another deacon prays. The congregation sings a song about "True Religion" that has many verses, one of which runs:

Where you going, Elias?
Where you going, I say?
Going to the River of Jordan?
You can't cross there.

They sing of the backsliders and cowards. The minister rises in excitement at the close and shouts, "That song is as true as my hand. It's true, true, true. There's not enough words to say it." He then extends an invitation to join the church; no one responds on this occasion. A deacon takes his place behind the collection table.

Whilst everybody is happy and enjoying this service, we come to you. We know you must have that true religion. But today we want $5.00. We want to get it right at once, quick. Now let everybody push hard while we sing. Let everybody give all he can to the service of the Lord.

The congregation sings a song with verses that could be extended indefinitely:

It's the walk that you take
That takes you home.
It's the prayer that you pray
That takes you home.

They raise $4.06. After three hours of this worship they go home.

* * *

One 13-year-old Bolivar County, Mississippi, girl said:

Sometimes I want to leave church and come home, 'cause looks like to me like the preacher don't be sayin' much. He do a lot of hollerin' and shoutin'. Maybe if I could understand what he was talking about I would like church better, but I can't see what he's tryin' to say.

One 17-year-old girl in the same county made the following comment:

I like the singing but I don't care much about the preachin' 'cause I can't understand what the preacher's talking about half the time. Seems like to me he's just sayin' a lot of words that just don't make sense. The older folks might understand them, though, 'cause they just shouts and hollers all the time he's preachin', but sometimes I wonder if even they know what it's all about.

Parental compulsion and community sentiment, rather than genuine interest in religion, bring these children to church each Sunday. A 13-year-old fifth-grade girl in Bolivar County said:

I have to go every Sunday because my father makes me, but I want to leave and come home, though, for the preacher don't be sayin' much, 'pears like to me.

Another 15-year-old girl from a well-to-do Negro family in Coahoma County, Mississippi, complained:

Mama takes me to church with her every Sunday. Church is all right, but you have to stay there so long, and I don't believe lots of what the preacher said.

In the same vein the 16-year-old son of a Mound Bayou filling station operator said:

Oh, Mom sees to it that I'm sitting up in church every Sunday. I don't mind going sometimes, but I don't feel like sitting up there all day every Sunday. Ain't nothing special be doing, and I just get tired of sitting in church.

34 White over Black in Green: 1940

The preparations for war evident in 1940 brought many more people into the military service, among them people joining for the sake of patriotism, for an opportunity to escape the seemingly endless frustration of the depression, and, for black people, sometimes the hope to break free of the cycle of racial and economic degradation. Their discovery, in the case of blacks, often came as a serious disillusionment since the military perpetuated the same system of segregation and subordination found in civil society. It was all the more disillusioning, though, since the bottom line experiences of the serviceman, to kill or die in the name of freedom, and the potential and the object of such service, seemed to negate in fact and ideal all color distinctions. The disillusionment experienced caused one black enlistee to voice his concern in the essay below, originally printed in 1940. Aside from the frustrations of a segregated army, which are obvious in retrospect and are mildly expressed by the anonymous author, there is another point touched on in his lament that deserves comment. "This is the age of science, of steel—of speed and modernization," he wrote, and in so doing revealed an important assumption that would come to be more and more important. It was, and perhaps remains, a materialistic age in which progress seemed to follow economic growth, which then generated new opportunities, not just for wealth but in social relations. Hardly a novel idea, the same notion had been crudely expressed by Lewis Harvie Blair in the 1880s, but in the wake of the New Deal, which emphasized power blocs in their economic and political manifestations and which seemed to identify the central need of the nation as that of material growth, the idea of modernization as the arrangement of social relationships in such a way as to facilitate smoother and greater productivity (or profitability) had indeed come of age. The promise of the market was a highly individualistic one that threatened to push aside caste. To attach one's hopes to the path of modernization could be almost irresistible. And then to discover that caste actually prevailed in those quarters where the government had the greatest opportunity to alter it could generate serious disillusionment. In time that disillusionment could broaden from a dissatisfaction with the army to a questioning of the ideas—such as freedom, or even modernization—that had been assumed to correspond with reality or to present worthy goals.

Source: A Negro Enlisted Man, "Jim Crow in the Army Camps," *The Crisis*, 47 (December, 1940): 385. Reprinted with the permission of the editor of *The Crisis*.

I am a newly enlisted soldier, stationed in the Northwest. I volunteered, as I knew I would eventually be forced into the Army by the draft, and I wanted a better chance than the draftee would have.

But, after being in the Army a short while, my military-inclined enthusiasm turned to a feeling of disgruntled surprise and sorrow. Why? I'll tell you why!

I had envisioned the Army as being a vast military machine, working with utmost precision. Instead I found it to be, for the Negro, a place impregnated with suppression and racial prejudice.

We have a War department theatre which shows the latest pictures. It is the size of a medium-class city theatre. It is for the military personnel and their families.

We have a Negro regiment stationed here, composed of approximately 300 men. And in the theatre, size aforementioned, there is a row of seats, seating not more than fifteen men, which is set aside for the Negro soldiers.

I ask you, is that the proper spirit for an army training to fight for democracy?

Whenever a Negro soldier sits in any seat other than the row set aside for Negroes, as I and many others have done upon their first visit to the theatre, he is rudely and loudly asked to move to the *Reserved For Colored* section. This practice arouses hatred where there would be none if we were treated as we should be treated.

Also in the library and the Post Exchange, and on the Post in general, the Negro is treated as if he isn't wanted. Many of the young men enlisted in the U. S. Army are thoroughly disgusted because of segregation. Many were faithfully promised, before enlisting, that they would have an opportunity to learn a trade, or continue with their previous studies. As yet there are no educational facilities for the Negro. Young men have enlisted to do their patriotic duty to America, and to learn some useful trade. The men have done their part. The question is: Will Uncle Sam do his Part?

Last, but far from least, is the way a Negro soldier is treated on the Army bus when he goes to town. It is far from any idea I ever had of Army life! When the Negro regiment was first organized here (it has only been stationed here a little more than a year) the Negro soldiers were asked to sit in the back of the bus, but since more and more have begun to ride the bus, they have begun to move forward and sit any place they please. Yet hardly a week passes without an altercation resulting from the word so many of the white race deem necessary to label us by.

Why is it we Negro soldiers who are as much a part of Uncle Sam's great military machine as any cannot be treated with equality and the respect due us? The same respect which white soldiers expect and demand from us?

This is the age of science, of steel—of speed and modernization. It is no time to let petty indifferences stand in the way of a nation in great need of defense, on the brink of a great crisis! There is great need for a drastic change in this man's Army! How can we be trained to protect America, which is called a free nation, when all around us rears the ugly head of segregation?

35 Housing For Sojourner Truth

One of the central issues raised by the in-migration of blacks into the cities and industrial centers of the North in search of wartime employment focused on housing. In places like Detroit, where housing was already a serious problem for blacks (see Document 32), the pressures of the new wave of growth seemed to approach the breaking point. In 1942, when a new housing project for blacks was built next to white residences the issue was squarely joined. What is noteworthy in this instance is not so much the resistance manifest in the white community but that, as the selection below indicates, the moral leaders of the community, of whom more could well be expected, derived their code of behavior from materialistic priorities. The reduction of social relations to materialistic formulas by those charged with the inculcation of a higher morality suggested how far the pattern of social change in America had moved in the direction of modernization.

Source: "Strangers That Sojourn," *The Commonweal*, 35 (March 20, 1942): 524-25. Reprinted with the permission of Commonweal Publishing Co., Inc.

Catholics—and particularly Polish-American Catholics—have little ground for pride in events recently reported from Detroit. Many months ago it was determined by the Federal Government that a housing unit should be built for Negroes in a certain section of that city. This section is a borderline section, very close to a district occupied by Negroes, although itself inhabited by white people. A considerable Negro patronage is enjoyed by the stores and churches of the neighborhood. The white population is mixed, but contains a very large number of persons of Polish origin. When this decision was announced, there was considerable protest, over a period of months, and the protestants enlisted the support of certain Southern congressmen in their effort to prevent the carrying through of the original pIan. It is reported that one of those active in organizing this movement of protest was a Catholic priest of the neighborhood.

Finally the pressure applied led the Federal Government to announce that the housing unit would be for white families. Then Negro pressure was brought to bear to restore the unit to the use for which it was originally planned, and again pressure won the day. The Office of Defense Housing Coordination designated "Sojourner Truth Homes" for Negro occupancy, and leases were duly executed with prospective Negro tenants. The buildings finally were completed, and February 28 was designated as the first day when occupancy could be taken. When the prospective tenants arrived upon the scene, they found a mob of nearly 1200 persons, armed with knives, clubs, rifles and shotguns (following the account in the New York *Times*), "ready to do battle in the street separating the project from a row of dwellings occupied by whitepersons." The result was a general fracas in which shots were fired, several persons were slashed, three policemen and about fifteen others, both white and Negro, were taken to hospitals. Attempts to calm the mob were unavailing. The night before, 150 white pickets had patrolled the project and burned a fiery cross. Three days later, Mayor Edward J. Jeffries, Jr., announced that occupancy of "Sojourner Truth Homes" would be postponed indefinitely.

Once again we are confronted with an appalling instance of official ineptness in handling what is at best a delicate situation. The vacillation of the government agency in charge of this housing unit can lead Negroes to only one conclusion— that the government has no policy based upon principle, but will yield to whatever pressure seems the greatest at the moment. The reasons for white opposition to Negro occupancy of this project are clear enough. On the material level, they are even understandable. It has become an established part—however unjust it may be—of the American pattern of living that white people and Negroes cannot live mixed together in the same section of a city, and when the Negroes come in, the whites feel that they must move out. Naturally this is inconvenient and sometimes means financial sacrifice, although such sacrifice is infrequent since, district for district, Negroes pay higher rents than whites. In the same way certain social institutions—notably churches—suffer when a district becomes Negro, and they do suffer in a financial way. Yet obviously there is a greater social good in the amelioration of Negro living conditions, which can only take place through the expansion and decentralization of Negro living districts, than there is social harm in the inconvience to the white families who feeI they have to move on. After all, it is a tradition of the American city that they will move on eventually anyway. And what is most shocking in the present instance is that those from whom the community should receive moral leadership were among the very organizers of a protest having as its principal purpose the preservation of purely material values.

36 Martial Law: The Only Alternative?

It is no accident that major racial violence has often erupted at those moments when both blacks and whites were beset with serious problems not of their own making and which eluded effective redress. The source of those difficulties—when diffused through an entire system in which power to make decisions rested in increasingly remote and obscure hands, yet responsibility to abide by those decisions devolved upon the many in their everyday lives—lay fundamentally in the responsiveness of the political economy to power instead of need. The powerless would often be left only the option of focusing on the most immediate manifestation and the most personalized form of their problems. When, as in the case of Detroit, those problems of the powerlessness of blacks and whites and an apparent lack of purpose in the very agencies designed to represent the people were accentuated by abrasive race relations, the pent-up tensions found release in racial violence. And, as in the case of Detroit, if the government would not act to remove those deeper frustrations generating the violence, it had but one option: the complete subjugation of all people in the city through martial law. In the future it would attempt to develop a midway approach through an interest group balance often termed pluralistic to further diffuse the source of the problem. The consequences of that approach would become evident most dramatically in this and other large cities of the nation a quarter of a century later.

Source: Francis Downing, ''Report from Detroit,'' *The Commonweal*, 38 (July 30, 1943): 361-63. Reprinted with the permission of Commonweal Publishing Co., Inc.

. . . Things like these riots run deeper, and to eradicate peculiar organizations is not to end the visceral character of their origin. Nor is it to end the basic economic insecurity and fear that make men hate one another and stain the civil streets with blood. Many things can be said about the riots, but this much is securely true: already workers are haunted by the apocalytic ghost of post-war employment. They are afraid that while they may lose their jobs others, whom they have been taught to regard as inferior, will take them. "Keep them in their place." "They know how to handle them down South." Everywhere one goes—on trains, on buses, on street-cars—one hears these ominous words. One has been hearing them for a long time. Nor has their echo died. But they do not verbalize—those words—a race hatred. They are visceral rationalizations of economic insecurity. Nothing so proves this as does the knowledge of the flaring resentment against the upgrading of Negro workers in our war plants.

Those who recall—historically, I mean—the draft riots run in New York City by the Irish in 1863, are familiar with this phenomenon. To fail to take into consideration this aspect of the riots in Detroit is, in my opinion, to fail to go to the heart of things. How to exorcize this ghost, how to eliminate this fear of post-war unemployment, how to dissolve this kind of fear is, naturally, something that I do not know anything about. But this I know: post-war planning that proceeds uncognizant of this is erecting a tower of Babel against the unattainable sky.

Then, of course, there is the business of housing. That, by way of complete honesty, is not a problem faced by the Negro alone. The fact is that there are simply not enough houses for all the additional people that war industry has brought to Detroit. The result is that the tensions incident to the sudden and close fusion of hitherto separated peoples has been increased. And until the housing situation is relieved, these tensions are likely to remain. Present schedules can take care of only 20,000 of the 46,000 families that have come to Detroit since the first of January. That is a statistic, and one has to live here, and to see conditions startling his own eyes before statistics are fleshed with life. But it will do, for the moment, to give the figure. It is not so stripped of meaning that you are unable to discover and construe its implications for yourself.

Recreational facilities are so bad here that they have hardly a nominal existence. The "latch key kids" that I read about in the New York papers are not exclusive to that city. And it was not an accident that teen-agers were participating in the riots.

Transportation is a factor. Even in New York people do not stand in single file for blocks to get on a bus. But they do in Detroit. In fact in Detroit one stands for almost everything. One stands and waits. If Harry James comes to the Paramount in New York, we know how difficult it is to get in. Or if there is an unusual picture at Radio City. Harry James does not need to come here. Nor do we require an unusual picture. A grade C picture, any band—the result is the same. You remember how you line up to get into Radio City; how you move along and, after what seems a week, you reach the ticket office. Then you slowly wind into the theater and up one flight of stairs. Then you suddenly realize that you have to wind up another flight of stairs. And when you get there, the chances are you and your girl shall have to see the picture separately. That is the kind of thing you and your girl do almost any night in the week in Detroit. And if you have taken her to a cafeteria for dinner before you go to the movies, the pair of you have stood in line to get into the cafeteria.

Needless to say you don't get a seat on a bus or a streetcar. And no one here seems to have the answer to why we are without a subway. Or if they know the answer, they do not regard me as old enough to be told. And people who work in the plants outside of Detroit—Willow Run, for example—many of them are living in trailer camps, in tents and in houses that scare you even to look at—much less raise a baby in.

Everybody has read, I take it, of homeowners like the people in Grosse Pointe, who refuse to open their houses to workers.

These are some of the reasons that constitute the background of tensions which spilled over into riot—into pillage and brutality and murder.

These are some of the reasons that there was martial law in Detroit. These are some of the reasons why a bus I rode home in on the Monday of the riots (they broke out on Sunday) had most of its windows smashed. And why the windshield looked like a collection of icicles. And why the floor was covered with splinters of broken glass. And why women clung with frozen fingers to the seat guards. And why the driver told us to duck as we went through one district. And why, as we rode through, little knots of men and women and teenagers were gathered together with sticks and stones in their hands. But they did not throw them on that trip—or I might not be writing this.

And these are some of the reasons why I saw soldiers camping on the grass of our little public parks, or on the lawn of our public library. And why I saw soldiers ride the town in jeeps. And why the soldiers carried guns. And why their bayonets were naked and shining in the noon-day sun. And why bars were closed. And the movie houses. And there was a curfew. I used to teach school, as they say. I used to teach history. And I talked about martial law. But I never knew what it was before. I know now. I do not want any more detailed knowledge on the subject.

But unless I am to get more knowledge, many things must be done. Places for people to live must be built. Places for people to play in must be increased. Detroit must cease trying to transport an increased war population with the services of a small New England town. Detroit must be made more than a place to work in. It must be made a place where men and women can live. And the whole basis of our emotional attitudes must change. But to talk about tolerance and education is to talk nonsense. Education and tolerance come, if they come, after the body has been cared for and the tension of the mind relieved.

Of course it is barely possible that the riots have humbled us—and that they shall not be repeated. They may have lowered the temperature, like a lightning storm. But that would be a foolish kind of belief to indulge. For all the factors that led to them are still here. Despite some of our alleged philosophers, there are still causes for things. And results are still their fruits.

37   The Only Alternative to Forceful Suppression?

The tension that erupted into full scale rioting in Detroit was manifest elsewhere as the social changes generated by World War II and the rhetoric of fighting for freedom against a racist government in Germany combined with the visible sacrifices being demanded of the public on every hand to create a less than united war effort. In the following account some of the blatant instances of discrimination directed against black soldiers off duty demonstrate the pervasiveness of the tension. The heart of the essay concerns the relationship between this kind of racial degradation and the violence that hit Harlem in August 1943. Perhaps equally suggestive in the analysis, though, is the comparison of the way officials in New York handled the riot with the pattern set by Detroit officialdom. Mayor Fiorello La Guardia in fact took an opposite course as he applied the basic lessons of modernization to quell the riot. Black and white Military Policemen were used to disperse the crowds, as opposed to using only white authority symbols. The "leaders of public opinion" were mobilized to set the strategy and the most influential and well known black leaders urged their people by way of sound trucks to return home. The alternative to martial law, an alternative, however, which was different because it was more subtle and sophisticated rather than because it addressed the real source of the problems, had been found. The gentler approach did work. At least it worked for the time being. As with Detroit, so too with Harlem: this approach would reach its limits in the 1960s.

Source: Walter White, "Behind the Harlem Riot," *The New Republic*, 109 (August 16, 1943): 220-22.

A few weeks before Harlem burst into flames on Sunday night, August l, a young Negro who had just received his gold bars from an Officers' Candidate

School in a Southern state came to see me. His face beamed with modest pride and love of country as he told of raising his hand to take the oath as an officer of the United States Army to protect his country with his life.

"Ten minutes later I boarded the bus to Washington along with some of my fellow officers—white boys from Georgia, Mississippi and Arkansas. We were all so excited and happy over winning our commissions that I forgot we were still in the South," he said. His trim, immaculately clad body sagged and a cloud came over his face as he told me of what happened then.

"Hey, all nigras sit in the back of the bus!" the bus driver yelled at him.

"I made up my mind right then that I had taken the last insult from crackers I was going to take," the Negro officer told me grimly.

"If I had to die for democracy, I decided that there was no better time or place than right then. I told the driver I was not going to sit in any jim-crow section and that if he was man enough to make me do so, he would have to do it. I sat down in the 'white' section and rode into Washington."

No clash or tragedy occurred in this instance, possibly because the white Southern companions of the Negro officer came to his defense. But multiply this episode by many thousands. Include in it the story of New York's famed 369th Regiment which had done an excellent job as an anti-aircraft unit "somewhere in the Pacific." Two hundred and twelve picked officers and men were returned to the United States to act as cadres in the training of new units. They were sent to Camp Stewart, Georgia, where, in the camp as well as on buses going into Savannah and in Savannah itself, a long succession of indignities were heaped upon these men to "teach these Northern Negroes their place."

Naturally these soldiers wrote to their relatives and friends in New York. Harlem newspapers published the stories. They became another segment of many other tales from Southern camps such as the killing by a Louisiana state policeman of Raymond Carr, a Negro MP, when Carr refused to leave his post of duty at the order of a white civil policeman. Only after enormous pressure was the policeman punished. His punishment consisted of a one-day suspension.

Last May 29 Judge William H. Hastie and Thurgood Marshall submitted a report on civilian violence against Negro soldiers to the National Lawyers' Guild, which in turn formally placed it before the War and Justice Departments. It was pointed out that recurrent violence in the civilian community directed against Negro members of the armed forces had increased in seriousness, in frequency and in the lack of any effective methods of control since a similar study had been made in November, 1942. The report grimly stated:

Civilian violence against the Negro in uniform is a recurrent phenomenon. It continues unabated. It may well be the greatest factor now operating to make 13,000,000 Negroes bitter and resentful and to undermine the fighting spirit of three-quarters of a million Negroes in arms. Yet, no effective steps are being taken and no vigorous, continuing and comprehensive program of action has been inaugurated by state or federal authorities to stamp out this evil. . . . To address a Negro soldier as 'nigger' is such a commonplace in the average Southern community that little is said about it. But the mounting rage of the soldier himself is far from commonplace. He may not express his feelings when he must wait until all the white passengers are accommodated before he can get transportation. He may even hold his tongue when he is forced to get out of the bus in which he is seated in order to make room for white passengers. But it is of such stuff that bitterness and hatred are made. In such a climate resentments grow until they burst forth in violent and unreasoning reprisal.

This prophetic statement is carefully documented with specific instances similar to the Raymond Carr case. Among them was recited the killing of Sgt. Thomas Foster, a Negro soldier, in March, 1943, by a city policeman in the streets of Little Rock, Arkansas. Foster was shot and killed while lying dazed on the gound. After killing Foster, the policeman calmly returned his revolver to its holster, took out his pipe and lit it. In July, 1942, city police officers of Beaumont, Texas, fired several shots into the body of a Negro soldier, Pvt. Charles Reco, who had been arrested on complaint of a bus driver because Reco sat under a sign dividing the seating between whites and Negroes. His body was behind the sign in the jim-crow section; his knees in front of it. To avoid trouble, Reco left the bus and was overtaken by the policeman, who hit him with a blackjack from behind and then fired into his prostrate body. Attorney General Francis Biddle issued a strong statement and promised vigorous federal action. But later the Department of Justice abandoned prosecution because there was "no prospect of conviction." The Guild report adds wryly: "This is not the first time that the Department of Justice has lost its ardor for action in Texas. In the circumstances, we can only hope that the extraordinary power of the Texas delegate to Congress has no relationship to the mental vagaries of the Department of Justice."

Other killings of Negro soldiers were cited in El Paso, Texas; Mobile, Alabama; Columbia, South Carolina; and other places.

It is out of this sad record that the shooting, not without justification, of Robert J. Bandy, a Negro MP, in a Harlem hotel by a white policeman on Sunday night, August 1, provided the spark which set off the explosion created by bitter, smoldering resentment against the mistreatment of Negro soldiers which was all the more dangerous because it had been pent up and frustrated. A five-minute shift in Private Bandy's movements that sultry Sunday might have averted one of the most destructive riots in American history, which took a toll of five lives, injured 307 and caused damage estimated to be in excess of $5,000,000. Bandy came to New York from a New Jersey camp to meet his mother, who had come down from Middletown, Connecticut, to spend Sunday with him and his fiancée. Bandy's mother checked out of the hotel around four o'clock in the afternoon and then set out with her son and his friend for dinner and a moving-picture show. It was an unfortunate, gratuitous circumstance that they returned to the hotel to pick up the mother's luggage just as an altercation developed when a policeman sought to eject an obstreperous Negro woman.

Bandy intervened, so that story goes, in an attempt to defend the woman. During the altercation he is alleged to have seized Policeman James Collins' night stick and to have struck the policeman across the cheekbone. He then turned away, refusing to obey the order to halt. The policeman drew his gun and fired, hitting Bandy in the left shoulder. Within a few minutes, the story had spread like wildfire throughout Harlem that a Negro soldier had been shot in the back and killed by a policeman in the presence of his mother. Blind, unreasoning fury swept the community with the speed of lightning. The available symbols of the oppressor, as was the case in Detroit's East Side, were the shining plate-glass windows of stores along One Hundred and Twenty-fifth Street. At the beginning, there was no looting. Nothing but blind fury was expressed. Later, from the more poverty-stricken areas of Harlem, poured those who entered the stores through the broken windows and began looting. Their acts were criminal and unforgivable But let him who would cricitize pause long enough to put himself in the place of the looters. Still barred from many defense industries in the area because of color, with dark memories of the depression years when 70 percent of Harlem was on relief because Negroes were hired last and there were not enough jobs for white workers, hemmed in a ghetto where they are forced to pay disproportionately high rents for rat and vermin-infested apartments, the Bigger Thomases of New York passed like a cloud of locusts over the stores of Harlem.

But the usual pattern of riots did not obtain. I spent the night touring the district with Mayor LaGuardia, Police commissioner Valentine and residents of the Harlem community. Mayor LaGuardia was on the scene a few minutes after the trouble started and remained there, as did Commissioner Valentine, without sleep or sufficient food until daybreak Tuesday.

The Mayor and the Police Commissioner did not content themselves with bringing in policemen and anti-mob paraphernalia. Even before the policemen poured in, Mayor LaGuardia called all the leaders of public opinion in Harlem who could be reached. A small board of strategy was set up. One of the first steps taken was to request the army to send Negro as well as white MP's into the area, and to have them perform their duties of rounding up military personnel in the riot area, in mixed units instead of separate ones. This had a calming effect on the community.

All during the night Negroes known to the people of Harlem broadcast from sound trucks exploding the false rumor that Bandy had been killed and urging the people to return to their homes and to stop vandalism and other violent acts. Coupled with this was the magnificent restraint and efficiency of the police. Daylight saw the diminution of violence. An exhausted community, its fury spent, was shocked at the damage done. Decent members of the community, most of whom had slept through the night unaware of what had taken place, were appalled. Condemnation far more severe than any person outside the community could utter was voiced in increasing volume throughout Harlem against the acts of irresponsible, criminal persons.

How different was Detroit! There a weak Mayor hid while Negroes were beaten on the steps of the City Hall itself. New York's Mayor was in the thick of the trouble, often at great personal risk. During the early morning hours, a report came to the Twenty-eighth Precinct in One Hundred and Twenty-third Street that a mob of whites was forming down near the New York Central's One Hundred and Twenty-fifth Street station. Refusing to wait long enough for Police Commissioner Valentine to supply him with a patrol car of policemen to protect him, the ebullient Mayor bundled me into a one-seater police car in which we were sped to the section. We found the rumor to be utterly false.

Returning, we came through Lenox Avenue, where there was looting. Regardless of personal danger, the Mayor shouted, "Put that stuff down," to a group of youthful vandals. Utterly startled, they dropped what they had in their hands and fled.

New York's Police Commissioner Lewis J. Valentine provided an equally sharp contrast to Detroit's Commissioner Witherspoon. Even more remarkable was the attitude of the police themselves. All during Sunday night and early Monday morning, thousands of police poured into the Twenty-eighth Precinct straight from eight hours of duty. Prior to being sent out on the streets they were herded into an insufferably hot squad room where a single drinking fountain served us all. During all those troubled hours, I heard not one word about "niggers," as I had heard so frequently in Detroit, nor was there any other manifestation of racial animosity. They were out to do a job of restoring order, and it was all in the day's work.

But though New York City acquitted itself nobly and established a pattern of procedure which should guide both it and other cities in future out breaks, stopping a riot quickly and efficiently is only a small part of the problem involved. The weight of sustained and unceasing public opinion must activate the federal government, and particularly the army, the navy and the Department of Justice, to stop, at whatever cost, the unchecked brutality against Negro servicemen which has cursed the country. Within the various cities themselves, ghettos must be abolished, along with the evils attendant upon segregation and proscription.

New York had another riot in 1935. Mayor LaGuardia appointed a bi-racial commission which held hearings and submitted a report which included recommendations that might have prevented, or at least made likely and less destructive, the riot of August 1, 1943. But unfortunately, the report was never made public and most of its recommendations were unheeded. It is to be hoped that this mistake will not be made again.

38 To What Shall We Return?

The following letter, written by a black army sergeant at Fort Leonard Wood, Missouri, in September 1944, indicates that the experiences of blacks in the military (and in civil society) had not dramatically changed despite the clamor, attention, and violence that they generated. Black soldiers were still segregated and their official treatment was as inferiors. One change was evident, whether in the streets of Detroit and Harlem or on the buses of the South or in the attitude of the black infantryman. The declared purpose of the war combined with the experiences of blacks, in the context of new potential opportunities in society due to the expanded economy, to strengthen the resolve to struggle for freedom at home. The new militance of blacks could be seen in the formation of new activist organizations like the Congress of Racial Equality in 1942 and the mushrooming of other organizations like the NAACP, which appeared more activist oriented. The legacy and lesson of A. Phillip Randolph's threatened march on Washington did not fade with the establishment of the Fair Employment Practices Commission. Curiously, the significance of the development of this new activism and insistence in the black community may have been a counterproductive one. As Mayor La Guardia had learned how to handle the angry rioters, so did more whites learn the same lesson. Not only would the Democratic leadership associated with Harry Truman come to the conclusion that such modernizing approaches could prove most effective in harnessing and disciplining what would become identified as the civil rights movement, but it would also learn that there was great political capital in a program that appealed especially to the concentrations of black people in the urban centers of the North. The problems in this assessment were, first, that these politicos often seemed more sensitive to civil rights as a political formula than as a fundamental issue of justice and, second, that even that support for civil rights tended to identify social problems in a fragmenting way—i.e., to perceive the problems of blacks, workers, women, or businessmen separately instead of exploring the common roots from which stemmed the whole range of problems. There is some justification for this approach, given a crucial assumption not uncommon among many sympathetic to the black population. That assumption was explicitly stated in this letter of 1944 when the black sergeant observed that blacks were forced to accept menial tasks while the white man encountered "no unjust limitation upon the advancements which he may attain." In keeping alive the myth that white people experienced complete freedom the seeds of racial tension would continue to grow.

Source: Sgt. Warren J. Brunson, "What a Negro Soldier Thinks About," letter to the editor, *St. Louis Post-Dispatch*. September 2, 1944.

Since enlisting in the Army in 1942, I have been stationed at three different posts, and have come in contact with many other colored soldiers from the different sections of our country. As a cadreman and instructor, I helped to train some of these men, most of whom are now in various theaters of active operation.

While in training with these soldiers, I studied them, their reactions and emotions. Therefore, in the following remarks I am sure I have expressed the sentiments of the Negro soldiers in America.

We all were inducted into or enlisted in the armed forces to subdue the ruthless enemies of our country, and to eliminate the loathsome foes of democracy and freedom. We have sought to liquidate the evil oppressors and aggressors and to liberate the peace-loving peoples who have felt the weight of the Axis heel. We know what it means to be an oppressed people, bounded in by many unjust restrictions; therefore we fight that liberty and freedom of all mankind may forever exist.

During our bitter struggles to accomplish the foregoing goals, we have encountered much bloodshed and suffering. Some of this has been by the hands of our own countrymen who have tried to deny us the very things for which our country fights—the Four Freedoms.

Those saboteurs on the home front who discriminate against us and our people in industry, and those in our armed forces who try to create confusion and hatred between the white and colored troops, by limiting our opportunities for advancement and by perpetuating evil discrimination are viewed by us as Nazis at heart, shielded by the cloak of American citizenship.

But we fight on to accomplish our military goals and to defeat our military enemies wherever they raise their heads. We have helped to rout them on many fronts, thereby assuring the world that democracy will have a military victory.

Now we are beginning to think about the peace, the home front and the day when we shall return victoriously from the fields of battle. To what kind of American home front shall we return?

Will it be a front on which democracy will have triumphed as well as it will have triumphed on the military fronts abroad? Or will it be one on which selfishness, greed for wealth and the recent prosperity enjoyed during the war have made the home folk forget, and have blinded them to the unimaginable suffering of human beings, and to the cause for which we fought?

Shall we return to a country of which a great section still will be fighting the ghost of the Civil War by denying us our rights to live as free men and free citizens? Or shall we return to a country in which every citizen is treated as a citizen, and where merit, not race, is the basis for opportunities and advancements?

Shall we return to a land where lynchers of Negroes may commit their horrible atrocities and then roam at will with little or no fear of being apprehended? Or shall we return to a land where all are afforded equal protection and justice by the law?

Shall we return to a country where every citizen, regardless of race, is afforded equal opportunities for training and education?

Or shall we return to a land where many thousands of us will be publicly robbed of our rights as citizens to vote?

These are the questions we are asking ourselves. These are the questions the American people must sincerely answer.

We have heard the famous quotation "with liberty and justice for all" time and time again. We have seen it in print often. Political speakers have uttered it vigorously over radio networks and before clamoring throngs. Too many say these words enthusiastically, but in their hearts they mean liberty and justice for all but the Negro.

As the score stands at present, regardless of the Negro's qualifications, he is flatly denied equal opporunties for economic advancement in practically all sections of our country. In a great majority of the cases, his low wage prevents him from adequately training and educating his children. Even when he does become fortunate enough to prepare his children or himself for certain skilled occupations, he finds the doors of opportunity closed.

Then, in his grave situation, he is forced to accept some menial task, while his white brother soars ahead, with no unjust limitation upon the advancements which he may attain. When such happens, a little imagination on the part of anybody with a brain capable of imagining or thinking will reveal the Negro's feelings and thoughts.

Except in the gutter positions, it has almost become a rule for the colored man to be the last hired and the first fired. Too often, he is forced by economic discrimination to perform at low wages the labor and domestic services for the families of the "bosses." Too often his children are denied adequate family relationship and home training, because his wife is too busy performing the housework of the boss' wife. She must do so in order to help her low-paid husband support their family.

Thus, the Negro housewife, to a great extent, is unable to help the public school teachers educate her children. Nevertheless, if any of these colored children become of age and fail to exhibit public conduct that is approved by society, unfair generalizations are made in regard to the race itself.

Is this truly "the land of the free and the home of the brave"? Or is that a myth, exploded by such evils as discrimination, segregation, economic isolation and many others, that it has become a joke?

We realize that all the kinks in our democracy cannot be straightened in the brief space of one or two years, but much greater progress and much longer strides can be taken toward this end. Russia has solved the problems of her minority groups. So can the people of our great nation.

When we return victoriously from the wreckage and the war-torn lands abroad, we wish no special favors, but as American citizens we want to be able to say, with exaltation and sincerity: Yes, this is America—mighty America, "the land of the free and the home of the brave." Yes, this is the land where "we hold these truths to be self-evident, that all men are created equal, that they are endowed by their Creator with certain inalienable rights, that among these rights are life, liberty and the pursuit of happiness."

Sgt. Warren T. Brunson
Fort Leonard Wood, Mo.

39 Baseball: The Main Arena

In the immediate postwar world of Americans the much hoped for racial equality was neither universal nor even on the horizon. The steps toward that opportunity were found not in new laws but in symbolic acts of everyday life. One of the most publicized steps came in baseball in 1947. In that year the front pages as well as the sports pages of the newspapers focused on the bold figure of Jackie Robinson, the new black first baseman for the Brooklyn Dodgers. He was the first black man to enter major league baseball. His reception was a mixed one since he was hailed by many as proof that ancient racial barriers could be overcome and at the same time was reviled by the taunts and jeers of others who found him threatening a white world. When Robinson came to Chicago to play in May the response was typical. The fear and rejection, the hopes and warmth, and the sheer curiosity generated by the event were effectively captured by Chicago columnist Mike Royko some twenty-five years later.

Source: Mike Royko, "Jackie's Debut a Unique Day," Chicago *Sun-Times*, October 25, 1972. Reprinted with the kind permission of Mike Royko.

All that Saturday, the wise men of the neighborhood, who sat in chairs on the sidewalk outside the tavern, had talked about what it would do to baseball.

I hung around and listened because baseball was about the most important thing in the world, and if anything was going to ruin it, I was worried.

Most of the things they said, I didn't understand, although it all sounded terrible. But could one man bring such ruin?

They said he could and he would. And the next day he was going to be in Wrigley Field for the first time, on the same diamond as Hack, Nicholson, Cavarretta, Schmidt, Pafko, and all my other idols.

I had to see Jackie Robinson, the man who was going to somehow wreck everything. So the next day, another kid and I started walking to the ball park early.

We always walked to save the streetcar fare. It was five or six miles, but I felt about baseball the way Abe Lincoln felt about education.

Usually, we could get there just at noon, find a seat in the grandstands, and watch some batting practice. But not that Sunday, May 18, 1947.

By noon, Wrigley Field was almost filled. The crowd outside spilled off the sidewalk and into the streets. Scalpers were asking top dollar for box seats and getting it.

I had never seen anything like it. Not just the size, although it was a new record, more than 47,000. But this was 25 years ago, and in 1947 few blacks were seen in the Loop, much less up on the white North Side at a Cub game.

That day, they came by the thousands, pouring off the northbound Ls and out of their cars.

They didn't wear baseball-game clothes. They had on church clothes and funeral clothes—suits, white shirts, ties, gleaming shoes, and straw hats. I've never seen so many straw hats.

As big as it was, the crowd was orderly. Almost unnaturally so. People didn't jostle each other.

The whites tried to look as if nothing unusual was happening, while the blacks tried to look casual and dignified. So everybody looked slightly ill at ease.

For most, it was probably the first time they had been that close to each other in such great numbers.

We managed to get in, scramble up a ramp, and find a place to stand behind the last row of grandstand seats. Then they shut the gates. No place remained to stand.

Robinson came up in the first inning. I remember the sound. It wasn't the shrill, teen-age cry you now hear, or an excited gut roar. They applauded, long, rolling applause. A tall, middle-aged black man stood next to me, a smile of almost painful joy on his face, beating his palms together so hard they must have hurt.

When Robinson stepped into the batter's box, it was as if someone had flicked a switch. The place went silent.

He swung at the first pitch and they erupted as if he had knocked it over the wall. But it was only a high foul that dropped into the box seats. I remember thinking it was strange that a foul could make that many people happy. When he struck out, the low moan was genuine.

I've forgotten most of the details of the game, other than that the Dodgers won and Robinson didn't get a hit or do anything special, although he was cheered on every swing and every routine play.

But two things happened I'll never forget. Robinson played first, and early in the game a Cub star hit a grounder and it was a close play.

Just before the Cub reached first, he swerved to his left. And as he got to the bag, he seemed to slam his foot down hard at Robinson's foot.

It was obvious to everyone that he was trying to run into him or spike him. Robinson took the throw and got clear at the last instant.

I was shocked. That Cub, a home-town boy, was my biggest hero. It was not only an unheroic stunt, but it seemed a rude thing to do in front of people who would cheer for a foul ball. I didn't understand why he had done it. It wasn't at all big league.

I didn't know that while the white fans were relatively polite, the Cubs and most other teams kept up a steady stream of racial abuse from the dugout. I thought that all they did down there was talk about how good Wheaties are.

Later in the game, Robinson was up again and he hit another foul ball. This time it came into the stands low and fast, in our direction. Somebody in the seats grabbed for it, but it caromed off his hand and kept coming. There was a flurry of arms as the ball kept bouncing, and suddenly it was between me and my pal. We both grabbed. I had a baseball.

The two of us stood there examining it and chortling. A genuine, major league baseball that had actually been gripped and thrown by a Cub pitcher, hit by a Dodger batter. What a possession.

Then I heard the voice say: "Would you consider selling that?"

It was the black man who had applauded so fiercely.

I mumbled something. I didn't want to sell it.

"I'll give you $10 for it," he said.

Ten dollars, I couldn't believe it. I didn't know what $10 could buy because I'd never had that much money. But I knew that a lot of men in the neighborhood considered $60 a week to be good pay.

I handed it to him, and he paid me with ten $1 bills.

When I left the ball park, with that much money in my pocket, I was sure that Jackie Robinson wasn't bad for the game.

Since then, I've regretted a few times that I didn't keep the ball. Or that I hadn't given it to him free. I didn't know, then, how hard he probably had to work for that $10.

But Tuesday I was glad I had sold it to him. And if that man is still around, and has that baseball, I'm sure he thinks it was worth every cent.

40 The Warriors in Peacetime

As many had anticipated, the circumstances to which many blacks returned after World War II did not differ dramatically from the prewar conditions. Some stayed in the military and others joined with the hope, once again, that it might provide the opportunity to break the cycle of degradation. Yet the military itself retained until the Korean War its segregated regimen and its less official racist practices. Some of both can be seen in the following selection, an autobiographical account of Larry King when he was in the army in the late 1940s. King was in an army that was just barely, and reluctantly, starting to move away from segregation in 1948. He was assigned the mission of escorting a black military prisoner from Shreveport, Louisiana, to Governor's Island, New York. The prisoner, a former staff sergeant named Hutchinson, had, as King recalls, "several years exemplary service" but had encountered a series of family problems common to military personnel resulting from family separations. After Hutchinson's third or fourth apprehension for being AWOL, each time having returned to his home in Louisiana, King arrived to take his prisoner. In the course of the train trip to New York, King learned more about discrimination in the military and in civil society. He also learned something that would take many a well-meaning sympathizer with blacks a long time to learn. He learned that blacks were not always overjoyed at the prospect of being recipients (whose desires had been assumed) of white sponsored and controlled largesse and integration.

Master Sergeant Bad ran his stockade much as I imagine Hitler commanded the Third Reich. He was broad, florid-faced, a ham-handed son of Ohio and a former deputy sheriff; one here had to revise upward one's estimations of the Army's talent for typecasting. He received me while relaxing among his private collection of handcuffs, zip guns, switchblade knives, and rubber truncheons artistically mounted on beaverboard behind his desk. He was drinking coffee served by an obsequious prisoner who bowed out of the room as if departing the odor of royalty. "Prisoners are shit!" Master Sergeant Bad thundered at the bowing lackey. "Sound off!" "Prisoners are shit!" the lackey obediently bawled.

Reading my orders M/Sgt. Bad said, "That's a smart-ass nigger you've come after, Sarjint." Well, I said, Hutchinson had been a good soldier before his family torments. "He tried that sob-sister shit on me," Bad said. "I told him if his old lady was humpin' outside the home he wasn't no worse off than half the white men I know and all the niggers."

He entertained me with stories of all the heads he had been privileged to knock in the service of his country. Criminal types could never be rehabilitated beyond their lower instincts: "They just like a bad buckin' bronco or a mean dawg. You got to clobber the puredee shit out of 'em often enough they'll remember who's boss." Niggers, he advised, were more troublesome than whites: they didn't feel as much pain, and they had shorter memories.

M/Sgt. Bad led me through three locks and past a cadre of guards. As we approached the bullpen where Hutchinson and other transient offenders bunked, he bellowed, "Prisoners *up!*" There was a wild stampede of nervous sweaty flesh; the prisoners sprinted into a single long rank facing the door and perhaps six feet from the bars. "You're drag-assin', you're drag-assin'," the sergeant accused. "Come again! Fall out!" The prisoners rushed back to their assigned bunks, straining and grunting. Some had not yet reached their proper places when their master thundered, "Prisoners, *up!*"—again inspiring the frantic scramble. Bad ran the prisoners through the exhausting exercise again and again, explaining in convenient asides his and the Pentagon's theory that the more miserable life is for a prisoner the less likely he is to repeat old offenses.

When the prisoners had lined up to his satisfaction M/Sgt. Bad spat, "Prisoner Six . . . *toe the line!*" Hutchinson leaped from the ranks as if kicked, his toes exactly touching a thin red line extending the length of the cell and ending no more than a foot from the bars. "They fuck up and step on that line or anticipate my command," Bad said, "and I treat 'em to a little practice with some ass-paddlin' on the side. We call it a piss party." He raised his voice, "Prisoners, do I give good piss parties? Sound off!"

"Yessir!" the prisoners shouted, with such enthusiasm one might have thought him a rival of Perle Mesta.

"Had one old jug-butted boy never did learn to toe the line without steppin' on it," the Sergeant said. "Dumb goddamn nigger! He come here weighing two hunnert pounds and left with a skinny ass didn't have nothing on it but calluses and blood." He chuckled, much cheered by the memory.

Hutchinson had unfortunately relaxed his West Point brace; just as he cut his eyes ever so slightly toward us, M/Sgt. Bad screamed, "What you wallin' them maroon eyes at, you burr-headed bastard? Goddamn your black hide, you're in my custody till I sign your release slip. I tell you to eat shit you eat it, right? Sound off!"

"Yessir!" Hutchison barked.

"You're a smartass runaway nigger, ain't you? Sound off!"

"Yessir!"

"You got shit for brains and piss in your blood. Sound off!"

"Yessir!"

Hutchinson was forced to affirm every insult M/Sgt. Bad was capable of delivering. Nothing was out of bounds: Hutchinson's race, sex habits, wife, and mother. Marching the prisoner to the office, his tormentor prodded him in the ribs with a nightstick—presumably the better to improve his inferior memory. While he signed papers to transfer the prisoner to my control, he warned Hutchinson what might happen to his black ass should it ever again know that particular stockade.

Hutchinson remained discreetly silent while a driver delivered us to the Shreveport train station. When we were alone he said, "Man, I'm gladder to see you than Christmas. That Sergeant Bad, he the meanest mutha in uniform. Especially if you Colored." Had he actually hit Hutchinson? "Name me a day he didn't," the black man said. (Later, when I delivered Hutchinson to Governors Island to await his next court-martial, and he was being stripped for processing, a ferret-faced white corporal grinned at welts and bumps on his back and shoulders. "I guess you got those falling in the shower, didn't you?" "Yessir!" Hutchinson said.)

Down in Louisiana, handcuffed to my prisoner as regulations prescribed, I had boarded the train; we took seats near the rear of a coach car. A conductor approached, apprehensively eying my sidearm. "You gonna have to take him to the Colored section," he said, pointing at Hutchinson. No, my prisoner would go where I went—and I was not going to any Colored section.

There was a delay while the Shreveport station sent reinforcements. A civilian with a public-relations smile and a squishy handshake was full of soft Southern assurances that he knew I would understand and sympathize with the railroad's position in honoring local customs. No, I did not, and would remain in place with my prisoner. The baffled railroaders, faced with conflicting authority, decided in favor of the man with the gun: "But really, suh, the dining car must be off limits. Any violations will unfortunately require the police."

Hutchinson slept or feigned sleep, arousing only to share the gummy sandwiches and tepid soft drinks purchased from an aisle barker, or to visit the washroom with his guard closely trailing. After each trip a black porter, called by the alert conductor, entered the washroom for purposes of fumigation. "Hello, Brother," he said in a whisper to Hutchinson on each occasion.

A skinny white man in a short-sleeved sport shirt, with the seedy look of a failed road drummer, a real-life Willy Loman working the Southern Territory, grew talkative as he siphoned off bourbon in the seat behind us. He leaned forward to cool our faces with whiskey breezes while telling how the white man had busted a gut to help the Nigra but the Nigra wouldn't help himself: refused work, stayed drunk or in jail, stole with more talent than Gypsies. "Don't you know that boy's closer to Heaven right now than most niggers ever get? Riding with white folks, havin' 'em look after him." When I replied that Hutchinson's care was provided at gunpoint, and therefore might not be fully appreciated, he looked on me with suspicion. Soon he began whispering around the car: why was that damned black nigger outlaw allowed to ride in the same coach with patriotic, God-fearing white people? A conductor moved the troublemaker to another car when I explained that should he further disturb me or my prisoner it would be both my sworn duty and my personal pleasure to shoot him.

At Washington the train became racially integrated. Hutchinson was vastly relieved: "Man, I'm glad to be rid of them peckerwoods. All that shit about me being in Heaven. . . ."

I apologized for the peckerwood's remarks, noting that I had silenced him and had him moved. You're back among friends, I said, so relax.

"You didn't do me no favors bringing me up on that white car, Sarjint," Hutchinson said. "I would rather have rode with my own people."

Such a possibility had not occurred to me.

41 "What Am I Fighting For?"

The military often served as a focal point for Americans concerned with racial equality since that institution, with its existing restrictions and regulations, could most quickly, as distinct from other areas of society, be transformed by deliberate effort. As such the military's racial practices appeared to many not just as a test of "society's" commitment to racial equality, itself a notion fraught with structural imprecision, but of the nation's leadership's commitment. In 1948 President Truman issued his famous order desegregating the armed forces. But as the following document reveals, the actual progress on that mandate was seriously limited even in the spring of 1951. This letter, written to the Senate Commerce Committee a dozen years later in support of pending civil rights legislation, recounts the experiences of a white officer leading predominantly black troops in Korea. Besides revealing the glacial speed of the process of desegregation the letter also indicates the basic social force at work in the process. Rather than through the deliberate efforts of commanders to alter the racial organization of the units, desegregation came about in the form of replacements of wounded infantry men. The lieutenant's ideas were in part motivated by sympathy since he saw the disparity between the sacrifices made for freedom and the realization of that freedom, and were in part more conservative (though the sympathy itself could often be rank paternalism) as he expressed his concern for the suffering in morale caused by prejudice and his hopes for a stronger defense of the nation with the elimination of this inequality. That these memories would linger so vividly with this white man for more than a decade and then cause him to push for equal treatment for blacks testifies to the intensity of the experience and suggests perhaps more the greater bitterness of blacks themselves.

Source: Letter from Nicholas G. Copadis to Senate Commerce Committee, August 6, 1963, printed in *Civil Rights: Public Accommodations*. Hearings Before the Committee on Commerce, U.S. Senate, 88th Congress, 1st Session, Part 2 (Washington, D.C., 1963), pp. 1281-82.

Manchester, N.H., August 6, 1963.

Committee on Commerce,
Washington, D.C.

Gentlemen: My sense of duty, both as a citizen and as a white retired infantry officer, compels me to go on record in favor of the civil rights public accommodations bill. This statement will not concern itself with the equal rights guaranteed under the Federal and various State Constitutions which, I am certain, have been thoroughly covered in the committee hearings by persons much more eminent than I.

This statement will cover my personal experiences with Negro troops which I commanded in Korea in 1951, and my strong belief that the fact these Negroes knew they were second-class citizens directly affected the combat effectiveness of my platoon and of the battalion itself.

I served as infantry rifle platoon leader in K Company, 19th Infantry Regiment, 2d Division, in Korea from March 1951 until June 2, 1951 when I was wounded. The battalion was composed entirely of Negroes except for a few white officers and replacements. From the moment I arrived until the moment I left, I could sense, and feel and see the results of the resentment of the men that they were frontline troops. After having spent many days on the line with them, during and after the Communist spring offensive in April of 1951, I had an opportunity to discuss this acute problem with them. I was deeply concerned because we had had our share of men absent without leave, deserters, and self-inflicted wounds.

On talking with these men, which included my platoon sergeant, Sgt. Cyrus Predow, Sergeant Coutee, and Corporal Hemphill, and asking them why the morale of the men was so low, why the men had to be prodded with a bayonet to keep them moving in an attack, the answers were the same. The men simply did not feel that they should be frontline infantrymen since they were considered second-class citizens at home. Predow said, and I remember it vividly: "What I am fighting for, to get my tail kicked to the back of the bus when I get home because I'm a nigger?" Others told me that, because they were Negroes, they couldn't attend certain events, couldn't shop where they wanted, had to go hungry because restaurants wouldn't serve them, and couldn't urinate for hours because there were no facilities for Negroes. Others told me they were knocked insensible in some cities because they happened to walk on the sidewalk. I personally have seen Negroes, combat infantry veterans, forced to leave post exchanges because of the rank, foul discrimination that exists in the South.

All this is not to say that the combat record of our outfit was not good. It was good, as evidenced by the Distinguished Unit Citation awarded for breaking the back of the Chinese offensive in April of 1951. However, there is no doubt in my mind that our combat effectiveness as a unit was seriously impaired by the fact that the Negroes knew they were relegated to the status of second-class citizens at home who were denied rights others enjoyed but still had to fight on the battlefield for the very persons who were denying them those rights. I strongly feel that unless the Negro in this country is afforded the same rights as other citizens, the same accommodations, then he should not be asked to perform the duties required of a citizen who enjoys those same rights.

As I led my men in the attacks and counterattacks in Korea through the decisive months of 1951 and saw them get hit by mortar fire, by 50 calibers, by burp-gun fire, by heavy artillery, and saw their red blood flow over their black skin, I could not help but feel an overwhelming sympathy for these men who, for a brief interval, served with me in our country's just cause.

In closing, I should like to quote parts of a letter sent to me by 1st Lt. Palmer K. Holk, who was my company commander. This letter was written after I was wounded in the attempt to secure a hill north of Inje, North Korea. It reads, in part: "We didn't secure the hill. Two days later we were relieved by the R.O.K.S. That day, 5 killed in action, 39 wounded in action. It got a little rough. Couldn't get any artillery fire and couldn't get the F.O. (forward observer) to move forward."

I quote Lieutenant Holk's letter to show the casualties suffered by this Negro company in one engagement. I would not be true to the memory of the men in my platoon who fought and died in those remote hills of Korea if I did not, at this time, make an earnest plea that the public accommodations bill be passed. The passage of such a bill would, in my humble opinion, strengthen our country internally, and at the same time would act as a fitting testimonial to those Negro war dead.

My sincere thanks to Senator John O. Pastore, and to the Committee on Commerce for allowing me to express my thoughts on this important legislation.

> Very truly yours,
> Nicholas G. Copadis.

42 Prophecies of Struggle

While race relations had always been susceptible to volatile outbursts and periodic intensification either in challenge or subjugation, the sheer institutional base for those relations and the frequent lack of optimism could normally weigh heavily enough to maintain, with notable exceptions, the status quo. But when the Supreme Court in 1954 and 1955 struck down the notion of separate but equal, one of the central institutional props supporting segregation disintegrated. The actual desegregation of the nation's schools would take years and even then with sometimes dubious effectiveness; the court battles would persist; legal maneuvering on the part of all litigants would abound; and Congress, the Presidency, and govermental bodies throughout the nation would inveigh mightily on the issue of desegregation and racial equality. Yet the major impact of the ruling may have been in another area. Like previous developments, whether a war labor shortage, an opportunity for freedom elsewhere, or more simply an increasingly despairing situation, this action of the Supreme Court provided a new stimulus to direct action by blacks themselves to alter the circumstances of their lives. And this time the stimulus would not fade with the end of a war or the shifting of political and economic winds since separate but equal could not be resurrected. In 1956 the public battle began to take shape in Montgomery, Alabama, when blacks inaugurated a boycott of streetcars in the city, which were requiring blacks to sit at the rear of buses that used white drivers, and which were the scenes of numerous instances of white abuses of black passengers. The boycott proved effective since blacks constituted a major portion of the passengers, and it was reinforced by a court order in November 1956, ordering the buses desegregated. But the issue had been joined and the battle would grow quickly to national dimensions.

The following letters to the editor of the Montgomery *Advertiser* indicate on one hand the hardening of lines among some whites in what would become a prolonged, frustrated, and bitter resistance to the erosion of their separatist society, and on the other hand the actual modest nature of the goals of the boycott. The first letter, published in July 1955, reveals that blacks in the community were already restive, making their presence and intentions known; it also shows the huge symbolic importance attached by some to challenges in any area of racial exclusion. The second letter, also in advance of the boycott, proposed to "fight fire with fire" by depriving blacks of employment in the South. Finally, the letter from one of the leaders of the Montgomery Improvement Association, which organized the boycott, is notable in that it indicates the basic role of religion—itself a traditional realm of black independence—in the movement, and for the ironic prophecy that resistance to this meager goal directed only at the city's buses would result in demands for total integration. The days of constitutionally supported segregation and inequality would never return.

Source: Letters to the editor, Montgomery *Advertiser*, on dates as indicated.

Editor, The Advertiser:

If we're going to continue to have segregation in Montgomery—in the South—let's have it and go all out for it, not be namby-pamby and go on halfway measures.

We've always had "separate but equal" facilities for Negroes and that's the way it should be. I have particular reference to that fact that some Negroes, probably this was instigated by the NAACP, went each day to the Parade of Homes in Gay Meadows.

One wonders why the Negroes would want to attend this, when by no stretch of their imagination or hope could they ever expect to buy or live in that section. They mingled freely with white people in going over these houses, registering alongside them, and I am of the opinion that had this event lasted longer, many more Negroes would have made their appearance each day.

I don't think these Negroes were interested in these homes. I believe it was a planned affair. One host at one of the homes when questioned about this, informed me that one reason no objection had been made to admitting the colored people was because he was of the opinion that was just what they had come for—to stir up trouble, to be asked out in other words, so that they could make an issue of it.

These homes are owned by private individuals, they would have the right to admit anyone or not to admit anyone and I believe it was a mistake to admit the colored people on this occasion. And as I said in the beginning, let's go all out for segregation, or else let the bars down and forget it, not give in inch by inch.

Mrs. J. B. McKinney.
Montgomery
[July 24, 1955]

Editor, The Advertiser:

This letter is written, in no unkind spirit, to the Negro race. I wish them well, among their own people. But now that they are attempting to push themselves into the innermost circle of the white man—his schools, churches, parks, colleges, restaurants. It seems to me we have only one recourse: to meet fire with fire, and fight this evil every step of the way. The mixing of the races is too serious to do otherwise.

To many the courses that have been suggested may seem hard. But this is no ordinary evil we have to fight. The suggestions are: To fire all Negroes from private jobs, firms and business houses, to withhold credit from Negroes.

They would find it hard to make a living down here and would migrate to the North and other sections to find work. No country that claims to be a democracy could possibly dictate to employers who they employed or refused to employ. So we have a weapon, and should (under the appalling conditions) plan to use it. It is a question of self-preservation with the white race.

Let the North prove its sincerity and that it is not using the Negro as a political pawn. Let us see how it will react to the impact of the Negro in the large numbers the South faces. It is the numbers that make it the huge problem it is. So far, the North has shown even worse violence when thrown into proximity with any migration—in housing, and so forth.

Ellen Mastin.
Mobile Highway, Montgomery
[July 15, 1955]

Editor, The Advertiser:

I have noticed that since the protest began there has been an avalanche of letters appearing in the Grandma columns urging that a compromise be reached. Some of these letters and suggestions came from people who are quite optimistic in their thinking; a few came from people who are realistic in their reasoning; but the majority of them came from people who are pessimistic in their belief.

Be it known, now, henceforth and forever, that the Negroes of Montgomery have no desire to compromise in this "bus situation." I have moved through the streets, and have been convinced beyond a shadow of a doubt that Negroes prefer walking rather than to go back to riding the buses.

Our request has been reasonable. These are the proposals:

—That assurance of more courtesy be extended the bus riders.

—That the seating of passengers will be on a "first-come, first-served" basis, with Negroes being seated from the rear to the front and whites being seated from the front toward the rear.

—That Negro bus drivers be employed on the bus lines serving predominately Negro areas.

On our side there can be no compromise with this principle envolved. In the first place this is a compromise to begin with. We should have demanded complete integration which does away with Jim Crow, and what our constitutional rights guarantee to all American citizens. It then seems to me that those who cry "compromise," should be courageously seeking ways to supplement these proposals.

The type of segregation, Jim Crow and discrimination being practiced here in the South is on its deathbed. There are some who are trying to keep it alive. But internal coercion and external pressure is sure to cause this personality to have an early funeral.

The Negro ministers have been charged by some as misusing religion and the Church. If there is any group of people who have come in personal contact with Jesus it certainly must be the Negro ministers. We don't teach people however, that the Bible teaches separation of the races. We teach them to believe in and live the life applicable to one who practices the brotherhood of man and the fatherhood of God. To under-estimate the Negro ministers is uncalled for, unjustifiable and absurd at the least. We believe in "good race relations" or as Mrs. Myron C. Lohman calls it "cordial relations between the races." However, I am quite sure we do not define the term alike. We believe that good race relations exist only when everyone is treated as an equal. This cannot be as long as there are laws preventing men of one race from enjoying the privileges and rights enjoyed by another race.

We shall never cease our struggle for equality until we gain firstclass citizenship and take it from me this is from a reliable source (the Negro citizens of Montgomery). We have no intention of compromising. Such unwarranted delay in granting our request may very well result in a demand for the annihilation of segregation which will result in complete integration.

(The Rev.) U. J. Fields, Minister Bell Street Baptist Church, Secretary of the Montgomery Improvement Association.

Montgomery
[July 5, 1956]

43 Little Rock

The crisis surrounding the desegregation of Central High School in Little Rock, Arkansas, in the fall of 1957 garnered the attention of the entire nation, as most observers agreed on the pivotal importance, one way or another, it would hold for the future. That importance and that significance proved to be much in the eye of the beholder. Many saw this as a test of the resolve of the nation's institutions, especially the federal government's commitment to the mandate of the courts, in the area of civil rights. Others saw Governor Orval Faubus trying to bolster his own political fortunes by appealing to a racial issue in summoning the Arkansas National Guard to prevent desegregation of the school. Still others would focus on President Dwight Eisenhower's nationalization of the National Guard to permit the nine black students to enroll as a vast and unwarranted expansion of the power of the federal government over the lives of citizens. Various discussions of plots hatched in Moscow, in the heart of the deep South, in the NAACP, or elsewhere added further portentous implications to whatever transpired in Little Rock.

The following letters from local citizens were addressed to the editor of the Arkansas *Gazette* and reveal some of the main themes of local sentiments and views of the matter. Little of the correspondence focused on explicit racial themes. Many writers considered the political circumstances peculiar to Arkansas and Little Rock in that year. The opposition to desegregation, which itself was often critical of Governor Faubus since he was ostensibly only delaying integration and not permanently blocking it, usually expressed a common theme of individual alienation from the institutions of government. The first three letters of the following group illustrate this. One puts the argument in terms of states' rights and the apparent usurpation of the powers of the state by the federal government while another moves quickly from the states' rights position to an attack on the process as one large step in a drift toward communism, identifying that system with the centralization of authority and the defiance of the public will, calling even for a national referendum on the issue of integration. Yet a third identifies the problem in George Orwell's terms as he sees the totalitarian society of 1984 descending on America. In so doing that correspondent observes that states rights provides a historic if not legal precedent which is being ignored by federal authority. In this general position of resistance to the centralization of authority it would no doubt be possible, as some have suggested, to see primarily a rationalization in legitimate terms of more racist oriented motivations. But the elitism assumed in that assessment is possibly equal to that attributed to those mounting the resistance to desegregation. What is especially interesting is that earlier generations would frequently voice their opposition to racial equality in ways that indicated an opposition to market intrusions, namely in their caste-dominated rhetoric and actions, at a time when, indeed, the market's influence sharply dominated the social context of their confrontations with blacks. It could well be that in the 1950s the centralization of power inherent in the modernization process and the subsequent loss of individual decision-making responsibilities as governments and economic institutions—be they business, labor, or the plethora of scarcity-oriented interest groups—assumed increasing authority over the individual, and had already created a very real pattern of cultural, and even physical, dispossession. Race relations proved to be the area of society where a stand would be taken, finally, to resist further change and hold on to an earlier way of life.

The other side of the debate sometimes voiced a bold congratulation that the nation was at last moving practice into line with historic ideals in racial equality and freedom. This often took the form of a righteous zeal that contrasted northern opportunities with southern oppression and condemned the bigotry of those who would keep the blacks from attending the white high school. Two of the letters printed below reflect this tendency. Others, especially parents of white students at the high school, while not enthusiastic about the desegregation of their schools, were inclined to accept the situation since they valued most of all education for their children. Indeed, they often viewed Faubus as the threat to freedom since he interfered with the desegregation plans of the local school board. A final argument, perhaps the least typical but maybe the most revealing, is found in a letter suggesting that the real problem in Little Rock was that decent people were afraid to express their true beliefs and that fear generated an atmosphere of repression and acquiescence to authority that was endangering blacks at that moment, but ultimately threatening everybody. In this cogent statement, again, a social context for the crisis in Little Rock can be found in which the other arguments also make sense. The issue of desegregation, especially as manifest in the instance of Little Rock—in which the confrontation came not only between black and white but between the community and the state and between the state and the federal government—provided a seemingly clear-cut issue and a sense of purpose in a nation where individual and local responsibility had been dissipating as power and responsibility gravitated to ever more centralized levels of business and government. For some it appears that in an increasingly centralized, bureaucratized, and depersonalized society where authority was, as Erich Fromm described it, anonymous and invisible, that central authority now suddenly became naked, visible, and personal, and thus could be attacked. For others, who found the pressure toward a conformity oriented around material growth both unfulfilling and unsatisfying, the cause of civil rights provided a sense of purpose. In fact there is the distinct possibility, certainly one with ample historical precedent, that a people that has lost its sense of purpose, mission, and goals could even find them in a negative way by ferreting out the enemy, be they witches or communists or simply people of different values and cultures. Whether they were for or against desegregation, the issue provided all kinds of people with a revitalized sense of purpose and mission that transcended the materialism of the American social structure. And it was exactly this stifling atmosphere of fear and conformity that the last correspondent lays bare. The tragedy was, of course, that once again such fulfillment could come only at the expense of setting peoples against one another, and again that the source of the frustration would escape, for a while, the accountability it thrust onto others. As this final letter seems to suggest, when people are afraid to speak out or unwilling to face the issue directly, then they have already lost their freedom.

Source: Letters to the editor, *The Arkansas Gazette,* on dates specified.

To the Editor of the Gazette:

The most important issue is not "shall we or shall we not have segregated schools." The issue is—do we still have sovereign states as provided by the Constitution, or do we have an all-powerful central government which has taken over the functions of our 48 states. Governor Faubus should be commended by all citizens for his courage in bringing this issue to the point where it may be determined once and for all if we the people of what we have believed to be a sovereign state, still have the power to operate our own public schools under what we have always considered to be power reserved to us by the Constitution of the United States.

Lloyd Godley.
Osceola
[September 19, 1957]

To the Editor of the Gazette:

If we don't stand for our state's rights we will become nothing but puppets of an all-powerful federal government. The first step in Communism is to take the authority from the hands of the many and put it in the hands of a few. Are we going to let a few, i.e., nine jurists or judges and a president usurp the authority of the will of the majority of our state?

I would and I believe all people would abide by a nation-wide vote on this question of integration. Why can't we have it? It is our inalienable right.

Elder E. R. Fitzgerald,
Pastor Pleasant Home
Baptist Church
Sheridan
[September 12, 1957]

To the Editor of the Gazette:

The late George Orwell, in his frightening and prophetic book, "1984," foresaw a police state in which history and all public opinion producing mass communication media were nothing more than tools for implementing the party line. Identities, beliefs and historical precedents were totally erased and more amenable ones substituted whenever a change in the party line so dictated.

Perhaps the only real tragedy in the current Central High School integration case is that we see Orwell's nightmare of 1984 materializing in 1957 from within our own ranks.

In the light of these thoughts may I present for our reflection the following trends evident in the current situation to any honest observer:

1. The changing interpretation of the federal Constitution by a Supreme Court which sheathes its dictates with its constitutionally ordained powers. Perhaps only Patrick Henry among the delegates to the constitutional convention foresaw the danger. On June 21, 1787, Henry told his fellow delegates: "It will be an empire of men and not of laws. Your rights and liberties rest upon men. Their wisdom and integrity may preserve you—but on the contrary, should they prove ambition, and designing, may they not flourish and triumph upon the ruins of their country?"

2. The use of federal force to execute these new interpretations posthaste in disregard of a plea for postponed but ultimate compliance.

3. The resultant destruction of states rights which have historical, if not legal, precedence over every federal law except the Constitution which gave it cognizance.

4. The biased and sometimes outrageous news coverage of the Little Rock story by the national press, radio, and TV.

To this "prejudiced, bigoted, misguided, wrong thinking segregationist and anarchist" the conclusion to be drawn from the facts per se is inescapable.

Howard Goggans.
Little Rock
[October 24, 1957]

To the Editor of the Gazette:

We recently left your city after living there approximately one-and one-half years. We chose to get to a less changeable climate and also to get away from the discrimination in the South. My husband is in the Air Force, so we can't always control our place of residence, but I just hope and pray that when our youngsters are of school age, that we are not in the South. I don't want them to grow up with the thick-headed bigotry that is so prevalent in cities such as yours.

Mrs. Robert Synarski.
Oxnard, Cal.
[September 11, 1957]

To the Editor of the Gazette:

I have been following avidly your editorials on the Little Rock school crisis and also the comments from the people of Arkansas. I want to add my voice to those who commend you on your Christian, enlightened stand in this matter. So many of us deplore this action of Governor Faubus and some of the more bigoted people of Little Rock, and we wish to thank you for standing firm in showing people throughout the country that we are really fair and human at heart. This fall I will be a freshman at a prominent Northern college. I have been looking forward to the opportunity to do some plugging for my home state, but I expect that I shall have to do some mighty earnest talking to counteract this incident and its results in the minds of the people I meet.

Ardent, Arkansas.
Hot Springs
[September 11, 1957]

To the Editor of the Gazette:

I am one of the 1,865 mothers of Central High School students who were not at the Governor's Mansion Saturday! Why were the other 1,864 mothers not there? Could it be that they agree with my reason for not being present! First, I do not believe it necessary to close our school; secondly, I want my child in school where he belongs.

Let me state here I am not in favor of integration. Neither am I criticizing these mothers for expressing their views, but they are only 135. Do they speak for all the parents of high school children?

I do not see a rosy situation without problems in integrated school, but I do feel that without interference our local School Board is capable of handling these problems.

Am I alone in thinking the students of Central High, most of these young people come from Christian homes with law-abiding parents, if given the chance can accept the situation for what it is—a law to abide with in good faith?

We are living in the age of One World, and I, for one, have enough faith in our young people to believe they can accept this challenge with the honor and dignity of good American citizens.

Elsie D. Jones.
Little Rock
[October 3, 1957]

To the Editor of the Gazette:

All this talk by "True American" and "Reader" about being too scared to say what they think and not being free, makes me sick at my stomach. There isn't anything to be scared of. My husband, who is a salesman, goes around the state saying exactly what he thinks, which is that Faubus is a fifth-rate politician who is willing to endanger the lives and schooling of other people's children just for his own selfish benefit. So far he hasn't had his throat cut, or even threatened, and he hasn't lost a sale.

I was talking to Robert C. Pierpoint, Far East bureau chief for CBS, the other day and he said that the people of Little Rock are the most frightened people he has ever seen. That must be pretty frightened, coming from a man who has been out of the country for 10 years. All the rest of the world is supposed to be worse off than we are. What are the citizens of Little Rock anyway, a bunch of spineless, gutless cowards?

Mr. Pierpoint said he tried for an hour to get a statement from Central High students, who only turned wordlessly away, until he got hold of my 13-year-old daughter from West Side. When my Central High daughter took it on herself to tear down offensive signs, she was warned repeatedly that she wouldn't have any friends, she might get killed, no one would dare to date her, etc. ad nauseam. One boy told her that the girls who walked out the morning of the big mob were disgusted with the Megaphone Girls Club who had been friendly with the colored girls. My daughter retorted that the Megaphone Girls were disgusted with the girls who walked out. The boy seemed surprised that my daughter wasn't crushed at the disapproval of a bunch of rabble. What I want to know is, "since when has the rabble and the white trash had the right to call the tune that rest of us dance to?"

Incidentally, my daughter hasn't been killed, hasn't lost any friends and [has] all of the dates that she can squeeze in.

What I want to know is, "what in the name of God are we afraid of?" A cheap politician that we can vote out of office next year, or impeach this year, and bunch of weak characters that have to have a mob behind them before they can work up courage enough to call children ugly names? This year it is the Negroes. Next year, it will be Jews or Catholics. The next year we will be so bound in the chains of our own fear that we will be at the mercy of a demagogue dictator and his Gestapo.

I have talked to several people who said that they felt as I did but they couldn't say so because of what their neighbors would think. What will their neighbors think? And why is what their neighbors think any more important than what they think?

What I think is that if we, the people for law and order and decency, don't stand up in public and say what we think then the thing which we greatly fear, loss of freedom, is going to come upon us.

(Mrs.) Merla Manor.
Little Rock
[October 23, 1957]

44 Sitting-In

As pressure mounted across the nation for blacks to receive equal treatment, the black community moved increasingly on its own to secure equality through a variety of activist approaches relying less on the formal legal avenues that would wend their way through the courts. Like the Montgomery bus boycott in 1956, the sit-in campaign inaugurated in Greensboro, North Carolina, in 1960 soon spread throughout the region. Seeking service at segregated establishments and then sitting and waiting, keeping the pressure there instead of leaving when refused, proved to be an effective tactic, as a number of businesses opened their doors to blacks; it was also a poignant way of dramatizing the issue of discrimination. It would be easy to over-emphasize the effectiveness of the sit-in, though, since many businesses would remain segregated establishments and would remain closed to blacks for years. But as a symbolic breakthrough the significance of the sit-in was enormous in revealing assumptions about race relations in various quarters.

The following letters to the editor of the Nashville *Tennesseean* focus on the sit-ins under way in that community in the spring of 1960, shortly after the Greensboro effort. The letter that condemns the action does so in terms that are instructive but hardly surprising. The paternalism that is evident in speaking for black people as the writer does, which is apparent in the belief that whites understand their interests better than the blacks themselves as well as in the traditional affirmation of white people that they "love our colored brethren and we want them to love us," is not altogether fabrication for political purposes; that paternalism was not only time honored and perpetuated but bespoke a social framework vastly different from the atomistic, individualistic society promised in various materialistic orientations. The sincerity of this pitch carries into another significant part of the defense of segregation from this onslaught.

Notably this additional feature of the argument stems not from reliance on the law as a sanctified standard for society, since the law had been deprived of much of its legitimacy in the eyes of white Southerners. Instead the basis of the argument centers on moral considerations incumbent on those who would "force themselves" upon others and the "irreparable animosity" which would result from such violations of the code of decency. The black students sitting-in at the lunch counters were unmannerly. The final point underlay the others: since such boldness is alien to this particular community surely it must be the product of outside influences. In one, literal, sense this is surely a mistake since the desire to be served at a lunch counter does not require a northern origin. But in another, symbolic, sense one wonders. Perhaps this society that prided itself on its manners and morality, even if at the expense of equity and individual justice, was in fact being undermined by powerful material forces that venerated a system which cared little for the color of a person's skin but at the same time cared much for the cash that crossed the counter, and that perhaps cared only for that cash.

The letters encouraging the desegregation of the businesses capture the passion and the overriding sense of justice and equality that became the hallmark of the civil rights movement. They also convey the aggressive but nonviolent spirit characteristic of the larger effort. At the same time, however, some assumptions emerge from their positions which, if carried logically further, could undermine some of their own goals. The reliance on the equality provided by the law may be one such notion. Since 1954 the highest law in the land was clearly on the side of these people. But what if the problem ran deeper than the law, into the very fabric and structure of society itself? It would not be long before many promoters of justice in the nation would find this focus on the law and the effort to make practice conform to the letter of the law too narrow and would discover that sometimes even the resolution of *de jure* problems only made the *de facto* problems in race relations that much more difficult to attack and indeed sometimes to perceive. The moral tone itself further suggests an ambiguity that would have to be confronted at some point. Sometimes the position would be frankly elitist, ascribing the opposition to various forms of bigotry and ignorance. Here only the presumption of objectivity and the attribution in one letter of "staid traditions and mores of a backward South" to the opposition even approaches that elitism. More important here is another component of the moral tone of the crusade. A substantial part of the value structure assumed turns out to be, upon closer reflection, the value structure of what many would call white middle class America. It could be that opening up the stores of downtown Nashville might be a major gain for the students at Fisk and Vanderbilt but would be of little relevance to those blacks in the community without the money to take advantage even if the potential of black purchasing power were recognized. How fundamentally this would meet the needs of the black community was more often assumed than addressed.

Source: Letters to the editor, Nashville *Tennesseean*, on dates specified.

To the Editor:

It is my recollection that the people of Nashville have never tried or wanted to force themselves in company or in places where it was quite obvious that they weren't welcomed or wanted.

Indeed, to do such a thing is to invite a brush with the law, not to mention the more serious aspects of the act, such as the irreparable animosity which would naturally result therefrom.

It is for this reason that we are at a loss to understand why local Negro college students are staging "restaurant sit-down strikes" in an effort to force these establishments to serve them right along with White customers.

Since Negroes weren't being served, it was, then, quite obvious that these establishments didn't want colored business, at least, not on an integrated basis, anyway.

These demonstrations are, to say the least, ill-conceived and are being directed by students who apparently have not the forethought to realize that the ultimate damage to racial relations will by far outweigh anything conceded them as a result of their seat-shining pranks.

These sitdown strikes are the brainstorms of Negroes who are not truly interested in the progress of their own race, else they would surely see that, in the end, their losses will by far outweigh their gains.

We people in Nashville love our colored brethren, and we want them to love us and since we have felt this way mutually to one-another for a long time, we are wondering if there aren't some outside interests trying to foment these disturbances.

C. Maurice Wain.
Nashville
[February 26, 1960]

To the Editor:

Much of the recent publicity concerning "sit in" demonstrations by Nashville Negro college students has failed to focus upon the real point at issue. Simply stated that point is whether the Negro whose purchasing power is encouraged in other areas of public stores is entitled to equal treatment at the lunch counter.

In the present disturbance let us take time out to review certain things. First of all, Nashville is a major Negro educational center. These institutions produce well trained graduates who see no reason why they should be relegated by tradition and blind prejudice to a position of inferiority to other groups in society less able than themselves. Their protest to such treatment in recent weeks has been non-violent in character yet their attempt to point up a moral issue to the community has resulted in attempts to completely ignore the real issue involved while picturing these students as part of a vast conspiracy second only to Russian communism.

A young man who had undoubtedly had a great deal of influence in these demonstrations is painted as a combination of all the worst traitors of our country's past. Here again the attempt is to cover up the real issue.

It is difficult for one who has all the rights and privileges he desires to sympathize with those who are striving to appropriate these rights to themselves. In times like these the majority of our society becomes either indifferent or champions of the "status quo." They assert that this is the best of all possible worlds and are determined that no one shall disturb it.

Nashville has not always withdrawn into the protective shell of preserving things just the way they are. In the past in the handling of desegregation in the public schools, in buses and in other areas responsible citizens have demanded imaginative leadership which has done an excellent job of securing racial harmony in our city. Other cities of the South have looked to Nashville's example and for this we should be justly proud. Are we then to give up such a position and return to hard shelled traditionalism? Friday morning's paper told of the appointment of a bi-racial committee to study the problem and offer a solution.

Despite all this let us hope and earnestly pray that the committee will be able to reach a workable solution which will once again demonstrate to the South Nashville's undisputed position of leadership in the area of race relations.

Lewis E. Moore Jr.
Nashville
[March 7, 1960]

To the Editor:

In Monday morning's issue, the editorial inferred that the Negro students were wrong in initiating the sitdowns in downtown stores, and that they should depend on the law and courts rather than provoking violence. May I call to your attention the fact that there have been no provocations by the students in any of these incidents. Always violence has come at the hands of the bystanders, of the whites.

If this is disbelieved, I kindly refer you to the newsreel report given on WLAC-TV's 6 P.M. news on Tuesday. I, along with thousands of other Negroes, question the rationality of this editorial, for through the past century the Negro and progeny have waited quite patiently for the law and courts to provide the civil liberties guaranteed each citizen by the Constitution of our United States. (Notice that I write OUR, for it is our U. S.)

Looking at this situation objectively, one must note that the courts of the South have been particularly lax in guaranteeing protection of and support to the Negro populace, and virtually no significant accomplishments have been made without an initial effort by the Negro to demand his inalienable liberties. Viewing the situation subjectively, why should the Negro, or any other minority group—be encouraged to expend finance in any institution or organization or business which provides humane privileges for a portion of the clientele and denies them to another portion?

To be sure, the American democratic way of living and the history of American whites is taught from day to day in the public school system to the Negro child—at the expense of history regarding his own people. Naturally, with this indoctrination of the American democratic society, the student will want to achieve that strata of existence on all levels, and not so much because someone else does but simply because it is his to enjoy. If democracy is the mode of government and society, it should be co-existent for all ethnic groups, barring none.

The day is now present when every person, irrespective of race or religion, must realize that the "good days" of ill-claimed and/or ill-gained glory is a thing of the past. Now is the time when all good men will come to the aid of the populace and decry the reprehensible and deplorable situation existent where law officers leave citizens to face the threats, insults, and bodily harm inflicted at the hand of ruthless, ignorant and undisciplined vandals.

The individual should be protected by law, according to your editorial. But when the law fails to do so, what should he do—stand by and suffer indignities inherent to the denial of privileges that are his by virtue of his being a citizen? Such is not representative of democracy; in fact, it is anything but, for democratic principles demand equality for every one.

These students are not provoking disturbances; rather, they are upsetting the staid traditions and mores of a backward South that stubbornly holds on to a fast declining, poorly grounded idea of a superior race. Their resistance is conducted in an orderly manner with no malevolence involved. As a consumer, a constituent and a Christian, I glory in the spunk of these students who fearlessly face the maddened wolves of this society armed only with a desire, a dream, an idea which is inherently theirs by right of the Constitution.

Mrs. N. E. Douglas
Nashville

[March 4, 1960]

45 Treason and Dark Fears: The Freedom Riders

In 1961 the concerted effort of a group of black people to ride buses through the South and to be served at stops along the way met not only protest and resistance but extensive violence as well. The freedom riders, like the sit-in protestors and bus boycotters before them, publicized the issue of discrimination perhaps more successfully than ever before. The issues dividing the protestors from the state authorities and the whites opposed to their demands for equality remained much the same. In the letters to newspaper editors printed below it is evident that the emphasis on law and order by these protestors may have been even greater than before. One letter in fact suggests that those individuals and authorities attempting to maintain segregation are guilty of treason since their actions undermine the nation. One's obligation, or allegiance, to the nation is being tested in this struggle. On the other hand, the antagonists of the civil rights effort assumed a certain moral position that was above the law, even terming it anarchy, in their struggle to prevent change. As usual the challenge could often be ascribed to "outside influences" and the violence itself ignored or justified by the seriousness of the challenge. That seriousness, the two letters attacking the freedom riders suggest, was greater than what was represented by buses and restaurants; it involved the mixing of the races. The dark fears of black sexuality seemed to be surfacing again, and with them the imagery of blacks as possessors of a separate culture. This perception circulated freely among white segregationists but was hotly denied again and again by civil rights advocates, who stressed the minimal difference between black and white, namely skin pigmentation. It seems that many whites came to the conclusion that once their domination of society through a caste system was removed and once their traditional standards and rules of behavior in social relations were also undermined, the only thing left, the "purity" of their race, would be sacrificed too. When they did so believe they were identifying, not the goal of the civil rights movement, but their own final bulwark of resistance, the only thing they felt they had left after the ravages of social change. And possibly they confused blood with culture.

Source: Letters to the editors, Winston-Salem *Sentinel* and Greensboro (N. C.) *Daily News*, on dates specified.

Dear Sir:

I feel that the editorial on the "freedom ride" incident, which appeared in your paper several days ago, needs some comment. The writer of the editorial expressed regret that the "shameful incident" had occurred, but went on to imply that the purpose of the "tests" seemed to have been to bring martyrdom to the victims of the assaults. I should like to remind the writer of the editoral, and other people holding similar views, that after long years of persecution, we, most assuredly, have accumulated enough martyrs to satisfy even the liveliest egos. We have only to resurrect a few of the histories of Negroes who have been lynched for "looking at a white woman," or who have been committed to mental institutions in the Deep South for "sassing" a white man.

It seems to be that instead of subtly suggesting to the Negro that he curb his demands for freedom in the Deep South, where he is sure to be opposed and which opposition will bring "shame" to our country, the editors of our newspapers might direct their pleas to the real offenders, the rabid segregationists of the South. True enough, the writer thought the offenders should be punished for their deeds. Let me remind the writer, however, that the deed of which these men are guilty is nothing less than treason against the country they profess to love. Article III, Section 3 of the Constitution of the United States declares: "Treason against the United States should consist only in levying war against them, *or in adhering to their enemies, giving them aid and comfort*." (emphasis supplied.) In the light of this definition, every act of violence which a so-called segregationist commits against a Negro, guilty only of the crime of 'color', is an act of treason; for by exposing to the whole world the "lie" which our country lives in the name of freedom and Democracy, he gives "aid and comfort" to the enemy.

It is time for us to face the facts squarely and try a different approach. It must be obvious to all by now that the Negro can no longer be intimidated by reminders of the dire consequences that will atttend his acts. The loss of a few more lives will not matter to a people who have already surrendered many lives without even the dignity of a struggle. It must also be obvious by now that the intelligent Negro is as embarrassed by our country's "lie" before the world as the intelligent white man, for, paradoxically enough, he has deep allegiance to the country which persistently refuses to grant him, in fact, the status of a first class citizen.

Daisy F. Balsley.
Winston-Salem Teachers College
Winston-Salem
[Winston-Salem *Sentinel*, May 23, 1961]

Editor of the Daily News:

If the editors who are deploring the reaction of Alabamans to the invasion of the "freedom riders" are sincere, why don't they start digging at the root of the trouble? Who started the mess down there, and why? If my information is correct, it was originated by a group of smart alecks, white and Negro, from a section of the country, far away from Alabama, who elected themselves monitors to supervise the social customs and conduct of Alabamans.

Anyone who tries to make it appear that only the riffraff of Montgomery seriously object to having outsiders try to regulate their customs is doing a poor service to Alabamans, or to any worthy cause.

Those eager beavers whose practical knowledge of conditions responsible for Southerners' objections to racial integration, who nevertheless presume to set themselves up in judgment, deserve to be given corrective treatment. People who through 300 years of close contact with Negroes prefer not to mix with them socially have at least as much right to demand that they keep their distance as the Negroes have to demand that the whites be forced to snuggle up to them.

It is silly for anyone to pretend that all the integrationists want and all they hope to gain is civil rights for Negroes. What the Negroes in the fight for integration really want and hope to force the white people in this country to accept is blood mixture of the races.

Whether this would be a good thing for us or not is beside the point. The point is, in so far as Southerners are concerned, that we prefer to remain Caucasian. And we believe that we have the right to defend our preference.

After all is said and done, the bald fact remains that the trouble in Montgomery would never have come up if the "freedom riders" had stayed home. If newspaper and magazine editors, instead of defending this caravan of meddlers, would advise that they be stopped and sent back where they belong and told to mind their own business, the gentlemen of the press would be doing the country a greater service than they are by berating the people who intercepted and manhandled those self-appointed "missionaries."

This is the Southern point of view in the case of racial integration.

Geo. D. Herring.
Asheboro
[Greensboro (N. C.) *Daily News*, May 29, 1961]

Editor of the Daily News:

In a recent letter to "Public Pulse" George D. Herring brought out two pertinent points in relation to the present wave of so-called "freedom riders" presently parading throughout the South.

First, he states in no uncertain terms that the blame for these irresponsible people, who are riding on the other fellow's money, viz. CORE and its associate members, are being promoted more by the publicity the news services are giving to them during these difficult times than by what they really are fighting for. Nothing pleases a spoiled child more than to get unnecessay attention or to hear many people tell of the cute things he said or did.

Second, he states his case more clearly when he says that the leaders of this silly movement are more bent on mixing blood with the whites than they are in receiving equal treatment by laws or even by pushing their way into positions they neither have earned nor are wanted. This is not to say that all people should not have equal protection under the laws of our Constitution. But to break down all state laws by force is to invite anarchy by mobs who are not always made up of the "riffraff" as some of our more eager reporters would have us believe.

The attorney general has asked for a cooling-off period for this present agitating mess in the South, but the Negroes and some puny white associates will have none of his advice. Well, perhaps they will carry this thing too far and wind up in the jug, such as in Mississippi. All these "tradition busters" could spend a better day at work on some constructive job near their own homes than by roving through the South with silent hate in their hearts and love on their tongues.

C. K. Fitzgerald.
Whitsett
[Greensboro (N. C.) *Daily News*, June 9, 1961]

46 A Discovery of Identity

The turmoil in race relations was not restricted to even a broadly defined notion of a civil rights movement. Some blacks, the most visible manifestations being the Black Muslims who followed Malcolm X and the militant and proud Black Panthers, rejected virtually every element of the civil rights movement from passive resistance to an anticipated integration into white society. In the following recollection of Lumumba Shakur, one of the Black Panthers' "New York 21," some of the faith that went into this new movement and some of the consequences of it can be seen. Aside from a positive revitalization of Afro-American cultural traditions and autonomy, this black nationalism could even provide the basis for bringing generations together, as Shakur and his father discovered. This would not be without its own perils, since that black identity was often resented by authorities in the prison system where Shakur was captive. It would also grow as Shakur and some of his fellow inmates later became Black Panthers with both a revolutionary ideology (sometimes) and a black identity.

Source: Kuwasi Balagoon *et al.*, *Look for Me in the Whirlwind: The Collective Autobiography of the New York 21* (New York, 1971), 240-43, 245. Reprinted with permission of Random House, Inc.

In 1962, the black inmates became aware of the so-called civil rights movement. We appreciated what Martin Luther King was doing, but we did not agree with his nonviolent approach toward the American system. Some blacks actually thought Martin Lurther King was setting up our people for genocide: niggers would be singing "We shall overcome" on the march to the gas chamber. Malcolm X won the black inmates' respect immediately. Malcolm X rehabilitated thousands of black inmates by just standing up to racist America and telling it like it is, educating his people about our reality—self defense—and our destiny. We all knew Malcolm X was one of the greatest men on this earth. A Puerto Rican brother in the cell next to mine would get the *New York Times* mailed to him every day. When the *Times* had something on Malcolm X, I would cut out the article and take it to the yard and show the article to other brothers. The brothers became very nationalistic in Comstock. When a brother in prison goes up to another brother and says, "The white man is a devil," no young brother would dispute or argue that issue, because in prison we felt and saw racism raw and buck-naked daily. In Comstock the ages were from sixteen to forty; only a black inmate in his late thirties would dispute or argue with the statement that "the white man is a devil." We would call the older brothers Uncle Toms and tell them that only uncivilized people and devils would run Comstock the way it was being administered. In the final analysis, when it was time to redress and change the racial conditions of Comstock, the older brothers who we called Uncle Tom told us we could not change the racial situation in Comstock. When the riot started, these older so-called brothers ran to their cells and locked themselves in.

In the summer of 1962, my father came to see me. He was telling me about the family, but he seemed reluctant about something. Then my father dropped it on me and it blew my mind, because I was thinking about how I was going to say the same thing to him. He asked me my opinion of Brother Malcolm X. I told my father that, "Malcolm X is a very beautiful brother and all the brothers in prison love Brother Malcolm X." I also told my father that I was a black nationalist and a Muslim but I could not relate to praying. I never before saw anything that affected my father like what I had just said. His facial expression became one of complete satisfaction. From that moment on, my father and I have kept an excellent communication that includes subjects both political and military in nature. My father told me he converted to Islam in 1960. He said he knew Malcolm X and that he went to hear Malcolm X educate blacks all of the time. Also, he said when Malcolm X was educating people, Malcolm said that "most of our young warriors are in prisons." My father said then that Malcolm X was a genius. We must have talked for about four hours. He mostly was telling me what was happening in the streets concerning the repression upon the black communities. He must have said about twenty times that it was beautiful to see that the devil didn't have my mind and it was good to see my spirits so high.

He left me a box with underwear, food, and a Muslim bean pie. When I was in the cell block, because everybody is locked in by 5:00 P.M., I was talking from my cell to the brothers about how my father had just blew my mind. First I said my father was down with the Muslims. The brothers responded with a typical, "Oh spare us, Shotgun." Then I said my father knows the good brother Malcolm X. The brothers said again, "Oh spare us, Shotgun." Then I said my father is going to change his slave name to Shakur (the Thankful) and I got to find a bad African first name. The brothers said, "Oh spare us, Shotgun, because you are always going to be Shotgun to us." I told the brothers I'm going to spare all of them from this big Muslim bean pie I got. "Shotgun, you wouldn't do that to your brothers." Everybody had heard about the Nation of Islam's bean pie, but very few had tasted one. About ten brothers ate that one bean pie like it was some kind of ritual. I related to the brothers just about everything my father had related to me. It blew the brothers' minds just like it had blown my mind to hear what was happening with black people and Malcolm X in New York City.

The Muslims and the nationalists began talking about formulating some kind of action to redress and change racial conditions of Comstock. I must confess that we talked about action for a year, because somebody would always disagree with any method of action. Esaw, Beany (Sekou Odinga), and Cheese were all in Comstock too by then. The four of us finally told everybody we were sick of talking, so when anybody wanted to get down with some action, call us.

* * *

When I was out, finally, I went to court and so-called-legally changed my slave name. All my family had done it already except Zayd, and he changed his slave name so-called-legally while he was in the navy—and when he did he immediately got interviews from the C.I.D. We all used religious, cultural, and ancestral reasons. I knew I would be making some babies soon and I felt that giving my child a racist, cracker's name would be like cussing the child. And I felt when my son got about eighteen years old, he would try to kick my ass for giving him a racist, cracker name. Today I have two sons and a daughter—two of them are twins. The boys are named Dingiswayo Mbiassi Abdul Shakur and Mtetwa Kieta Shakur. My daughter's name is Sekyiwa Jamilla Shakur. I have never heard of a white person naming their children African, Asian, or American Indian names. Every white person I ever heard of, including socialists, radicals, revolutionaries, communists and all progressives, have given their children European names. I wonder why?

47 Crusade in Mississippi

In the years following the initiation of protest through sit-ins, freedom rides, and other activities designed to challenge racial discrimination, a large movement grew with a focus on voting rights for blacks, especially in the state of Mississippi. Quite literally and openly this consisted of efforts by many white college students from the North who went into the South to encourage and instruct black residents in the matter of voter registration. In so doing they worked closely with local civil rights leaders and the sometimes competing agencies of the NAACP, SNCC, and CORE combined in the Council of Federated Organizations (COFO) to direct the effort. The ultimate product of the effort, despite setbacks and frustrations, was the Mississippi Freedom Democratic Party, which traveled to Atlantic City in 1964 to challenge the regular delegation from that state at the Democratic National Convention.

The following letters, written by some of the activists in 1964, reflect some subtle developments within the movement and some shrewd insights about the future of race relations. One immediate quality is the questioning evident among some of them about the efficacy of nonviolence. While this spirit had sustained civil rights activists for some time, in 1964 many had their doubts and concerns; the immediate result of that stance too often was an open vulnerability to violent reprisal. And that violence from their white adversaries came frequently and even with the tolerance or participation of law enforcement authorities. The FBI itself refused to offer protection in deference to their investigative mission. Other important aspects of this correspondence include information about the actual strategy and technique of voter registration and the discovery for many of genuine black culture, usually in the form of religion. The violence, the erosion of enthusiasm for passive resistance, and the realization of cultural differences could have been taken to be portentous: the foundations of civil rights activism were crumbling. The relatively minor (compared to earlier and later incidents) riot in Harlem in 1964 mentioned by one of the correspondents indicated the same thing: the rioting response of blacks, anywhere, was completely understandable to this person committed to nonviolence. That violence should erupt at all perhaps indicated other limitations of the civil rights movement: more and more blacks lived in the North, not the South; the Civil Rights Act of 1964 had not solved the *de facto* problems of discrimination; violence was being countered with violence. One of the students who returned North to Chicago at the end of the summer found his assumed friendship with black people not reciprocated when he encountered a black leader in his own town. The distrust by blacks of the white man perhaps was greater. Indeed, the failure of the Johnson administration to support the Mississippi Freedom Democratic Party at the Democratic Convention confirmed to many blacks that white paternalism existed, as always, among those who called themselves with touching sincerity their friends. The future of the civil rights movement was a clouded one in 1964.

Source: Elizabeth Sutherland, ed., *Letters from Mississippi* (New York, 1965), pp. 29-30, 50-52, 69-70, 120-21, 148, 182-83, 231-32. Copyright © 1965, McGraw-Hill Book Company. Used with the permission of McGraw-Hill Book Company.

Dear Folks:

Yesterday was non-violence day here. In the morning we heard Jim Lawson of Nashville, who gave us the word on non-violence as a way of life. Lawson speaks of a moral confrontation with one's enemies, catching the other guy's eye, speaking to him with love, if possible, and so on . . . "Violence always brings more harm to the people who use it; economic and political forces have no place in the Movement . . . etc." These are the things Lawson came up with. . .I feel very strongly that he does NOT represent the Movement.

Stokely Carmichael of SNCC rebutted him in the afternoon session: Nonviolence used to work because (1) it was new; (2) the newspapers gave it top coverage week after week, and most important (3) the demands were minor and the resistance to change was not hard-core. Now the North is tired of demonstrations, a very vigorous backlash has emerged, and the papers will only report major violence. Now we are responsible for what we do, and have to explain the stall-in instead of having it welcomed on the front pages of the press. Again most important, the movement has grown up, and is now aiming at the places where the white society really feels threatened—at jobs and at voting.

There comes a point when you get tired of being beaten and going back the next day for your beating for 5 days in a row. You get tired of being asked whether you are a Negro or a nigger, and ending up on the floor of the police station screaming at the top of your lungs that yes, you are a nigger, boss. You get tired of seeing young women smashed in the face right in front of your eyes. Stokely does not advocate violence. No SNCC workers are armed, nor are there guns in any SNCC office. What he is saying is that love and moral confrontations have no place in front of a brute who beats you till you cry nigger.

My feeling, and I think these are common, is that non-violence is a perverted way of life, but a necessary tactic and technique. It is harmful to the human person to feel that he must love a man who has a foot in his face. The only reason that I will not hit back is because then I will be in the hospital two weeks instead of one, and will be useless to the movement during that extra week when I can only read Gandhi's latest book on how to win friends and influence people . . .

                                                                                                        Bill

                                                                                    Holly Springs, July 6
. . . Sunday I went to a real whoop and holler church, with people shouting, screaming and stomping. The sermon began as a talk and ended as a song. The preacher jumped up and down and had tears running down his face. He finally was overcome by the sheer power of his word and started to sing 'This Little Light of Mine' in the middle of a sentence. We joined him, and people came up to grab his hands. I was one of them. This was the only House of God I had ever run into in my life. Amen! It was real, powerful and glorious.

                                                                                                Vicksburg
I went to church today, the third time since I've been here . . . It's just like the scene in *Go Tell it on The Mountain*—but it's real—there's a direct tie between every person in that church and God, and every person with me and I with them.

Tonight was different from the first time . . . I left the church, wondering the eternal question of God, which we so easily answer with terms of science and evolution and theories of the Beginning . . . I cannot say God, I cannot think God, yet I cannot so easily dismiss the thought of some higher order of things— and after so long I cannot accept it and I want to run to some Wise One and plead "Tell me, tell me—what is the answer?" And there is no Wise One to answer me—and now I shall never know and I am afraid to read again what I am writing to you now with such speed because I know two weeks later, I will say to you—well, I was very tired when I wrote this to you and I will forget how I felt and I will sink back into that middle class existence you and I and our clan live in. No—I do not mean that exactly, for we do think and really wonder and worry and hope and weep and feel—but it's sort of a rut. For we think more or less in the context in which we were brought up—Aye, liberal and thought-provoking though it is, it is still enslaving us . . .

                                                                                    Moss Point, July 8
. . . On Sunday I heard a very fine preacher in a little ramshackle church down the road. A congregation of about twelve adults and a few children, scattered around to look like more, in flowered hats, little girls in bright pink dresses, sat listening and mostly fanning themselves with stiff carboard fans which said "Friendly Funeral Home" on the back. This one gesture I would pick to show a big piece of Mississippi life; this slow fanning in the heat, the head cocked sideways, eyes half-closed, lazy, feeling the wind on wet skin . . .

The preacher was a visiting bishop, a great orator, almost a black nationalist, shouting out about Africa...no Uncle Tom he, and Pharaoh he said was "not a man, but the symbol of a government, a system, like Uncle Sam, the man with the long beard, always there even if the President gets shot." He spoke like this, loudly and earnestly, to the little fanning congregation, which answered now and then with a quiet "oyeslord" and "ain't it the truth" to the rhythm of their fanning.

Gulfport, July 8

Canvassing, the main technique in voter registration, is an art, and like an art, it is not a scheduled thing. You don't work from 9 to 5. There is no such thing as a completed job until everyone is registered. When you cheat and take a lunch hour (and it feels like cheating) you suddenly find yourself reviewing a failure or a success to discover the whys: maybe I should have bullied him slightly, or maybe I should have talked less—and relied on silences. Did I rush him? Should I never have mentioned registering at all, and just tried to make friends and set him at ease? It goes on and on. . . .

Techniques and approaches vary. Mine is often like this:

Hi. My name is Steve M. (shake hands, having gotten name, address, from a mailbox). I'm with COFO. There are a lot of us working in this area, going from house to house trying to encourage people to go down and register to vote. (Pause). Are you registered to vote? (This is the direct technique. Often people, being afraid, will lie and say yes, but you can usually tell, because they will be very proud.) Are you planning on going down soon? (This makes them declare themselves. Usually they say "yes" or "I hadn't thought about it much." The other answer is "No, I ain't going down at all.") "Well, I have a sample of the registration form." (Take it out and hand it to them.) "You know, some people are a little afraid to go down because they don't quite know what they're getting into. It's something new and different, and they're not sure about it."

Then I go on, "You know, it is so important that everyone get the vote. As it stands now, that man downtown in charge of roads doesn't have to listen to the Negroes. They can't put him out of office. He should be working for you." (Much gossip, chatter, mutual questions through all this).

Then pull out the Freedom Democratic Party application.

"This is a protest party. Anyone can join to protest the laws about voter registration and the way elections are carried out."

You get the picture. It goes on, 10 hours a day, 6 days a week. On Sundays we rest by working at other things. We go to church. Since all visitors are allotted time to speak, I relate voter registration to God. I have become a pretty good preacher. . . .

Moss Point, July 9

On Monday night we had a mass meeting, and the fifth district director, Lawrence Guyot, gave a terrific speech. The gist of his speech was that people say Moss Point is an easy area, "we have nice white folks here," that everyone has what they want already. But we don't have such nice white folks here, he said, and even if we did it shouldn't make us apathetic, it should make us want to take advantage of that extra little space . . . He kept saying, "What will it take to make you people move? A rape? A shooting? A murder? What will it take?"

At the very end of the meeting we were singing the last verse of "We Shall Overcome," 300 people in a huge circle. Suddenly there were gunshots, and all these people including me, hit the floor in a wave . . . A few seconds later we all got up trembling. A car of whites had gone by on the road outside and fired three shots through the open door. One Negro girl was hit in the side. She is in the hospital and is going to be all right, but nobody knew that at the time. The whole thing was additionally frightening because during the confusion when everybody was taking cover under tables etc., a piece of wire or something got caught in an electric fan and made a noise like a machine gun.

All during the meeting, the deputy sheriff was sitting there and the police patrol outside. The sheriff left shortly before the meeting was over and with him the police protection. At the time of the shooting there was no police anywhere around. Instead, they came fifteen minutes later, long after the whites had gotten away. . . .

. . . The boy who had been standing next to her, just outside the door of the meeting hall, said that there were four white men in the car. Kids were walking around saying, "They can't do that to us any more." It was only with much persuasion on the part of some of their friends and the COFO workers that they calmed down a little and went home. That night, the police arrested five Negro men. No white men! These five had gone home for their guns and gone out to see if they could find the car from the description given. They saw what they thought to be the car. Some men in the car apparently fired at the Negroes. The five stopped at a gas station to tell some policemen what had happened. The police searched them, arrested them on charges of carrying "concealed weapons" and never followed the suspicious car. . . .

Bolivar County, July 28

Dear Everybody

. . . Harlem riots have really been spread all over the newspapers down here. After living in a Negro community for a while it is a lot easier to see why riots occur . . . Nobody had to "agitate" Negroes to make them dissatisfied. All it takes is something to trigger it off. . . .

Medgar Evers wrote that in his younger days he wanted to start a guerrilla war in Mississippi. Some of the young people here have come close to advocating the same thing—"Some of the guys, they don't buy this nonviolent stuff. We want to get out and DO something." After facing a few bombings, beatings and jailings some of the summer volunteers felt like throwing a few bombs back themselves . . .

Yours for freedom,

Robert H.

August 2

So much has been happening that my arrest seems like a small bit of information that I should pass on.

Three different cars tried to run me down when I was in a parking lot of a large supermarket registering people. A whole bunch of the not so non-violent youth started taunting a white man in one of those cars. He got out of the car and started threatening them with a knife. At this point Clarence McGhee stepped onto the scene, the big brother of the two kids who have been down to the theatre. He stands well over six feet. He understands the need for non-violence, and has helped us calm some of the kids down a couple of times. But if somebody touches him—look out! Well, with thirty screaming kids standing around, daring the white man on, Clarence just stood there with a little smile on his lips, his head cocked slightly to one side, and waited for the guy. He didn't shout or taunt or anything, he just stood there and stated the facts: "You've got the knife, come and get me." The yellow peckerwood turned away, of course. The sight of Clarence standing there certainly was the prettiest sight I have seen so far in the state.

Well, then we all walked down the street, the kids still going strong, and me trying to calm them down somewhat. A cop came along and five helmeted police jumped out and told us to stop and started warning us that they would arrest the whole bunch of us if we gave them any more trouble. Just at that point a white man ran out from a store, and fingered me: "He's the one, he's the agitator, he's been causing trouble all day." They put me under arrest, frisked me, and started strong-arming me toward the car on the other side of the street. I tried to ask what the charge was, but they were shouting back at the man, asking him if he would testify, and telling what time the hearing would be. Half way across the street one of the cops hit me hard in the right rib. I thought it was a fist, but people on the street said that it was a club. I slumped down in the street, and the cop who had my arm twisted behind my back dragged me along the rest of the way and threw me sideways into the car. As we went down to the station, one of the cops turned around in his seat and suddenly reached over and pulled a fistfull of hair out of my arm. Later he yanked my snick pin off and jabbed me in the leg with it. Real kid stuff—absolutely senseless.

Two FBI men came around to the jail later and asked if I had been brutally beaten. The first bit of humor so far. I told them no, not brutally.... Finally Chief Larry came into the cell and said I could go.

Great trick we could have pulled on the FBI, but forgot to do. Our office was shot into [just after I got out of jail]. The FBI came and got up on a ladder to check the bullet marks. He was sort of nervous up there, and the people down below kept on making comments about cars on the street and so on. The ladder apparently began to shake visibly, and the FBI asked whether people were watching the street all right. Dottie says she should have said at this point: "Sorry, we are not in the protection business, we will, however, investigate the matter to see if any Federal Law has been violated." That, brother, is a perfect analogy of how we feel all the time: up a ladder with your pants down, and FBI's running saying that they really can't do anything until we are messed up and something has been violated....

Looking forward to seeing you all soon. Write more.

Yours in the struggle,

Bill

My first day back, I found a group from Downtown CORE raising funds for Mississippi on the corner of 8th Street. I stopped to talk with one of the fellows and after a few minutes I began to feel odd...Suddenly I realized what it was: he was a Negro, and we were on a corner crowded with white people. If we'd been in the white section of Hattiesburg, there would have been real danger.

A few days later, I was headed for the "downtown" train—in Hattiesburg that meant the white business district.

I've felt depressed since I've returned. I don't know how much is personal, and how much it is reaction to that place and the people I've left behind, and a heightened awareness of so much that is wrong up here....

Chicago

As we got into our car a lean Negro squatted down by the window next to me and warned us not to leave. This was his territory, he boasted. "We may be bums, but if you want some wild excitement we can find it for you." When we told him that we were just looking for some friends, he changed his pitch. "See those guys down there," he pointed to a gang at the end of the block, "there's Eskimo, and that's Shorty and Johnny. I'm Blackboy. I'm the boss." In a moment of innocence I stuck out my hand. Blackboy ignored it.

"As long as you're with us," he continued, "you're safe anytime you come down here. We'll even watch your car for you. Ask anybody for Blackboy. But mostly just look for this"—he held his wrist up to the window, baring a silver studded leather strap. . . . "You won't see another one like it around here. Just give us seventy cents for a drink." Blackboy was in his middle thirties. He wore a blue windbreaker and blue jeans. I gave him a quarter and a half dollar, and we were allowed to leave.

Blackboy rules the four blocks south of Ohio Street on Clark Avenue in Chicago. In Mississippi we might at least have communicated. One friend of mine remarked that he was upset every time he passed a Negro—they don't come to embrace you for what you've done, and up here you can't even wave without being counted queer. But Blackboy is real too....

48   Whose Needs Met?

The antagonism generated by the volunteers helping to organize the blacks proved to involve more than the local white populace. Sometimes the very blacks whom they hoped to aid felt less than grateful to these missionaries of change. The following interview with Linda Jenkins in 1969 focuses on her activities as a SNCC worker in 1964 in Indianola, Mississippi. As such she was one of the two natives of the area to serve on the staff there. The disappointment generated by misplaced confidence and then the exodus of the crusaders from the area, leaving the locals to face the problems alone, caused a natural resentment. In fact, in retrospect she viewed the motivations of those freedom volunteers with a measure of disdain as some kind of ego trip, or at least feared that they were more concerned with their own problems than with the problems of those they presumed to help.

Source: Transcript of tape-recorded interview with Linda Jenkins by Robert Wright, at Indianola, Mississippi, July 13, 1969, pp. 1-3; compiled by the Civil Rights Documentation Project. The transcript is located in the Ralph J. Bunche Oral History Collection, Moorland-Spingarn Research Center, Howard University, and is used with the permission of the acting director of the center.

WRIGHT: Linny do you know—remember when the movement first started in Indianola?

JENKINS: Well, when it first started I wasn't there for about three months afterwards. I came in about December.

WRIGHT: What year?

JENKINS: 64. And things were going, you know, good here. It was a lot of our state people working and everybody had confidence—really that's what happened. Most of the people had too much confidence in the staff workers.

They didn't have confidence in themselves they just had it in the staff workers only.

WRIGHT: Now, your sister Eunice, made some criticisms about the students that came down here. She said they were trying to work out their own hang-ups. What was your opinion?

JENKINS: I'll say about three or four that was here knew what they were doing.

WRIGHT: Only about four? Three or four?

JENKINS: Yeah. And the others were just around. Maybe they was lost. Or I would say, maybe they weren't accepted at home and thought they would come somewhere and be accepted. Or they didn't shine, you know. When they got here they were somebody important. And when they were at home they weren't important; so they would come here. And really, I don't think a lot of them really know what purpose they were here for. You know, they were just here saying, well, we gonna help the black poor people and that's it.

WRIGHT: So you think this was a detriment to the movement here?

JENKINS: It hurt, because a lot of them came in. They were here long enough to get the people's confidence. Then you notice being in the South, that if you white a lot of Negroes gonna believe you or they gonna take your word. So they were believing these people; they disappoint them and then they left. And now these people are still left out there, you know. You can't get their confidence anymore because these students left them. They had a lot of faith. At least, they had too much faith in them, you know.

WRIGHT: Are you saying they shouldn't have come at all? Or they didn't organize correctly when they were here, so that people would be prepared to take over when they left?

JENKINS: I'm saying they should have came with a different attitude. They should have organized things different while they was here. Ok, while they was here, it was only two local people on SNCC's staff, Otis Brown and myself. Everybody else was from out of town. Well see, I think they should have let more people from here took part on the staff, you know; let them know what was going on in the office. And they would have been just out to help give us outside information. But instead they played the important role. So when they left, the thing was hungup. There was Otis and myself and maybe one or two more, that only knew what was happening when these people left.

49 A Cleansing, Revolutionary Laugh

The civil rights coalition, which was already crumbling, began to fall apart even more in 1965. One signal development indicated the change in direction of black America. In the summer of 1965 a riot erupted in Watts, an area of Los Angeles, that attracted national attention for its violence, tenacity, and boldness. The disillusionment with the opportunities for either cultural or individual fulfillment in a white dominated society and with leaders who urged peaceful protest and gradual change grew to explosive proportions. Indeed, the guerrilla activities in the city bore a striking resemblance to those in Vietnam—with a similar legitimation. The violence may have been, in other words, not just a protest of the conditions of existence in urban areas like Watts, but a rejection of the social system itself, including its reformist channels and potentials. While whites reacted to the rioting with feelings that ranged from disbelief or masochistic satisfaction among those who had espoused the cause of civil rights, to calls for race war or pride in seeing a prophecy fulfilled by those who had long been insensitive to the problems of the black population, blacks themselves were divided in their responses to the phenomenon of urban rioting. Some, the more conservative, saw this as a definite setback and loss of consensual legitimacy for blacks; it would be that much more difficult to secure equality if blacks were identified with violence and disorder. Others, like Eldridge Cleaver, who was then serving time at Folsom Prison, saw a different significance. Viewing the ghetto as the modern extension of slavery, this rioting was in fact a revolutionary act with all the legitimacy of a slave revolt. But it was even more because it contained in it a newfound sense of pride and liberation. The political efficacy of passive resistance aside, the psychology of sitting and waiting for *others* to change the situation of your own existence could only be a self-abnegating experience.

To act instead of being acted upon could hence be liberating. Cleaver effectively captures this significant insight in the following passage.

Source: Eldridge Cleaver, *Soul on Ice* (New York, 1968), 37-38.

Folsom Prison
August 16, 1965

As we left the Mess Hall Sunday morning and milled around in the prison yard, after four days of abortive uprising in Watts, a group of low riders from Watts assembled on the basketball court. They were wearing jubilant, triumphant smiles, animated by a vicarious spirit by which they, too, were in the thick of the uprising taking place hundreds of miles away to the south in the Watts ghetto.

"Man," said one, "what they doing out there? Break it down for me, Baby."

They slapped each other's outstretched palms in a cool salute and burst out laughing with joy.

"Home boy, them Brothers is taking care of Business!" shrieked another ecstatically.

Then one low rider, stepping into the center of the circle formed by the others, rared back on his legs and swaggered, hunching his belt up with his forearms as he'd seen James Cagney and George Raft do in too many gangster movies. I joined the circle. Sensing a creative moment in the offing, we all got very quiet, very still, and others passing by joined the circle and did likewise.

"Baby," he said, "They walking in fours and kicking in doors; dropping Reds and busting heads; drinking wine and committing crime, shooting and looting; high-siding and low-riding, setting fires and slashing tires; turning over cars and burning down bars; making Parker mad and making me glad; putting an end to that 'go slow' crap and putting sweet Watts on the map—my black ass is in Folsom this morning but my black heart is in Watts!" Tears of joy were rolling from his eyes.

It was a cleansing, revolutionary laugh we all shared, something we have not often had occasion for.

50 Something Bigger Than Us

While the arena in which the struggle for racial equality was being waged changed from the South to the urban areas of the North and West, changes were still coming to that area that had been the initial focus of the civil rights movement. In many ways the triumph of desegregation in the public accommodations of the South represented a hollow victory as the discontent elsewhere suggested, but the change was nonetheless momentous for those involved. The following account of a Georgia storekeeper in 1965 indicates some of this. This man, who ran a drugstore, had resisted efforts at desegregation successfully until the Civil Rights Act of 1964 forced a change. The following year he admitted blacks. In this account, which he provided psychologist Robert Coles, it is clear that while the victory may have been limited, or even empty, the defeat was hard to take.

Source: Robert Coles, *Children of Crisis: A Study of Courage and Fear* (Boston, 1964), pp. 287-88.

"When I saw them come in I shuddered again, just like before. They weren't the same nigras, and I thought they might get tough or violent. But they didn't. They just moved in on those counter chairs and asked for coffee. My countergirl looked scared, and confused. She turned to me and asked me with a look what she should do. I didn't say a word. I just nodded to her. She knew what I meant. She started pouring. They didn't seem to want to stay long. They drank a bit, then they got up and left. The three white people at the counter just sat there. They had stopped drinking their coffee out of curiosity. We all looked at one another, then one of the customers said to me: 'A store is a store, I guess; and you have to serve whatever walks in from the street.'

"That wasn't the way he talked last year, I remember. But it wasn't the way I did either. It's changing down here, that's what's happening, and the man in the street, he has to keep up with it, even if he doesn't always go along with it. I suppose that comes later, agreeing with what's already happened. some of my friends say that if we had fought this battle harder, the integration people never would have won. I tell them that we did fight once, and lost. No one ever let us vote on this. We're all segregationists, the white people of Georgia; or most of us are. But we've got caught up in something that's bigger than us, and we've got to live with it, the way I see it. There's no choice. When I say that to them, they agree with me, no matter how much they talk of killing every nigger in sight, so I guess most people make their peace with things as they are."

51 La Plus Ça Change ...

The white store owner and his white customers may have felt defeat in the process of desegregation, but the black population was not universally victorious in even this limited area. For many of them the circumstances of life had not changed demonstrably. The noted black writer Louis Lomax returned to his native town of Valdosta, Georgia, and published his account of the changes that had come about since he left to make his way in the wider world. He perceptively observed, on the one hand, how much things remained the same for the masses of blacks in the South and, on the other hand, how it was mainly the black bourgeoisie that benefited from changes in race relations.

Source: Louis E. Lomax, "Georgia Boy Goes Home," *Harper's*, 230 (April 1965): 157, 158.

I found no tension whatsoever in the Valdosta Negro community. The Negro masses undulate along the streets, oblivious to what is going on in the Congo, in Red China, or in Mississippi. The county hospital has been completely integrated, and the authorities have shut down the old back entrance marked "colored." Yet despite the fact that the leaders have told local Negroes to use the front door, one witnesses the pathetic spectacle of their going to the same place to find a back way in. What mainly struck me is that there are more of them, and that they are growing in geometric proportions. They are the citizens of "Niggertown," the habitués of juke joints, of pig-foot alley and crumbling shanties. Their children pour into school, only to drop out. Talking with these dropouts one comes away knowing that they never really dropped in. They don't know anything; they can't do anything. Here, among the black masses, is the greatest monument to my town's—the South's—wickedness. It is a society which continues to grind out hundreds, thousands, millions who are totally defeated, who are alienated from that society from the day they are born.

* * *

Meanwhile, the Valdosta black bourgeoisie are becoming more and more comfortable, their world more and more secure. They are the ones who can afford to dress up and go out for dinner once a week to a previously "white only" restaurant, who can travel during their vacations and take advantage of the integrated motels, hotels, and travel facilities. Yet few of them have actually contributed to the Negro revolution that has made these things possible. The Valdosta black bourgeoisie are largely schoolteachers. Despite their new freedom, they must plod away in schoolrooms that are still separate and unequal; they must keep quiet about integration or be fired.

52 The War on Poverty: Rhode Island

The battle against racial discrimination seemed to take a new form and, to many, to actually reach the core of the problem when President Johnson secured enactment of his programs designed to wage a war on poverty. The legislative and administrative effort was large indeed and the ostensible goal laudable. The "war" was to be waged by retraining impoverished people to enable them to qualify for employment in particular skills, to increase black and poor participation in the decision-making process through community action programs, and to tackle fundamental problems in the American welfare system. Yet for all the bluster, the problem of poverty remained unsolved in the United States, and the programs themselves were subject to serious criticism. Not the least of the problems in the waging of this "war" was that the enemy, poverty, was never adequately defined. Instead of focusing on the maldistribution of wealth, the essence of poverty itself, the administration directed its attention at procedural areas. As Theodore Lowi has pointed out, the administration deemed the problem of poverty to be mainly the result of inadequate participation in the decision-making process (instead of perhaps the cause of such inadequate participation) because of weak organization in the poorer parts of society. Therefore, new organizations were encouraged (under the Community Action Program) and poor people were encouraged to help themselves in the competition for limited federal largesse. The result of the action can be seen partly in the testimony offered below in congressional hearings on the War on Poverty in 1967. The bureaucratic expansion and confusion was visible to virtually any observer. The creation of jobs in the program itself formed a major component of the war's effort. The competition for power in the program emerged often and the resultant bitterness was understandable since the efforts often perpetuated a form of paternalism that placed the poorest of the poor in the lowest positions and therefore assigned them the least power and influence in an effort designed to fight poverty. It further weakened the power of blacks and the poor generally by stimulating the fratricide and power jockeying common to a fragmented community. In this, a complete application of the principles of modernization, the victory in the war may have been most evident. The victory came not so much in the elimination of poverty but in the defusing of the radical critique offered by blacks and poor people alike. And the victory came without touching the central problem: the maldistribution of wealth and power in the nation.

Source: *Examination of the War on Poverty*. Hearings before the Subcommittee on Employment, Manpower, and Poverty of the Committee on Labor and Public Welfare, United States Senate, Part 5, Providence, Rhode Island, May 1, 1967, pp. 1965-68.

[STATEMENT OF MRS. MADELINE McCARREN, PROVIDENCE, R.I.]

Now, the programs, the training programs, the concept of these programs was to help the people to become self-sustained, to help people reactivate old skills and learn new skills and the primary goal was that these people would gain the self-respect that is due them. This has not been accomplished in any area that I have seen. The parent aids in the schools, the only thing they do or don't do that they have to at home is to change diapers and wash dishes. I haven't seen any programs that help these people to go out in the technical fields. I haven't seen any that learned machining, typing or a business course. If it is necessary to pay them and train them, pay them. I find that when a position pays a salary of $5,000, the poverty criteria is so that the job specifications change to suit the person, not the job. People in the program drive around in blue Jaguars registered in Vermont. Are they committed to poverty? I think its downing the name of poverty."

SENATOR PELL: In reply to the new Jaguars—

MRS McCARREN: There are two.

SENATOR PELL: What are their names?

MRS. McCARREN: Well, they are better able to speak for themselves. I think they are here.

SENATOR PELL: What are their names?

MRS. McCARREN: Mr. James Manson with a salary of $10,000 and the other one is Sandra Rich.

SENATOR PELL: Are they both driving Jaguars registered in Vermont?

MRS. McCARREN: That is correct, as of last week.

VOICE FROM THE AUDIENCE: That is incorrect. My car is registered in Rhode Island.

MRS. McCARREN: Well, you must have just done it because you knew I was going to say it. Now, I am also a member of the Personnel Committee. I don't think that anyone can ask me what my politics are, but I will say I most certainly voted under the star. I, as a member of the personnel committee, pointed to a name on the staff that was included in the organization and changing of it. I was told that although we were given raises for reorganization and change of title that this person was not included and would not be. I was told that person would be finished if I continued to press for this person's change of salary. My notes, in several instances, do not remotely resemble the meeting unless I fell asleep at the meeting. Now, that was tabled too. I would now like to answer Mr. Freeman Soares, he spoke about the policymaking positions. I really think he is holding a policymaking position. Mrs. Patterson is one person that he spoke about. Mrs. Patterson was chosen by advisory committee, six out of nine, not Progress for Providence, and I might say that I was instrumental in doing this because I felt she was a neighborhood person capable of filling that position as an interim appointment and I called the chairman of the committee and suggested if they felt this way they should hold a meeting and vote. This is how Mrs. Patterson got the position, certainly not any patronage through Progress for Providence. That is the end of my short note. Thank you.

53 The War on Poverty: Mississippi

The issues surrounding the efforts of the War on Poverty remained similar, whether in the urban Northeast or the rural South. The following testimony, taken in Jackson, Mississippi, paralleled that given in other areas. The competition between different branches of the program, such as the Mississippi Action for Progress, the Child Development Group of Mississippi, the Community Action Projects, Project HEADSTART, and other agencies, occupied much of the attention of the committee conducting the hearings. Often those testifying before the committee would point to the injustices done to the group they represented, complaining that they were being shorted funding which they saw going to other groups; that they lacked administrative support which went to other groups; or even that other groups were moving in on their territory. The testimony of Mrs. Unita Blackwell from Issaquena County was, however, particularly pointed in its probing of the larger problems confronting the effort at uplift. Her testimony, and the following testimony by Mrs. Fannie Lou Hamer (whose name was consistently recorded in the hearings as Hammer) of Sunflower County, a nationally known leader of the Mississippi Freedom Democratic Party, indicated that the weaknesses of the war were fundamental. Among the problems noted were the competition between food stamps and commodity programs (earlier testimony had in fact produced substantial arguments in favor of, and in opposition to, each program); the need for genuine local participation; the oft voiced lament that welfare, at least in the form in which it was encountered, destroyed dignity; the humiliation and frustration of bureaucratic demands on local operations; and the observation that sometimes the War on Poverty programs were simply doing work that the county government should be assuming responsibility for.

Source: *Examination of the War on Poverty*. Hearings before the Subcommittee on Employment, Manpower, and Poverty of the Committee on Labor and Public Welfare, United States Senate, Part 2, Jackson, Mississippi, April 10, 1967, pp. 592-95.

SENATOR KENNEDY OF NEW YORK: Do you think that the poverty program is accomplishing its objective and if not how can it be improved?

MRS. BLACKWELL: Well, I think it has done a great deal to help people, to understand that there is something they can do for themselves. I still think folks have to be made to feel and they do feel since this program has started that they can do something to help themselves. This is very important. We need more money in the State to strengthen the program. We need to strengthen the program. We have got to have, we just must have participation on the local level and I am not talking about the local level of the same power structure, what I call power structure of the plantation owners and board of supervisors who have kept us in this bad shape all the time. It has to be people that is involved themselves in the program, the recipients of the program. Also the people who have tried to stand up and talk to people and tell them what their rights are, these kind of people must be down at the bottom making some decisions for themselves. I think one of the weaknesses of the program, going back now to qualifications, I am worried about what these qualifications are because now we've got some forms to fill out that come down from OEO and I'm telling you the truth it takes a lawyer to go over it and fill out the application. These kind of things something has to be done about. I also think what could be done in the program that we put more money into training people, and if we do have people with administrative ability, people can be trained into those abilities. I found out folks can be trained, really trained, to do a lot of things, and here's one sitting here. I used to chop cotton and pick it, and I have come a long ways.

SENATOR KENNEDY OF NEW YORK: Thank you. I don't want to take any more of my colleague's time.

SENATOR CLARK: Senator Javits?

SENATOR JAVITS: I would like to address a question to the panel and then let whoever desires to answer it. Which of the programs do you consider the most important, bearing in mind that we can't get everything in terms of practicality and money in the Congress; do you consider the Headstart program, that is the program for very young children, the most important, or is there some other priority that anyone would like to suggest?

MRS. HAMMER: I think, Senator Javits, that the Headstart program is one of the most important factors in Mississippi now, because not only does it give the children a headstart but also it will give the adults a headstart.

SENATOR JAVITS: And may I point out that it right now gets a very large part of the funds which are available here, very much more than, for example, the training of adults through adult basic education. I gather that it's general agreement—would anyone on the panel dissent from the idea that starting with the youngest children is really the highest priority in the program?

SENATOR CLARK: I want to suggest some of you people, I have no views myself, might disagree with that, who would feel that the STAR program, adult literacy, and some of these other programs which tend to upgrade the work opportunity and job opportunity of older people might have an equally high priority, but I don't know whether you think that or not. Does anybody want to respond to that?

MRS. HAMMER: Senator Clark, I would like to speak to the adult education that has been conducted again in Sunflower County. Some of the people that have attended the adult school there—I don't know anything about STAR because STAR works in the city and the rural area is without that kind of program but I think it would be beneficial.

SENATOR CLARK: How about the neighborhood youth corps?

MRS. HAMMER: Well, I don't know too much about that other than I did see a lot of kids out on the highway with corns in their hands for cutting grass and doing the things that the board of supervisors should have had done by the county.

SENATOR JAVITS: I gather, then, unless somebody demurs, that there is general agreement, in view of the tremendous load of woe which has been carried here for so many tens of years, that it is best to give the highest priority to the very young.

54 Victory in the War on Poverty

The War on Poverty generated a number of changes, many of them substantial improvements in the circumstances of black people, but it also made other changes that much more difficult to achieve. By pitting blacks against blacks, poor against poor, many previously united communities began the process of disintegration, and cooperation sometimes became that much more difficult. By offering new material accomplishments, and by offering and making available more money to the black community, the single most visible end product of racial discrimination was not eliminated, but its severity was sometimes reduced. The result often proved to be a fading, or at least a reformulation, of the activism evident in previous years. The following assessment of this impact is offered by Linda Jenkins, a former SNCC worker and native Mississippian, in 1969. The Mississippi Freedom Democratic Party, which itself served as an institutional testament both to the betrayal of blacks by the white liberals in Lyndon Johnson's Democratic Party and to the ascendancy of blacks to domination of their own movement, was now effectively dead. That effort fell victim to the forces unleashed by the reforms of the Great Society.

Source: Transcript of tape-recorded interview with Linda Jenkins by Robert Wright, at Indianola, Mississippi, July 13, 1969, pp. ll-12; compiled by the Civil Rights Documentation Project. The transcript is located in the Ralph J. Bunche Oral History Collection, Moorland-Spingarn Research Center, Howard University, and is used with the permission of the acting director of the center.

JENKINS: I think the MFDP is dead in this county at the present time. They are trying to get another kick-off; to get it going. But right now it's not very active. Like they say, when the poverty program came in, a lot of people that had been active was out for the dollar. They lost interest in everything except the dollar. And this was the thing.

WRIGHT: So you think the poverty program killed the MFDP? Or did people stop participating?

JENKINS: It didn't kill it. I will say it played a great part. You know how people are, money is attractive. These people never had any money before. Maybe some people, all they ever had was going in the field making $15.00 a week or either working in a white woman's kitchen for $15.00 a week. But when the poverty program came along, you just think, now he could get him a job making $90.00 a week. You know, everything was taboo except the program and his dollars. So MFDP died. So many people just pulled off and left it.

55 Redefining the Problem of Racial Equality

Aside from the immediate impact of government programs, the course of the black population in America had shifted direction and had achieved a certain momentum of its own by the mid and late sixties. The following interview with Ancusto Butler, a leader of three black activist organizations in Cleveland, Job Seekers, Freedom Fighters, and United Freedom Movement, reveals some of the contours of this redefined black movement. Indeed, the circumstances in Cleveland, with its large, concentrated black population, a history of racial friction, and the presence of a variety of heavy industries, typified the plight of blacks in modern America in many ways. Accordingly, the views expressed by Butler, and his observations about his fellow black people in the ghetto, go well beyond the goals set by the civil rights activists a decade before or even sooner, and in fact are sometimes explicitly hostile to the continued efforts (or lack thereof) of organizations like the NAACP, the Urban League, and even the Southern Christian Leadership Conference. Those groups appeared to be inadequate partly for their reluctance to enter into the issues many blacks saw as immediate and meaningful. More relevant was the rhetoric of Black Power advocates like Stokely Carmichael and H. Rap Brown. Integration was not the goal it once had been; according to Butler, it was even a problem for blacks, as exemplified in the white rush to the lurid attractions of the black community at night. Education, something almost sacred to generations of earlier activists, appeared almost suspect because of white domination of the educational process and its tendency to mitigate race pride or encourage race shame by the propagation of white styles of life and dress. The wearing of the hair could even betray one as an enemy to his people or reveal one's pride in his race. The issues that mattered were jobs, poverty, medical care, and homes. Throughout, the needs of the black people seemed to be dignity and economic independence, goals that ran counter to the efforts of the best intentioned of the white friends of the blacks as well as their most ardent antagonists. One final shrewd observation made by Butler is especially relevant since it not only confirmed the tendencies of the past, but possibly offered a prophetic warning for the future: personal gain would always be the nemesis of the effort to secure racial equality.

Source: Transcript of tape-recorded interview with Ancusto Butler by John Britton, at Cleveland, Ohio, November 14, 1967, pp. 10-ll, 20-26, 34, 38-39, 44; compiled by the Civil Rights Documentation Project. The transcript is located in the Ralph J. Bunche Oral History Collection, Moorland-Spingarn Research Center, Howard University, and is used with the kind permission of the acting director of the center.

BRITTON: What are negotiating sessions like with these companies that really don't want to come in. For instance, you mentioned Procter & Gamble. When you negotiate with these people what are some of the things that are said in these meetings, the give and take?

BUTLER: Well these meetings get very hot under the collar, and not only under the collar you feel like sometimes sitting in on these meetings, getting up throwing blow for blow. Some of these fellows can come out with some of the weirdest ideas, they can come out with the story that we just can't find no Negroes qualified, or no Negroes apply, when we know sometimes before we even hold a meeting with this company, we will send at least ten qualified Negroes to this company to apply for jobs. Then at the meeting we ask them to—could we see those applications. We know so-and-so has been here at a certain time, Miss so-and-so was here at a certain time. Then they start to squirm. Well those applications we don't keep those on file, we renew our file every so often. They come up with some of the most horrible things that you've ever heard in your life, in these meetings.

BRITTON: Well how do you counter their arguments?

BUTLER: Well the only thing, we make it plain to them. We don't go in to threaten them, either you do or you don't. It's just that simple. We're not going to beg you for anything. It's one thing that the white man is going to have to get up off of, and I'm not Rap Brown, and I'm not Stokely Carmichael. But, God knows this is true, the white man for years and years and hundreds of years, has always put the Negro in a position the minute he get up and put on his shoes in the morning, he's got to prove himself until the day he lays down and dies, he's got to prove himself. This is something that the white community is going to have to get away from. This Negro has got to prove himself. This is what they want you to do, prove yourself all the time. I can't buy that philosophy any more and I won't accept it.

* * *

BRITTON: What has been your relationship, and the relationship of your relatively new civil rights organization to the old organizations like the Urban League and the NAACP, what has been the relationship between you and them?

BUTLER: Well I feel this way, I try not to criticize any organization, and I don't publicly, but privately I give them hell. Because there are so many things that each organization could do. Some of the older organizations, I know they got this go slow tactic I don't believe in going slow because every Sunday morning, I see the dogs, the cats, the bears, and the mice that's on television, and yet, there is no Negro that I know of that has a nationwide television show. This bugs me in my own livingroom. So I don't believe in go slow policies, but some of these older organizations do. This is why I give them hell when I get in a meeting with these people or even run up on one of the leaders in the street. What are you doing to support us in this particular issue? Now you have your own ideas, I'm not going to try to change your basic philosophy, but something, if it's no more than criticize me publicly, do something. But apparently, some of the older organizations, they're tied by the apron strings or the city's former administration downtown.

BRITTON: What about the churches, I know in the South the churches were the backbone of the civil rights movement there. In a big city like Cleveland, were the churches of any help to your particular organization?

BUTLER: A lot of various churches have given its support. But let's face it, there's five big churches in the city of Cleveland has done nothing period. Nothing period. And I'm not biased or prejudiced when I use that word. They have done nothing period.

BRITTON: You're speaking of the five largest Negro churches?

BUTLER: That's right.

BRITTON: Let's go back to last year just recently, the whole world has read by now of the rebellion, the riot here in Cleveland. Were you in the streets those nights?

BUTLER: I was in the middle of the riot. I watched kids, 10 and 12, maybe 15 years old tell the cops to shoot me whitey, you so-and-so, I have nothing to live for anyway. Shoot me. I've seen those kids throw firebombs. I've seen those kids walk out in front of machine guns. You didn't see this on television, you didn't read about this. But, I seen this with my own two eyes. I don't know myself what the Negroes are thinking in the city of Cleveland, and I do know this, during the riot, I have seen some of the most brazen Negroes, that I have ever seen in my life in a street fight. I've seen them brave in the eyes of a cop with machine guns, billy clubs, shotguns, they wasn't afraid.

Now I don't know what the city of Cleveland is coming to, unless the white people take a different outlook on life insofar as the Negro life, there is no life. Like when you go into these old buildings in the Huff area, where the riots started at, you see this nasty four-letter word, which some people would say nasty. But to me all these kids is doing is expressing themselves. Feed us colored kids. This is what they're saying, but some people perhaps would look at that as a nasty word when it's wrote in the four-letter term. But to me that's what it means. Now these kids they're out in the streets, some of these kids didn't have clothes and shoes. But when the riot came, they got these clothes and shoes and food. I would say in the city of Cleveland there are some awful brave black people here.

BRITTON: Can you perceive that there has been any difference in attitudes among whites since the riot. I mean are they treating Negro people any differently now than they were before the riots?

BUTLER: They ain't treating you too much different, but let's put it this way, they have a more of a cunning way of doing things. They don't talk out and say hey boy, hey you, it's Mr. now because Charlie don't want his business wiped out, let's face it. And you see these kids, just about any kids on the street now, knows how to make a bomb. How they learned it, I don't know, but they do know how to make a bomb.

BRITTON: So then you're saying really, that the looting that took place and so forth was not just kids out for a lark, they were out for necessity.

BUTLER: No, some of these kids actually needed food, clothing, this I do know. And some of these kids that were out there in the street, they didn't care if they lived or died. And the riot in the city of Cleveland was caused by white individuals that had this nigger attitude, go to hell so-and-so, you're no good, you'll either be a boy or I'll kill you. This is the attitude of so many whites in this city. And it was all created by our former administration at city hall.

BRITTON: During that riot, several people were killed, do you, of your own knowledge, know what has happened to the families of these men, their wives and their children?

BUTLER: Well, Mrs. Tony, she is living at the present on two hundred and some dollars a month. Five boys left. Her husband was gunned down on Euclid Avenue right off Euclid. This particular family is existing today, there was another family that was shot up. They were a young couple, that was shot up for no reason at all, none whatsoever. But the policemen you see, they're trigger happy, anything black they're ready to shoot, shoot, and the city administration is the blame for this because they set up this kind of document at city hall. A nigger is no more than a dog, perhaps less, because after all they do have their fancy dog sitting up on the car seats and everything. They feed these dogs, they give them the best medical care, but here we have all these Negro kids that needs care, they don't get it because the city administration will not provide, so I would say that these families that have been hurt by the riots are just existing.

BRITTON: Does Mrs. Tony Foster live on welfare now.

BUTLER: Mrs. Tony will not receive welfare, she will not accept it. Mrs. Tony lives on her dead husband's social security. This is the sole way—this is the only income that she has, let's put it that way.

BRITTON: Do you have any idea what happened to the guys who were arrested during this rioting, overall could you take a stab at telling us whether they were put in jail, under the jail, or what?

BUTLER: Well, some of them—they would like to put them under the jail. Some of them were arrested, some of them were cleared, some of them received a little time, because there's always got to be some guinea pigs. You got to blame the riot on somebody. They wanted to blame it on the Communists, they wanted to blame it on Lewis Robinson, they wanted to blame it on so many different Negroes. But when it comes down to the final analysis they could not because the court must follow a guide line, and by following that guide line they had to clear most of these people.

* * *

BRITTON: If it came to a choice, if the people in the ghetto had to make a choice who they would follow tomorrow morning to solve the problems they have, based upon your contact, would you say that they would be Rap Brown and Stokely, or would they follow Martin Luther King, or would they follow Roy Wilkins?

BUTLER: Rap Brown, all the way Rap—and Stokely, that's right. The reason why I say they would follow those men is because, the broken promises, the failure of the power structure to meet these people's needs.

* * *

BUTLER: This is something that I think we should emphasize a little right here. Most of your Negro athletes, they are very informed people, they're not stupid. You'll find most of your rock and roll entertainers, when you see these fellows with their hair slicked down all on their head and they're all slicked up—their hair. Now these people, in my way of thinking, is not truly what you would call a black man. Because he's ashamed of his nappy hair, he's ashamed of being a black person, he don't want to be a black person he can't be white, so what is he. But you'll find most of your jazz musicians, most of your athletics in the black field, and the black people, you'll find that they don't dress like this. They don't have their hair all did up like a lady or something. You'll find that these people are very informed, and just be looking at a Negro by the way his hair is, it tells me something. That this man cares about his people. And, you'll find this with mostly all of your Negro athletes.

BRITTON: Tell me, among the people you have contact with in the ghetto area, and you yourself, do you find that integration with the standard definition of Negroes trying to break into white society, do you find that integration is still the goal of people in these areas? Are they more influenced by the theory that says regroup in you own community and come out powerful?

BUTLER: Now, first of all, let's emphasize on one thing. Now this is something that might be changed, several discothesques just a bit, but at night—at night and I want to say this very clearly, at night, there is total integration in the ghetto areas; at night total integration. The white man comes down off the hill at night to pick up my women at night. He pays their price, at night. Now it's hard for a black man to even talk to a Negro lady in the ghetto areas at night. But when daylight comes, this white man cannot stand a Negro person, but as soon as the sun goes down, it's total integration in the city of Cleveland. Integrated by night and day time hate. That's the way we live in the city of Cleveland. Now so far as integration, we have that at night, we don't need any more integration, we need jobs and homes for people to live in. We need more medical care for the ladies that don't have husbands, and I'm very concerned about this.

* * *

BUTLER: Do you realize what the NAACP, the Urban League, and a few of these other large organizations that have financial power, do you realize what they could do if we could all unite and fight together? Do you realize what we could really do for our people? But it's always the type of man, you'll always find this type of man in any organization. Apparently, sometimes they think more of themselves than they do of the people. They can only see personal gain in so many things. This is what has held us down so much. And the word when you become educated, it seems to me like they're—the higher educated Negro, seems to me like he thinks more like a white man, really than a white man is. And why I don't know. I guess this is what an education is, you think like a white man.

56 A Community of Their Own

The assassination in April 1968 of Martin Luther King, the most noted black leader of the civil rights effort and the proponent of a gospel of nonviolence, triggered a new wave of unrest in the black community. Blacks in city after city took to the streets, and the burning and looting of major cities was under way. To many people who thought significant progress had been made since the days of Watts, this phenomenon came as a complete shock. Many black leaders as well as white spokesmen derided it for its violence and potential of alienating even more whites. The administration of President Lyndon Johnson reacted with disbelief; after all, studies had already been done of previous instances of "civil disorders" in the nation; programs had been enacted; and if there was white culpability here it was in large measure that of the governing bodies of the cities, which had not developed the appropriate crisis management techniques and ways of mollifying the anger of blacks in their ghettoes. And to many this seemed an inappropriate way of expressing disapproval of the assassination of a spokesman for nonviolence.

Yet the rampage was intense and met with considerable support within those ghetto populations that witnessed the destruction. The following interview with one of the rioters in the Washington, D.C., riot in April 1968 makes more comprehensible exactly what was happening in the smoke and dark of the night. The looting often took large dimensions and was something that the news media especially focused upon. Yet in this interview it is readily apparent that the looting had real limits, and that it was often highly selective in the target stores and in the goods being taken. This anonymous person admits to having looted a sponge. While it would be an overstatement to suggest that all or even most of the participants in the looting were similarly motivated, clearly a different set of values than what many people were accustomed to recognizing in society was evident, namely the priority given utility over profit. That is only part of the explanation of the course of developments in these urban riots. Many were taking what they in fact needed.

This blended with another phenomenon, namely the ascendancy of a new militance—not by black leaders, most of whom pleaded with the rioters to stop the destruction, but by the black people themselves. Two aspects of this militance are revealed in this interview. First, the actual circumstances that produced the turmoil go far in helping to explain the militance. The death of King suggested to many that the main reward for working for change nonviolently through the existing system, a system already much tainted by unresponsiveness or tokenism, was an early grave. Militance seemed entirely appropriate to them. Second, the opportunities created by the beginning of the rioting and the inability of city officials to cope with these problems demonstrated that militance had more satisfactory rewards. And those rewards were not simply material. New feelings of pride and of cooperation emerged spontaneously in ways that confirm many ideas on the psychology of resistance and liberation developed by Frantz Fanon. And throughout, one additional element seemed to have enormous significance. When this participant discussed the problems facing black people, he was careful to make a distinction between the symptoms of the problems— the living conditions they know in the ghetto—and the substance of the problems, the forces that create those conditions. In itself this perception came much closer to assessing the problem of racial equality than had any government agency, even in the most indirect way. The logic of it was clear: if living conditions were improved, but the forces that made some people continually vulnerable remained, the problems of modern America would remain unsolved. And that insight, perhaps more than the destruction of the institutions of oppression in the ghetto, signalled the true revolutionary nature of the uprisings.

Source: Transcript of tape-recorded interview with Anonymous Participant "A" in the riot in Washington, D.C., April 4-8, 1968, by James M. Mosby, in Washington, D.C., April 26, 1968, pp. 4-7, 9, 19-20, 21; compiled by the Civil Rights Documentation Project. The transcript is located in the Ralph J. Bunche Oral History Collection, Moorland-Spingarn Research Center, Howard University, and is used with the permission of the acting director of the center.

MOSBY: When you say mild looting, what do you mean?

A: Well, although I entered a number of stores that had been broken into, my looting was of the nature of taking things which I felt I could use or things I felt I wanted, rather than just taking that which was in sight. This didn't seem to be the attitude that most of the people had. They just went into the stores and took whatever happened to be available to them at the time. I guess I might call myself a rational looter. I went into the stores as though I was shopping.

MOSBY: Selecting.

A: Yes, selecting something which I could use. I remember watching some fellows go into Pep Boys. I was standing right there when the store was first broken into and a number of fellows had come out with tires and lawn mowers, air conditioners. I stood in front of the store and tried to think of what I could use. I went into the store and came out with a big sponge because I knew I needed something to wash the dishes with.

MOSBY: A sponge?

A: A sponge.

MOSBY: You mean you looted a fifteen cent sponge?

A: One sponge, not even two, just one.

MOSBY: Back up a little. What motivated you to loot?

A: What motivated me to loot?

MOSBY: Yes.

A: That's a rather difficult question to answer. I suppose there are a number of predisposing factors. Perhaps my attitude at that particular time, the feeling that Martin Luther King had been assassinated, an advocate of nonviolence and perhaps the best liaison between government and ghetto people or black people, a man who was preaching nonviolence but nevertheless met death as a result of an assassin's bullet, which is by no means nonviolent. This sort of thing seemed to bring up a hell of a lot of conflict and contradiction. It affected me in such a way that I felt, "Well gee, here's a man preaching nonviolence and nevertheless he was shot down. It seems as though I have no alternative but to take on some militant strives because nonviolence doesn't seem to be the answer."

MOSBY: This militancy that you're referring to is looting and burning?

A: Yes, that's one form of it.

MOSBY: I mean that's one form of militancy that you took part in?

A: Yes. Getting back to the question of what motivated me, that's part of it and also, I guess, the fact that there were a number of people out on the street, a considerable number, a crowd which was large enough to make the police department somewhat ineffective. The stores were accessible to go into.

MOSBY: You mean it was safe to loot?

A: No, it wasn't really safe. I at no time thought it was safe to loot. There was always the risk involved. But I felt that in view of the circumstances, the risk of perhaps being apprehended or penalized for the looting was small enough to chance going in and taking those things which I felt I could use. My attitude changed during the time in which the looting was going on. After seeing the people out on the street and listening to a lot of people talking, it aroused a certain feeling of militancy within me. I felt that for some reason or another this was the proper thing to do at that particular time—taking from the white merchants those things which I felt brothers had been denied of because of oppression and a number of other factors that have made difficult the success or liberation of the black man.

MOSBY: You said your attitude changed. To what? I don't understand.

A: My attitude changed from an attitude of complacency to one of militancy.

MOSBY: Do you still uphold this attitude today, or has it subsided with the riots?

A: Well, I think you might say that today my attitude is still somewhat militant. I don't think that it will ever change from being militant and go over into the area of being complacent. Even if the black man were given the rights that he should have, I still can't see where I will change and become a complacent individual.

* * *

A: I was cautious. I was what you might call a cautious looter and I was also—again using the term—mild. I was thinking on a small-term basis, just about things that I could use at that particular time. Another example of this is the fact that I'm more or less a heavy smoker. I spoke approximately a package of cigarettes a day. And that was the last item stealable—two or three packages of cigarettes. There were a number of cartons of cigarettes available, but I had only taken two or three packages.

MOSBY: It seems sort of strange. Why were you so moderate in looting?

A: I don't know. Perhaps because I'm a rather moderate person.

MOSBY: Did guilt play a part in it, do you think?

A: No, I can't say that there's any guilt involved at all.

MOSBY: Did you consider looting as something to do or consider it as a fight against they system—taking out revenge on the white man—or what?

A: I think it was a form of fighting the system by all means. I had hoped to see as many of the establishments go down as did go down. As a matter of fact, I advocated the burning of all the stores in the area, all of the grocery stores, delicatessens and liquor stores and other forms of business establishments that the ghetto area was saturated with.

* * *

A: Well, whenever a decision was made to hit a store, you would have a number within a certain group who would play certain roles. You'd have some people who would look out for the cops. You'd have other people who would further the break. You had other people who were going to go into the stores, and you had those who were just going to stand outside and watch and notify the people whenever the cops were coming.

MOSBY: You mean most of the people never knew one another before, probably had never seen one anothher before?

A: Right. And that was the extent of the organization.

* * *

MOSBY: So what is happening in the community today? How do people feel? What do you think the mood is?

A: I think for the most part the mood has been relaxed a bit. The people, of course, are not as tense now as they were during the time in which the looting and burning was taking place. But by the same token, the people are not complacent either. They feel that they have done something which they should have done quite some time ago, and now that it's been done that it's all over and forgotten. The people, I feel, could do the same thing again a week from now or ten months from now, simply because of the fact that the reason why this thing took place is something which is not just present within the community. It's not the fact that the people are living in run-down, rat-infested houses, but because of why they are living in these houses. And for the most part, they are still living under these conditions. They still can't get good jobs, and I don't mean jobs pushing a broom where they can make $65 or $70 a week. They want opportunities. They want the same opportunities that the whites have, and they don't have them. They don't have those opportunities.

* * *

MOSBY: Someone told me a couple days ago that during the rioting and looting, he felt that black people felt proud of what they were doing, that most felt, "This is my time to really get the white man, beat the system, and I like what I'm doing." How do you feel about this?

A: Well, the key word in that is pride and I've sensed the development of the great deal of pride in the Negroes in the area.

MOSBY: Because of the riots?

A: Because of the riots. I've noticed now that a lot of the brothers are walking around and speaking to one another and calling one another brother, and if there's anything that they can do to assist another brother, such as accommodating someone who has been burned out or sharing food or even in the case of goods that were looted, there's been a lot of trading going on. A fellow has pants in size 36 and he wears 32. He's been able to negotiate a trade with someone else who wears 36 and has 32.

Some pride has been elevated in Negroes. They feel that this is a way of letting the white man know that they really don't want him in the area, that they want to develop a community of their own involving their own people.

57 Where Do We Go from Here?

The following interview with another participant in the Washington riot in 1968 confirms some of the suggestions developed in the previous document. Especially significant is this person's understanding of the relationship of the riot to the life and death of Martin Luther King. But he also moves beyond that statement as he places greater emphasis on the attack directed at the symbols and institutions of oppression in the looting and arson during the riot. The object was to hit the system hard, so hard in fact that it would be difficult or impossible for the same institutions to return the ghetto to resume their exploitative practices. The arson is especially intriguing in this description not because it was novel or restricted to the conditions of urban life, but because it had always been an important method of redressing certain social grievances. Because it is a crime that destroys the evidence in its very commission, it is also an act that is very difficult to prove. The coordination of the arson efforts among people living in a particular area is what gives this action a modern significance and a revolutionary flavor. And once again, this participant points to the subtle relationship between violence and pride that has been noted before.

Of special import in this interview is the participant's tendency to overestimate the accomplishments of the riot and to underestimate the resilience of the power structure. He was quite confident that those institutions that were burned out would not be able to return unless they changed their policies dramatically, and that if they did not they would be burned out again. This was too much optimism. More significant and fateful, though, was his response to the question, Where do we go from here? Once the initiative had been gained by the people themselves, the tendency too often proved irresistible to pass it back to the "sociologists, social scientists, you know, the psychologists, the Urban League people, the Urban Redevelopment people, the government administrators, Congress." Since these were precisely the same people and agencies who in some measure bore responsibility for the circumstances leading up to the riot, this would prove to be an act of abdication.

Source: Transcript of tape-recorded interview with Anonymous Participant "B" in the Race Riot in Washington, D.C., April 4-6, 1968, by James Mosby, in Washington, D.C., April 24, 1968, pp. 8-9, ll-13, 15-19, 25-28; compiled by the Civil Rights Documentation Project. The transcript is located in the Ralph J. Bunche Oral History Collection, Moorland-Spingarn Research Center, Howard University, and is used with the permission of the acting director of the center.

A: Yes, I felt it was a chance I could be caught, and thinking this way I decided not to do anything. I didn't really see where it was to my advantage. We hadn't really thought about it. We had never thought, well if there's a riot, what are we going to do? You know, we had never really given it much consideration. So the first night, we didn't really take part in any looting, but we decided—as a matter of fact, at that point I had thought that I wouldn't do any looting, I wasn't too interested in looting although everyone could dig something free. But primarily what I was thinking about was burning some stores.

MOSBY: You wanted to burn instead of loot?

A: Right.

MOSBY: Why burn?

A: Why burn? Well, for two reasons. One, because if you hit the man in his pocketbook you really hurt him. And if you burn him . . . you see when you loot a store and maybe you destroy some windows and break up a few shelves and stuff, he can restock his store, he can raise his prices and boom, a lot of people are going to go right back there and let him continue to work them out.

MOSBY: Can't he rebuild if he was burned? Can't he just rebuild again?

A: It's possible to rebuild, but by the time he does rebuild, he would have realized a sizeable loss.

MOSBY: Did you do any burning this particular night?

A: Yes.

MOSBY: On the 4th?

A: Right.

* * *

MOSBY: Okay. Lets get back to burning. You stopped burning and started looting?

A: Well, no, it wasn't a question of really stopping burning. We burned, like I said because we wanted to really put the man out of business. We wanted to gut his store and get rid of him. It's as simple as that. Now the burning took place that night and its much easier to pull things off at night when you aren't seen.

You see, you have to realize that we were working from two . . . we had two things in mind when we were burning. There were two things that we had to consider. First of all, we had to look out for the cops, and secondly, we had to watch out for the people. Even though there was a lot of people who were taking part and there were many others who were watching, who were in sympathy. You can't really trust people, see. You can't be sure of what people are going to do or what they are going to say. A lot of people were worried that they didn't want us to burn one particular store because they lived next door to it, and they were afraid that we were going to burn their crib—by crib, I mean house—so we got a lot of static from them and plus . . . see these people around, they'll tell on you, they're afraid of authorities. First, as soon as they see a blue coat or a badge they get scared and before they know what they're saying, they're telling who you are and where you are, you know.

MOSBY: Did you burn this particular establishment that people were trying to keep you from burning?

A: Yes, well we were coming by Pep Boys and we reached in and took a couple of cans of turpentine, which is highly flammable and we brought it back here and we made some cocktails . . . we went down and we burned a store.

MOSBY: When you burned that store, did the fire spread to the living quarters of these black people?

A: No, but very . . . a very funny thing happened. There were three of us and we all went and we all had gallon jugs with varsol and turpentine and detergent in them and the rag which was soaked with the turpentine and varsol and we lit them. And I threw mine and the other guy threw his but the third guy, and he's the one who had done a lot of the talking to the people trying to reassure them that everything would be alright, his slipped off his hand and landed right on these people's front porch, and it started burning. But two things were fortunate. One, there were steps, a lot of steps and they went way up and when it hit, it started coming back down so that it was burning but the fire was not going toward the house and secondly, the whole establishment was brick, so that kept that from really burning too, because in order for something to have really gone down, the fire would have had to take place inside where there were objects that could burn.

But we split and we went back a few minutes later and explained to the people that it was a mistake and tried to get them to understand that we felt that there was no risk involved if we burned the store next to them. So we went back again about half an hour later—we made some more cocktails—and we went back again, and when we got back somebody had already started a small fire at the store. So we got close and fired our cocktails off and got the fire really going.

* * *

MOSBY: How did you feel about Dr. King before his death?

A: All right I dug King from the standpoint that I knew that he was working for us, black people, and I dug him as our most eloquent spokesman, and as a man who did get things done, maybe not always I wanted him to and maybe not always with the results I wanted but he did get things done. And for that, I dug him and for that, everybody who was in the street dug him. Maybe half the people out there really didn't agree with King or were not non-violent people, but the fact that he was killed, a lot of people have poo-pooed this thing about the riots being in the name of King. Well no one really said that it was in the name of King, not ... King was—you might say, the catalyst or the trigger— but this thing has been brewing for a long time, a long time and it wasn't just because King was killed, you see what I'm saying? It was because of the fact that all the other things piled up and then this, because people out in the street, you know people who have been fighting the man all their lives have had it tough. They're saying, "Well damn, if you'll off King then you'll off me in a minute because what have you got to lose offing me. If you can get away with offing King, then you can off me. I may as well get out of here and jam you up as quick as I can, because I'm pissed-off, you know."

You don't sit down and think and use logic and reasoning and rationale when a man is shot. You don't stop and think: well, boom, this will happen, that will happen, the law will take its course; there must be a reason. Everyone isn't like that, you can't . . . we aren't that cold, we're emotional as people. And its just like having someone in our family offed, really with most people by offing King. Like I said, everybody might not agree with him, I'm not non-violent myself. But King was definitely in touch with the people because he had changed his stand, he had become more militant and everyone could see this. And because of this and all the other things he had done for us, just about everybody dug him whether they agreed with him or not.

MOSBY: Well, did you feel in looting and burning that you would help honor the memory of Dr. King, or that you would disfigure that memory?

A: No, to tell you the truth, no one really stopped and thought about this at the time. I feel this way. I know I didn't. I can really only speak for myself. But I don't think anyone stopped and said, "Well now, what will this do to the Kings—the Kings of the future and the people who will take King's place in the present?" No one stopped and considered what the consequences could be in terms of how white America would approach it—any future Kings or those who would take his place—but afterward with all the rhetoric being ... revolving around this aspect as an aftermath of the riot, I thought about it and I tried to assess in my mind what would be the ... what kind of damage this . . . the riots would have done to say, a person like King or other people who would take his place and support the same principles. And it seems to me that really, really for those people who are interested—who are truly interested in furthering race relations and in furthering the rights of people in getting rid of ghettos and slums and uplifting people economically, socially, etc., it won't make a great deal of difference. It really won't. People who are looking for excuses, some of these phony liberals and these guiding the right-wing honkies who sit at home with their rifles and get worried that the rioting and looting might spread out their way, this is just an excuse for people to say, "Well, to hell with the black man because he doesn't honor anybody. He went out there and burned in the name of King and King was non-violent."

This is really to me, illogical. It's very illogical for the very fact that while King was non-violent these rioters do not have to be connected with King. They may have used King's name and I think that's all well and good if they did, because they were pissed-off that he was killed. But the fact is that while many people use King as an excuse to riot or he was a catalyst or trigger for rioting, these same right-wingers who're talking about this scarred his memory. These are the people that often use that as an excuse to stop whatever gains could possibly be made in the future as far as civil rights are concerned.

MOSBY: What do you feel that the riots did for the black community, the black people in the ghetto?

A: Well, in terms of intangibles, it engendered pride for one thing. Pride and dignity, its a peculiar type of pride or dignity that one gets from destroying property that belongs to the enemy, you know? And the white man is our enemy. It's as simple as that, you know.

This is a curious country because people in this country equate, for example— if I can get off the track just slightly to make a point. People in this country equate Communism with evil, not everyone, but you have that element. That right-wing element again, who equate communism with evil; the John Birchers, the Minutemen, these kind of people. Communism is evil, you dig. So they make that equation very simply and very easily. Anything connected with Communism is evil. That's why we're in Vietnam, to stop Communism and this kind of thing. You see what I'm saying? Well, okay, by the same token without going into details in this analogy, we equate the white man with evil and as the enemy. We see him very simply as the enemy, and so its a curious type of pride and really great feeling to be able to destroy anything that he is either symbolic of or representative in any kind of way.

MOSBY: Do you see any other way of fighting the system, a more effective way maybe?

A: Well let's put it this way, this is just a way of fighting. Violence isn't the only answer. Anyone who will stop and think about it and just be reasonably open-minded, know that violence isn't the only way, just like non-violence isn't the only way. But you'd be surprised at the number of doors that were opened up when people become violent, you know. People are pissed-off, people are tired of living the way they're living. They're tired of being kicked and trampled. See, you've got these people that always talk about the Negro has to work for what he gets. He had to bring himself up, just like we did, just like the Irish did, just like the Italians did; just like they did, just like I did, you know. But that's a lot of bull for one reason, all these people had a head start on us. When they came to this country they were able to right away start pursuing whatever goals they wanted. Even though they ran into discrimination—and I don't discount that for a moment—but they were able to start pursuing their goals right away, even though a lot of these people came and moved into the ghettos themselves, like the Irish or the Italians. You know they were crowded in segregated neighborhoods, but we were here 300 years before we had our chance and then after we got our chance, so to speak—it really wasn't a chance—but after we got, lets say freedom which was really nothing but a word at the time and maybe still is, when we got our chance we had so many things going against us. We had to have laws passed just to allow us to vote and if we're equal—a man down on 14th Street the other day said, "If we're so equal and if the white man looks upon us as just like himself, then why did we need these laws to vote, laws to go and eat at lunch counters. Why did we need a civil rights bill if we're so equal? Why do we need it? It should just be taken for granted that we automatically can have all the rights that the white man has."

* * *

MOSBY: You say they're better off now?

A: I think they'll be better off. I think that from where they'll go from here . . . hell, for one thing when a lot of these places are going to be rebuilt, they'll be rebuilt a hell of a lot nicer. And these people won't have to live in rat and roach infested cribs and where you got to be content with all kinds of garbage odors and this kind of thing, you know.

MOSBY: What changes would there really be if all owners returned to their burned out stores and they rebuilt them and they rebuilt the apartments above the stores?

A: Well, that's interesting and that's part of where do we go from here. Because for one thing if a lot of these store-owners try and move back here, they're going to be burnt back out. It's as simple as that, they're going to be burnt back out. That's all there is to it, they're going to be burnt down again—smashed, looted, burnt down.

Now the thing is this, there will be some white owners who will rebuild back here and they might manage to stay. But those who do are going to have to demonstrate two things to the community. One, that they're not trying to gyp the community—and by gyp I don't mean just like, for example, a store, here's a guy that builds a store and opens some apartments and his prices are . . . we realize, at least I realize—let's put it that way—their prices are going to be a little higher than Safeway, say, for example, or some chain stores, but the thing is this, he's going to have to demonstrate that he's not out to gyp people, that he's not out to just make his money and run back out to Prince Georges County and Montgomery County or wherever the cracker lives and sit back there and watch his TV and sit in his home and talk about how fair he is and how liberal he is. He's going to have to put some of that money into this community for whatever projects come up—block projects, block parties, and what-have-you, because the thing is he was here before we were. All the people who lived here, they moved out. They ran out, they didn't want to be bothered with niggers, so they ran out. So he stayed here and started cheating us and exploiting us and making money off us and then he ran out to Prince Georges County at night—every night— and put his money in his favorite home or his bank out there and sat back while this neighborhood continued to deteriorate.

So this is the problem as it's been going down, not to mention the gyp artist and the people who charge high prices for rotten meat and old food and all kinds of other crap that they try to pawn off on the blood of the neighborhood. And don't make any mistake about it, they tell you how fair they've been. That's a lot of bull, the majority of them are crooked. They try to beat you for anything they can. They underpay the blood that work for them and they cheat the bloods who are their customers.

MOSBY: I see. What do you think of. . .

A: Let me finish answering your question. First of all, you say where do we go from here. I really can't answer that. That's a question for sociologists, social scientists, you know, the psychologists, the Urban League people, the Urban Redevelopment people, the government administrators, Congress. All these different people, not just Congress, or not just the Urban League or S.C.L.C., but everyone has to get together as is universally recognized I'm sure, and initiate programs. I'm not talking about just big, elaborate crap that never comes off. I'm talking about real down to earth stuff that really gets to the people, you dig, and pull this thing off. See, Congress can jump up and pass a riot bill in six months, they can jump up and appropriate money and send a man to the moon. They can jump up and do anything they want, just like that. But when it comes to us, when it comes to us they jam us up, you dig it. Now over half the Senate is Democratic. Over half the Congress is Democratic, you dig it. And as Malcolm said, "That 's the party the black people backs", you dig it. We back. . .black people voted predominantly Democratic Senate and House in the last three elections. . .last two elections, for sure I know of, dig it. And we backed these people. We put them first; they put us last. They've been bull-shitting with this open housing crap for three or four years now. They've been bull-shitting with voting rights and civil rights. They finally passed that crap. Tokenism, that's all it was, so Goddam we should have been able to vote as soon as we were considered citizens.

The Malaise of Race and Society
in Modern America

58 A Total Disaffection

In the years immediately following the great hopes and monumental despair generated by the political system in 1968 and the persistent war in Vietnam, the vigorous protest that had been the province of militant blacks assumed a broader base as many whites, especially college and draft-age youths, began to feel the same frustration and alienation that previously had disaffected blacks. Indeed, it was the same party that had betrayed black activists through its paternalistic, bureaucratic, and modernizing proposals that now generated the broader discontent. The implications of this development were many. On the one hand, blacks now were no longer alone in their quest for justice in society, and their allies in the effort came not out of sympathy or condescension but out of similar experiences. While this could effectively spell the end of paternalism and give the protest a revolutionary potential, it could also erode the distinctiveness of black militance as race relations became submerged in a vast movement of protest against exploitative and alienating institutions and relations. While many whites, as the following personal account suggests, came to this movement after working in the civil rights movement, this was a far different kind of protest and the goals reached much deeper and broader into the whole system of power in the nation. Clearly one era was over and another was beginning.

Source: Michael Useem, *Conscription, Protest. and Social Conflict: The Life and Death of a Draft Resistance Movement* (New York, 1973), pp. 181-82. The bracketed material is contained in the original published interview.

Although I had been in some sit-ins during the civil rights days, I was hardly political and was strongly dedicated to privatism. It was really the war that woke me up. I knew about the [David] Miller, [David] O'Brien [one of the 1966 resisters who received extensive publicity] and Sheep's Meadow events [draft card burnings in Central Park, April 15, 1967], but I didn't visualize myself doing it. It took a real depression about the war which was rapidly becoming an obsessional thing. I couldn't sleep well and nightmares about the war were frequent when I could sleep. . . . I have a metaphysical bent which can isolate acts through my imagination. If you take the fact of one child or soldier dying 12,000 miles away, it seemed that the distance was arbitrary and it was as if it were happening in my backyard to those I loved. The war became personalized through an extrapolation of the perception of senseless death, steel, and bullets. LBJ could rain death down on innocent millions. The enormity of the crime was terrible. . . . I felt a total disaffection with America, it had betrayed me, and I could think of no other solution except resistance.

59 "Don't You Feel . . . ?"

Exactly how responsive the government was and would be to popular needs remained a question that could generate little optimism. In the following testimony concerning federal food programs Simpson Willis, of East St. Louis, suggested that this form of assistance not only failed to solve the problems at hand but in fact generated other problems. Indeed, the suggestion runs, the programs were counterproductive. In order to receive welfare the individuals could not hold a job; thus the program encouraged unemployment by requiring people not to work. In order to receive the payments for Aid to Dependent Children the parents could not live together; thus the program actually encouraged family separations. It should be remembered that this system of welfare was perhaps the area where the system worked at its best, not at its worst, since at least there was some intent of helping out victims of the system. That the presumed beneficiaries of the program should be so critical of the operation of the system indicates the broad disenchantment with the arrangement of power and rewards and responsiveness in the modern political economy. Before one concludes, however, that the following testimony is a sign of growing attentiveness on the part of Congress to such problems, the tone and substance of Senator Percy's questions should be considered. The condescension in the questions ranges from the tone in which the questions are put, to the broad suggestion that this barely literate person with twelve children whom he is unable to feed is the expected result of such a system, and makes clear that the fight for dignity had not yet been won. So, too, observe the Senator's habit of making pious statements about the problem and seeking affirmation from the man providing testimony by asking "Don't you feel . . . ?" That much had remained unchanged in centuries, at least in the halls of power.

Source: *Nutrition and Human Needs*. Hearings before the Select Committee on Nutrition

and Human Needs of the United States Senate, 90th Congress, 2d Session, and 91st Congress, 1st Session. Part 10, Washington, D.C., May 14, and East St. Louis, Illinois, June 27, 1969, pp. 3315-17.

SENATOR PERCY. Can you tell me how much education you have?

MR. WILLIS. I ain't got too much.

SENATOR PERCY. Does the lack of education hinder your getting further work?

MR. WILLIS. Yes, sir.

SENATOR PERCY. Can you tell us what brought about your not getting enough education so that you could get a job and hold a job?

MR. WILLIS. Well, when I was at home I had to work. I have no brothers, my dad was old, and I had to help him work.

SENATOR PERCY. Would you feel it too late in life to go to school, if education was provided to you to get the ability to read and write? Do you work for a gas station?

MR. WILLIS. No. I work for a clothes cleaner, a laundry.

SENATOR PERCY. But for almost any job, you need to read want ads and fill out an application blank, don't you?

MR. WILLIS. That's right.

SENATOR PERCY. Is it too late in life for you? Or is it just too difficult with 12 children to go back to school and try to get that basic education which might enable you to get a higher paying job?

MR. WILLIS. I was going to school. My eyes bother me, and they wouldn't give me no glasses.

SENATOR PERCY. But you'd be willing to go to school if you could get glasses, then?

MR. WILLIS. Yes. I wouldn't mind going to school, because I know I need a higher education than I got.

SENATOR PERCY. Do you feel that the lack of nourishment that your children suffer now impairs their ability to learn in school? If they go to school with an empty stomach, do you thing they are going to fill their mind as well, or are they going to be thinking about that empty stomach?

MR. WILLIS. Well, I'm going to tell you, mine aren't going to go hungry. I will kill and rob before I do that. Mine ain't gonna go hungry. I am going to die first. The only reason I got this job at $50 a week, I didn't want to get and bum. I don't want to kill anybody or take nothing, and that's the reason I got the $50 job, but it ain't enough.

* * *

SENATOR PERCY. . . . When you went to work and got a job, you were penalized because they said you've got a job, and are not eligible for these other programs.

MR. WILLIS. They told my wife I had enough to take care of myself.

SENATOR PERCY. In other words, the welfare system places an incentive on you not to work. You might be better off if you didn't work.

MR. WILLIS. You're right about it.

SENATOR PERCY. Well, now, don't you feel that's the kind of thing as legislators we ought to try to correct? This present rule that if there was a man in the family they couldn't get any ADC assistance, gives an incentive to a man to say goodbye to his family. Don't you think we, as legislators, have to put sense back into these welfare programs elements that take into account human nature and human reactions?

60 The Decline of the Family

One unmistakable fact quickly reveals a fundamental contour of black life in modern America. Between 1940 and 1975 the proportion of black families maintained by a woman without a husband present doubled, jumping from 18 percent of all black families in 1940 to 35 percent in 1975. Or, put another way that narrows the period of dramatic change considerably, the number of black children living with both parents declined from around three-fourths of the children under eighteen in 1960 to around one-half in 1975.

That the family was in serious trouble in modern society had been evident in many quarters for some time. Indeed, Daniel Patrick Moynihan had suggested in the mid-sixties that the matrifocal family so characteristic of blacks lay at the bottom of the weakness of the black community, a weakness which thereby contributed to racial unrest in the cities. While for many Moynihan's analysis of the problem served mainly to divert attention from political and economic inequities, and for others to demonstrate the pervasiveness of white middle class values in the assessment of black social arrangements, the fact remained that blacks were living together in two-parent families with decreasing regularity. Part of the significance of the disintegration of the family is evident in the comparison with white families; although white families were suffering too, the decline was far greater among blacks. It was, thus, part of a larger process of social disintegration in the nation and one that afflicted blacks with particular severity.

It would no doubt be an exaggeration to attribute this process to the system of welfare payments, as some were quick to do. The growth of the system may provide the key, however, as the activist state and economy in the 1960s and 1970s increasingly performed services once provided by the family, which both undermined the family structure by removing part of its reason for existence and debilitated individuals by discouraging individual autonomy. This disintegration shows the impact of modernization on the family, perhaps the last refuge in slavery or freedom, from impersonal and powerful forces; or, in Christopher Lasch's words, "the disintegrating impact on the family of a dangerous environment, in which the struggle to survive creates an atmosphere of chronic antagonism, and friendship, love, and marriage are sustained only with great difficulty." It could well be that at some point in this period since the 1960s the goal of equity became redefined from that of creating a new world to holding on to what good was already there.

Source: United States Bureau of the Census, *The Social and Economic Status of the Black Population in the United States: An Historical View, 1790-1978*, Current Population Reports; Special Studies Series P-23, No. 80 (Washington, D.C., n.d.), Table 74, p. 103.

Percent Distribution of Families by Type: 1940 to 1970 and 1971 to 1975

Year and Race	All Families (thousands)	Total	Husband-Wife	Male Head, No Wife Present	Female Head, No Husband Present[1]
Black					
1940[2]	2,699	100.0	77.1	5.0	17.9
1950[3]	3,432	100.0	77.7	4.7	17.6
1960	3,950	100.0	74.1	4.1	21.7
1970	4,774	100.0	68.1	3.7	28.3
1971	4,928	100.0	65.6	3.8	30.6
1972	5,157	100.0	63.8	4.4	31.8
1973	5,265	100.0	61.4	4.0	34.6
1974	5,440	100.0	61.8	4.2	34.0
1975	5,498	100.0	60.9	3.9	35.3
White					
1940[2]	28,740	100.0	85.5	4.4	10.1
1950	35,021	100.0	88.0	3.5	8.5
1960	40,873	100.0	89.2	2.7	8.1
1970	46,022	100.0	88.7	2.3	9.1
1971	46,535	100.0	88.3	2.3	9.4
1972	47,641	100.0	88.2	2.3	9.4
1973	48,477	100.0	87.8	2.5	9.6
1974	48,919	100.0	87.7	2.4	9.9
1975	49,451	100.0	86.9	2.6	10.5

[1] Includes widowed, divorced, and single women, women whose husbands are in the armed forces or otherwise away from home involuntarily, as well as those separated from their husbands through marital discord.

[2] Data revised to exclude one-person families.

[3] Data include families of "other" races.

61 The Limits of Political Participation

While the broadening of the franchise in the 1960s to permit more blacks to vote resulted in an immediate increase in black electoral participation, the revolution was short-lived. In 1968, the first presidential election in which many blacks were able to cast a ballot brought out nearly 58 percent of the blacks of voting age. That compared to the 42 percent that voted in the congressional elections in 1966. In the South, where the change was most notable, 44 per cent of the blacks of voting age had voted in the presidential election of 1964 (an election held before the enactment of the Voting Rights Act of 1965), 33 percent in the congressional elections of 1966, and 52 percent in the presidential election of 1968. By 1974, however, after the distressing electoral choices offered in 1968 and 1972, and after the resignation of Richard Nixon resulting from his complicity in the Watergate scandal, the electoral and political system seemed even more tainted than it had been in the midst of the crises of the late sixties and early seventies. While both black and white participation declined in 1974, blacks voted in smaller proportions than had been the case even when many were disfranchised in the South before the civil rights reforms. In 1974, 30 percent of the blacks of voting age turned out at the polls, nearly one-third less than the proportion in 1964. Only 46 percent of the white population voted in 1974, compared with 71 percent in 1964, again a drop of around one-third.

In a way it was like emancipation: the blacks had been freed, this time to vote, but with what choices and hopes? Upon examination of the reasons offered by those who chose not to vote, the analogy becomes more vivid. In 1974, 42 percent of the blacks who were not registered indicated that their interest had not been stimulated sufficiently by the political process to register. Among those who were registered, the largest group of those who did not vote (except

for those who said they were unable to go to the polls because of
illness, work, and emergencies or other reasons) likewise consisted
of those who were not interested, and the next largest group actually
"dislike[d] politics." It would not be unreasonable to suggest that
many of these people were actually voting "no" on the system itself
when they stayed away from the polls in 1974. Given the very recent
and intense struggle for political freedom that remained fresh in the
memories of many blacks, and given the equally vivid recollections
of repression and intimidation that had been invoked to prevent
blacks from voting in the South, a distinct appreciation for the limits
of the political process seems evident.

Source: United States Bureau of the Census, *The Social and Economic Status of the Black
Population in the United States, An Historical View 1790-1978*, Current Population Reports;
Special Studies Series P-23, No. 80 (Washington, D.C., n.d.), Table 104, p. 15l; United
States Bureau of the Census, *The Social and Economic Status of the Black Population in the
United States 1974*, Current Population Reports; Special Studies Series P-23, No. 54
(Washington, D.C., 1975), Table 97, p. 148.

Reported Voter Participation of Persons of Voting Age, by Region for General Elections: 1964 to 1974
(Numbers in thousands)

Subject	Presidential Election			Congressional Election		
	1964	1968	1972	1966	1970	1974
Black						
Number who reported that they voted:						
United States	6,048	6,300	7,033	4,398	4,992	4,786
South	2,576*	3,094	3,324	1,870	2,278	2,219
North and West	3,891*	3,206	3,707	2,528	2,724	2,567
Percent of voting-age population who reported that they voted:						
United States	58	58	52	42	44	34
South	44*	52	48	33	37	30
North and West	72*	65	57	52	51	38
Percent of registered population who reported that they voted:						
United States	NA	87	80	69	72	62
South	NA	84	75	62	64	54
North and West	NA	90	85	76	80	70
White						
Number who reported that they voted:						
United States	70,204	72,213	78,167	57,757	60,426	57,918
South	15,813	17,853	20,201	12,922	14,313	13,850
North and West	54,392	54,362	57,966	44,835	46,113	44,069
Percent of voting-age population who reported that they voted:						
United States	71	69	64	57	56	46
South	59	62	57	45	46	37
North and West	75	72	68	62	60	50
Percent of registered population who reported that they voted:						
United States	NA	92	88	80	81	73
South	NA	87	82	70	71	61
North and West	NA	93	90	83	84	77

NA = Not available
* Includes persons of "other" races.

Reasons for Not Voting or Registering for Persons Who Reported That They Did Not Vote, by Region: 1974
(Numbers in thousands)

Reason for Not Voting or Registering	Black United States	Black South	Black North and West	White United States	White South	White North and West
Total persons who reported that they did not vote[1]	9,389	5,182	4,206	67,213	23,224	43,989
Persons reported registered but not voting[2]	2,577	1,657	920	19,755	8,016	11,739
Reported reason for not voting:						
Percent	100	100	100	100	100	100
Not interested	22	21	23	20	22	19
Dislikes politics	9	7	13	15	13	16
Unable to go to polls	45	47	41	33	33	33
Out of town or away from home	8	8	7	16	15	16
Other reasons[3]	17	17	17	17	18	16
Persons reported not registered[4]	5,169	2,794	2,375	38,622	12,667	25,954
Reported reason for not registering:						
Percent	100	100	100	100	100	100
Not a citizen, resident requirement not satisfied	6	3	8	13	10	14
Not interested	42	46	38	37	43	34
Dislikes politics	6	3	9	10	7	11
Unable to register	8	10	7	4	4	4
Registration inconvenient or didn't know how	8	9	7	7	7	8
Recently moved, has not registered	7	4	10	11	10	12
Other reasons	14	14	14	12	13	11

[1] Includes 1,228,000 blacks and 7,020,000 whites in the United States (not shown separately) who did not report on registration.

[2] Includes only those who reported a reason for not voting; excludes 415,000 blacks and 1,816,000 whites who did not know or report a reason.

[3] Includes a negligible number of persons who reported "machines not working or lines too long," and "didn't know of election."

[4] Includes 497,000 blacks and 2,036,000 whites (not shown separately) who did not know or report a reason for not registering.

62 Busing the Issue Away

Perhaps no single development reflected the extent to which issues of racial equality and political and economic democracy had become blurred in the 1970s more than the court ordered busing of students to other, sometimes distant, schools instead of promoting the *de facto* segregation of school systems. The efforts to desegregate the Boston area schools proved to be among the most volatile in the entire program. There, busing orders stimulated boycotts of schools, and the violence that accompanied the bus arrivals at schools received nationwide publicity. To many it was the Little Rock desegregation crisis all over again. And, indeed, the arguments sounded familiar. Those who defended the effort, even like some below who initially opposed busing, often did so in the name of education for the children. Those who resisted were prone, like their predecessors of the 1950s, to speak in terms of an expansive federal bureaucracy imposing its will on peaceful citizens. The rhetoric, the violence, and the tensions flared, but it seemed that the lessons of two decades had gone unlearned. So clouded were the issues that "freedom" and "community" could be identified in some quarters with racism, and "racial equality" could be equated with efforts to override the popular will. By pitting racial equality against notions of freedom and neighborhood—or even racial integrity—each cause became tainted; and the actual issues that made these people so vulnerable to the intensified feelings of dispossession—the issues of culture and neighborhood, and the values associated with them, such as education and commitments to children—became that much more mired. It would not be possible to honor commitments to all quarters at once in the context in which the issues were posed by the government, or more broadly, by the structure of power in America. The original issue, which involved equal educational opportunity for all, an idea which few would oppose, had been placed in such a narrowed context that to seek greater opportunity for some would of necessity threaten others. In this way the busing issue demonstrated the persistence of broader racial issues as diversions in the 1970s just as they had been for centuries.

In the testimony offered before the United States Civil Rights Commission in Boston in June 1975, following the year's experience with busing, one quality evident among the supporters of busing is the contrast between original negative responses to busing and later acquiescence to the system of authority. Related to this is no doubt a common dilemma faced by many. As Ms. Peggy Coughlin related a phone call to her from a woman trying to figure out what to do amidst the conflicting pressures and options, the central difficulty became evident: "I really felt this woman was looking for someone to tell her what to do . . . ." Such confusion and cónflict were only natural and such seeking for direction, when given only artificial, tainted, and divisive choices, could only be expected. Of course, at the same time, this seeking for direction was also the logical result of the loss of autonomy and individuality in the nation. It was the voice of powerlessness.

Source: U.S. Commission on Civil Rights, *Hearing before the United States Commission on Civil Rights*: Hearing Held in Boston, Massachusetts, June 16-20, 1975 (Washington, D.C., 1978), 300-315.

MR. ALEXANDER. Mrs. Coughlin, to go back a moment now to when you heard that the school system in South Boston was to be desegregated. You've had several children in the local schools. Is that not correct?

MS. COUGHLIN. Yes, it is.

MR. ALEXANDER. What was your reaction?

MS. COUGHLIN. I didn't like it. I didn't—it's not so much that I cared if people came into our schools, if the blacks came into our schools, but I was very, very much against forced busing, and I didn't want our kids to have to go out of the area.

MR. ALEXANDER. Did your children attend school at the beginning of school, this year?

MS. COUGHLIN. No, I went along with the boycott for the first 2 weeks. We were asked to boycott, and I did say that I would for 2 weeks, but please don't ask me any longer, because I did want the kids to go to school.

MR. ALEXANDER. So after the 2 weeks did your child go back to school?

MS. COUGHLIN. Yes.

MR. ALEXANDER. To the South Boston High School?

MS. COUGHLIN. Yes. I have just one up in high school. I have one that was supposed to go to Roxbury, but I did the cowardly thing. I sent her to a private school.

MR. ALEXANDER. What happened in South Boston High School with your son's class while he was there? Did he continue to go?

MS. COUGHLIN. Yes, he did.

MR. ALEXANDER. What happened in the December-January period at South Boston High School?

MS. COUGHLIN. Well, that was—it was pretty hectic. I had, as a matter of fact, way back in August was when I really first got involved. I was so upset over the problem with Judge Garrity I had sent quite a long letter to him, and after not getting an answer from him, I went down to our local paper and I had the letter put in the paper, which in turn, of course, caused a big paper to come and interview me, and actually, I certainly didn't think I said anything wrong, but at that time we did get some threatening phone calls to myself, my family, and to my youngest daughter.

So—we had had a bad tragedy in the family and my husband had been sick, so he said to me, "For God's sake, keep your mouth shut and stay out of things." And I really did. I stayed completely out, except for the sending the kids back to school after the time was up. And then—

MR. ALEXANDER. What happened to bring you back in?

MS. COUGHLIN. The idea of closing the high school was just—I thought it was just so terrible to want to close South Boston High School. It's been open since right after 1900, and I have had children up in the high school for 18 consecutive years, so I should have them for the next 6, but—you know, I don't know what's going to happen.

MR. ALEXANDER. What in fact did you do when you learned that South Boston High School might well be closed down?

MS. COUGHLIN. Well, I had heard, someone had called and said that there were going to be a couple of different committee meetings, school committee meetings, which I had gone in and attend. One was at an elementary level, or rather middle level, which they call now. And like, they heard the elementary and then the middle, and then the high school, and I did have one in the elementary—I mean in the middle class, and one also in the high school, so I was able—you know—to speak. I didn't have that much to say, other than the fact that I thought the schools should be open.

Then it kind of died down again until January 1, when it came up that Judge Garrity was planning on speaking to some of the parents, and I was called and asked if I would go over to the Federal Building and see if I could talk.

Well, I didn't want to take any chances, so I made a call to School Committeewomen Kathleen Sullivan, and I asked her, "You know, if I'm going to spend my time, I want to be heard," you know. And I went over there, but actually we weren't heard. We were ordered the next day to give a deposition for the judge, which was actually a waste of time. And that's why even with this subpena, which I can see now is not the same thing, not run the same way—we did no more, practically than just say our name and address and that we did have a child in the school, but other than that I think they were more concerned with all the—what the big shots had to say, not what just the average parent had to say.

MR. ALEXANDER. Did you as an "average parent" do anything in particular to try to keep South Boston High School open?

MS. COUGHLIN. Yes. As a matter of fact, the day we made the deposition, we were invited up—I was one of the ones who was invited up to Superintendent Leary's office, and on the agenda for that meeting was the closing of South Boston High School. And to say I got panicky was—you know—upset about the whole thing, and when it came down to the question, what would the parents do in order to help to solve the situation—so at that time it came to me that I knew I could get enough parents who were willing, if the police couldn't provide protection, I felt that the parents could keep things under control. And—which seemed like a good idea at the time. Nobody objected or anything else.

So I spent the next 2 days completely on the telephone trying to get parents who were willing to go into the school and—I didn't know what they were going to do, I really didn't. Just to patrol the corridor, or just to give the kids moral support, to let them know that the parents were with them and that they wanted them to continue their education. And such as it was, it was a bad year, as everybody knows, and you can't deny that.

MR. ALEXANDER. How many people were you able to contact who were willing to do this?

MS. COUGHLIN. I had—from late Friday night when I got home until early Sunday evening, I had close to 120 parents.

MR. ALEXANDER. Now, were these parents who were in favor of the desegregation of schools, or were these parents who were strongly opposed to the school desegregation?

MS. COUGHLIN. I would say we were all opposed.

You know, I feel so middle-of-the-roadish, you know? I think that we were opposed to it, but at the same time, we didn't want any trouble. We didn't want any kids to get hurt, and were willing to go in and have students, both black and white, receive their education without any violence, if we could help in any way.

MR. ALEXANDER. I gather that parent committee was never actually utilized when the—and that the State police, etc., were brought into South Boston High School.

MS. COUGHLIN. Well, not completely. Actually, when they found out—I had no idea this was going to boomerang like it did, the day that—as a matter of fact, Sunday night, Miss Sullivan called me up and asked me if I would go over and let the school committee know how well I was doing getting people, you know, involved. And I had no idea that it was going to be on television and that it was going to make such a big impression on people. All I was concerned with was impressing the kids, so that they would go back to school and they would know that in this short time we had that many parents who were willing to do—and stand by them 100 percent.

This was my whole idea, certainly not being on television or being interviewed. That was the furthest thing from my mind. But it just sort of—I didn't know I was—I didn't know I was being, like, positive in my thinking, because I was only thinking of the kids. I wasn't thinking of anything nationally or anything else.

MR. ALEXANDER. Did you encounter a great deal of community criticism for your position?

MS.COUGHLIN. I did. I did.

MR. ALEXANDER. Would you still be willing, let's say for Phase II, to organize parents to protect the school system, to protect the buses coming in, to protect the children walking from the buses to the classroom door, if such were achievable?

MS. COUGHLIN. Yes, I would. But the funny thing is, though, we did—I had called Mr. Reid, our principal, and I told him about the parents that I had had, which he was very pleased. So he said to me, "Mrs. Coughlin, do you have any black parents?" And of course I had to say no. I didn't know any black parents. So he said, "I can't bring just white parents into the school. We have to bring both black and white." So he said, "I will be willing to go to the Freedom House and get black parents who are also willing to give their time and go," and he did. And actually, we went up there on just two occasions, and we found out that we really weren't needed at all.

I think the fact that the kids knew that we were behind them, and that people did really care, we were not needed. And Mr. Reid gave us—well, as a matter of fact, he took us from the basement up to the top, in every room we went by. And nobody was aware that we were coming, classes were being conducted, and I don't know what, but it was particularly orderly on the day that we were there, and—but I think that we—and even as far as lunch, he had us go down to the lunch room that day so that we wouldn't be—you know, because that's where most of the disturbances had occurred, was in the lunchroom.

MR. ALEXANDER. When you became known in the community from the television appearances; did you start receiving, either on a name basis or on an anonymous basis, requests from other parents for help of any sort?

MS. COUGHLIN. Yes, I had one in particular. I still don't know who the woman is to this day, that called me up, and she was quite upset about boycotting her children up until that time, and she says, "Why are you telling us to send our children back, when others are telling us to keep them home?"

And I said, "I'm not telling you to send your children back. That decision has to be yours and your husband's, certainly not mine." I said, "I'm just—the ones I was referring to, which I thought I had made myself clear, were the ones who were in school, to please go back, and, you know, we'd try to make things work out for them."

But she really—I really felt that this woman was looking for someone to tell her what to do, so I said "The only thing I could suggest to you is to go to both schools and speak to the principal and ask him to bring you through the school and let you and your husband decide for yourself, because I cannot make the decision for you."

About 2 weeks later, the woman did call me back and thank me for my time and said that she did send her children back to school.

Index

About the Author

MICHAEL J. CASSITY received his Ph.D. from the University of Missouri-Columbia and has been a professor in the History Departments at the University of Missouri-Columbia, the University of Kansas, and the University of Georgia. In 1981 he served as Director of the Wyoming Historical Survey in the History Department of the University of Wyoming. His articles on American social history have appeared in the *Journal of American History*, the *Southwest Review*, and a variety of other journals and magazines, and he has recently completed a book-length analysis of social change in a nineteenth-century community.